- HAVE A -

HAPPY WEEKEND

1 YEAR - 52 DESTINATIONS
- ALL OVER EUROPE -

+KUNTH+

It's summer in the city of Paris; this is at its prettiest under the sunlight and the people enjoy the "savoir-vivre" along the Seine.

Spring in Budapest when Cherry Blossom trees are blooming on the shores of the Danube above the Freedom Bridge, which was inaugurated in the year 1884.

HAVE A
HAPPY WEEKEND!

MONDAYS COME AND GO LIKE CLOCKWORK, AND A LOT OF US OFTEN FEEL DESPONDENT BY SUNDAY AFTERNOON. BE THAT AS IT MAY, WE DO HAVE TO FACE A "MONDAY", AT LEAST 52 TIMES A YEAR. HOWEVER, THIS ALSO MEANS THAT WE HAVE 52 WEEKENDS, SO WHY NOT MAKE ALL - IF NOT MOST - OF THEM A HAPPY WEEKEND?! WITH CONTINENTAL EUROPE AT YOUR DOORSTEP, YOU HAVE 52 SATURDAYS AND SUNDAYS, AND SOME ARE LONG WEEKENDS, THAT BECKON FOR A TRIP TO SOME OF THE MOST ATTRACTIVE CITIES AND REGIONS IN THE WORLD. A BREAK FROM THE MUNDANE; A LITTLE ADVENTURE; NEW DISCOVERIES; NEW EXPERIENCES; OR, SIMPLY RELAX AND ENJOY THE FRESH AIR OFF THE SWISS ALPS, OR GO FOR AN AUTUMN SWIM ONE SATURDAY AFTERNOON IN DUBROVNIK, WHERE THE WATER IS STILL WARM AND STUNNINGLY INVITING. FOR A SHORT TRIP TO BE SUCCESSFUL, PLANNING IS KEY. YOU SHOULD DECIDE BEFOREHAND WHICH CITY AND WHAT YOU WANT TO DO ONCE THERE. THE 52 WEEKENDS RUN ACROSS ALL SEASONS. EACH SEASON OFFERS EACH CITY A CHANCE TO FLAUNT ITS SPECIAL CHARACTER DIFFERENTLY. SPRING IS CELEBRATED IN MANY PLACES: ROME HAS ITS CITY BIRTHDAY; AMSTERDAM CELEBRATES THE KING'S DAY; AND VALENCIA SAYS FAREWELL TO WINTER WITH A LARGE EXTRAVAGANT FESTIVAL. AUTUMN PRESENTS MAJORCA IN A FANTASY WORLD OF SOFT PINK WHEN THE ALMOND TREES BLOOM; AND, ON ST. PATRICK'S DAY, IT IS THE GREEN THAT DOMINATES DUBLIN. SUMMER IS CASUAL, PEOPLE RELAX AND SIT OUTSIDE DURING THE WHITE NIGHTS IN THE CITIES OF THE BALTIC SEA ENJOYING THE LONG DAYS; OR FOLLOW THE DELICIOUS AROMA OF GRILLED SARDINES THROUGH THE STREETS OF LISBON. THERE ARE SO MANY HISTORICAL COMPETITIONS IN TUSCANY; WHILE IN VERONA, YOU CAN LISTEN TO OPERA AT AN ANCIENT AMPHITHEATRE UNDER FLICKERING CANDLES. PROVENCE PRESENTS THE WORLD IN A SEA OF PURPLE FROM ITS FIELDS OF FRAGRANT LAVENDER. AUTUMN LURES YOU TO EXPERIENCE THE GLAMOROUS FASHION WEEK IN MILAN; THE CRAZY PARTIES IN IBIZA; OR, SEE THE AMAZING HUMAN TOWERS AT THE FESTA DE LA MERCÉ IN BARCELONA. AUTUMN IS ALSO THE BEST TIME FOR A LITTLE HIKE IN CORSICA AND WITNESS THE BIRD MIGRATIONS IN TALLINN. AND OF COURSE, PEOPLE CELEBRATE ECSTATICALLY AND WILDLY AT THE BIGGEST FOLK FESTIVAL IN MUNICH! THEN COMES THE WINTER WITH THE CHRISTMAS MARKETS IN STRASBOURG, AND INNSBRUCK SPARKLE WITH FESTIVE ATMOSPHERE, JUST LIKE THE COSTUMES AT THE CARNIVALS IN COLOGNE AND VENICE. THE BEAUTIFUL WALZ IS ONLY DANCED PROPERLY IN VIENNA; AND THE VAST SKY OVER LAPLAND COMES ALIVE WITH THE POLAR LIGHTS DANCING IN THEIR INCREDIBLY MESMERIZING COLOURS.

THIS BOOK SHOWCASES 52 CITIES AND TOWNS IN EUROPE AT THEIR MOST EXCITING, CAPTIVATING AND STUNNING DISPLAY - ALL OF THEM ARE INVITING YOU TO POP IN, SAY "HELLO" AND HAVE A HAPPY WEEKEND!

Left: A ride on the London Eye is one of the activities that should not be missed in the great British capital.

Upper right: The Princes Street Garden of Edinburgh invites you for a walk during summertime.

Lower right: The Campo de' Fiori in Rome becomes lively every morning when the market is opened.

CONTENTS

Right: Sitting at a street café and absorbing the relaxed atmosphere of a small city and leaving the everyday life behind – that's what Calvi in Corsica has to offer.

SPRING

Isolated rocks and islets off the coast of Cornwall with lighthouses, like the one here on Godrevy Island, are not uncommon.

#01   AMSTERDAM

AN OLD TOWN ENTIRELY BUILT ON WOODEN POSTS, 80 KILOMETRES OF WATERWAYS, HUNDREDS OF BRIDGES AND A RED LIGHT DISTRICT AROUND A GOTHIC CHURCH: AMSTERDAM IS TRULY UNIQUE. THE GREAT PERIOD OF AMSTERDAM WAS THE 17TH CENTURY, THE GOLDEN AGE OF THE NETHERLANDS, WHICH AT THAT TIME BECAME THE LEADING NAVAL AND ECONOMIC POWER, ESTABLISHING COLONIES AND TRADING POSTS AROUND THE WORLD. THE COUNTRY GAINED MUCH MONEY, AND THE CITIZENS OF AMSTERDAM INVESTED IT IN THE BEAUTY OF THEIR CITY. BUT THEY TRIED TO BE PRACTICAL AT THE SAME TIME AND PUT THE CANAL BELT AROUND THE CITY TO BE ABLE TO TRANSPORT THE GOODS DIRECTLY TO THE TRADING HOUSES. TODAY, THE CANALS WITH THEIR HISTORIC ROWS OF HOUSES AND BRIDGES ARE THE SYMBOL OF ROMANTIC AMSTERDAM.

Above: The tall, narrow canal houses on the Amstel are built tightly together.

Left: The "Southern Church" rises at Zuiderkerkhof Square in the vicinity of Nieuw market and Rembrandt House.

Right: The Amsterdam Rijksmuseum is the largest museum of art and history in the Netherlands. In particular, its extensive collection of Dutch masters enjoys a worldwide reputation.

○ RIJKSMUSEUM

The museum was founded in 1800. Since then it has grown steadily and now presents mainly Dutch masters in a neo-renaissance building. Rembrandt's "The Night Watch" can be found here. In addition to other world-famous masters such as Ruisdael and Vermeer, more than seven million works of art from all periods, genres and provenances can be seen in the museum.

○ ANNE FRANK HOUSE

A visit to the Prinsengracht is mandatory. The famous Anne Frank and her family lived in one of the rear buildings. The place in which they hid from the Nazis can be visited, where personal items and photographs can still be viewed.

○ DAM SQUARE AND ROYAL PALACE

The Dam is an extensive square in front of the Royal Palace. The nucleus of the city which also gave it it's name. The square was created on a dam in the river Amstel. In the royal palace wall paintings and noble furniture can be viewed, if the royal family is not present.

WHY VISIT IN SPRING?

A SEA OF SEVEN MILLION CHERRY-RED TULIPS GENTLY ROCKING THEIR HEADS IN THE SOFT DUTCH WIND ... WITH THIS IMAGE, KEUKENHOF, THE LARGEST FLOWER GARDEN IN THE WORLD, GREETS ITS VISITORS EVERY YEAR AT THE OPENING OF THE SPRING SEASON. FROM MARCH 20 UNTIL LATE MAY CUSTOMERS CAN WANDER THROUGH THE INDIVIDUAL THEME GARDENS AND CAN BUY FLOWER BULBS. IT IS WONDERFUL TO GO THERE BY BIKE AS KEUKENHOF IS ONLY 35 KILOMETRES FROM AMSTERDAM.
KING'S DAY AT THE END OF APRIL IS THE LARGEST NATIONAL EVENT IN HOLLAND, AND IS CELEBRATED WITH STREET PARTIES AND TRADITIONAL ORANGE CLOTHING.

Left: Spring is welcomed on the tulip fields of the Keukenhof. The flowers extend endlessly.

At the top: Patrician houses line the Herengracht. Their small width is deceptive, as the houses extend far to the rear.

Above: On water is the best way to explore Amsterdam. Numerous travel agencies organize guided boat tours.

Right: Evening mood at the Kloveniersburgwal, also called "de Kloof", one of the oldest canals in the city.

○ CANALS

Similar to ring roads, Amsterdam's canals surround the old town centre. Wealthy merchants settled here. In the past plants were delivered by boat on the Singelgracht and sold here directly. Although today the goods arrive by truck, they are still mostly offered for sale on houseboats. Besides the Singelgracht, the Prinsengracht, the Keizersgracht and the Herengracht are of particular importance.

○ JORDAAN

Exceptionally colourful is the old artisan and poor people quarter Jordaan west of the Prinsengracht. It owes its homely charm to the many houseboats along the quays and the Hofjes, winding, often green residential courts.

○ RED LIGHT DISTRICT

The Rossebuurt, as the Dutch call it, is located in the old town. The ladies in the shop windows, however, may not be photographed! There are even good restaurants and a condominium here, as well as informative and amusing tours. In the middle of the red light district you will find one of Amsterdam's oldest buildings, the Oude Kerk. It was built around 1300 and is now used as an exhibition space.

○ VAN-GOGH MUSEUM

This museam boasts the world's largest collection of Vincent van Gogh's works.

○ BEGINENHOF

The narrow, sometimes somewhat askew-looking houses with courtyards are among the oldest buildings. Once upon a time, single women lived here in a religious community.

○ REMBRANDT HOUSE

Rembrandt lived and worked in this house for nearly 20 years. You can see a reconstructed interior, an old printing press and small sketches of the master.

○ NIEUWMARKT

Where once a canal flowed, a place was created in 1614, which still today hosts a daily market. The old streets around the market include Amsterdam's Chinatown.

GOING OUT

Restaurant De Kas // You will hardly be able to eat fresher food anywhere else in Amsterdam as the elegant restaurant is located directly in its own large greenhouse, where the ingredients for the daily changing dishes are grown.

// www.restaurantdekas.nl

Restaurant Greetje // Although Amsterdam is well-known for its multi-cultural cuisine, traditional dishes are still popular in some places, with the Greetje in the Nieuwmarkt en Lastage neighborhood being outstanding.

// www.restaurantgreetje.nl

Café de Jaren // Modern and flooded with light is one of the most popular of the so-called Grand Cafés. In order to enjoy the first rays of sunshine in spring, it is worth reserving a place on the terrace, which, with views of the Amstel, is located directly on the water of the Kloveniersburgwal.

// www.cafedejaren.nl

SHOPPING

○ **BOEKENMARKT OUDEMANHUISPOORT**

Nestled between historic university buildings, a small bookmarket is open daily, apart from Sundays. It is also suitable for rainy days, because the stands are protected by arcades.

○ **KAASHUIS TROMP**

No visit to Amsterdam is complete without a trip to an authentic cheese shop! Kaashuis Tromp offers regional products as well as varieties from all over the world, for example from New Zealand or from South Africa.

// www.kaashuistromp.nl

○ **BIJENKORF**

Directly on the Dam you will find this luxury department store with its magnificent building. Excellant service, the largest selection of jeans and award-winning restaurants. Sometimes even the Queen shops here.

// www.debijenkorf.nl

DAYTRIPS

○ **ZANDVOORT**

This seaside resort is the beach for Amsterdam citizens seeking a break from the city. In addition to pretty pavilions by the sea there is also a charming dune landscape and quiet national parks. On your way to the North Sea be sure stop in the picturesque old town of Haarlem.

○ **IJSSELMEER**

Between Friesland and North Holland you can find the largest lake in the Netherlands, the IJsselmeer. A combination of pretty fishing villages, beautiful natural surroundings and at the same time a great sailing area. The region is very easy to reach by bicycle from Amsterdam.

Left: Next to the futuristic facade, the Conversatorium Hotel offers a cosy outdoor terrace.

WHERE TO STAY

Hotel The Exchange // If you have a taste for the extraordinary, chose one of the individual rooms in this hotel. All rooms were literally "dressed" by Amsterdam fashion students.

// www.hoteltheexchange.nl

Motel One Amsterdam // The colorful Motel One is dedicated to the two things that are classically associated with the Netherlands: bicycles and tulips. Without being tacky, it's one of the more economy designer hotels.

// www.motel-one.com/hotels/ amsterdam/hotel-amsterdam

Conservatorium Hotel // In the past the conservatory used the magnificent building for its purposes, today it is an elegant luxury hotel, which not only impresses with its great acoustics. The hotel was designed by award-winning architect Piero Lissoni and combines a modern elegance with the building's musical past.

// www.conservatoriumhotel.com

NOT TO BE MISSED

OBSERVING 15 BRIDGES FROM THE MAGERE BRUG

The narrow old retractable bridge made of wood - built in 1617 and renewed in 1871 - is a great photo opportunity in the evenings when lit up by 1,200 lightbulbs. Thanks to its location, above the Amstel at the top of church street, it is also a good vantage point - 15 bridges can be viewed from here at the same time. It connects the banks over the Amstel between Kaisergracht and Prinzengracht. Every year - usually in the presence of the King - a concert is held here on the anniversary of the "Victory in Europe Day". In addition, the bridge was the backdrop of numerous films, such as the James Bond movie "Diamonds are Forever."

VISITING A "BROWN CAFÉ"

Bruin Cafés are authentic Amsterdam establishments. Incidentally, these are pubs that share the same dark style, old interiors. The best way to disconnect from the hustle and bustle of the city and get to know locals. Try for example the Café Oosterling or the , t Smalle, which was opened in the 18th century as a Genever (Dutch Juniper Gin) tasting room.

TAKE A BOAT TRIP ON THE CANALS

The canals occupy a large part of the city area. By boat you can get to see important sights and every-day life. Very handy: Hop-on-hop-off boats.

SHOPPING FOR ANTIQUES WATERLOOPLEIN

This market is open from Monday to Saturday. But do not be fooled by the name, because this is a flea market, with second hand articles to clutter, not just antiques. Nevertheless, the atmosphere is unique and you can surely find a few hidden gems.

DISCOVER A FREE LUNCH CONCERT IN THE CONCERTGEBOUW

A highlight of this concert hall with its two ballrooms, that have been in existence since 1888, is the organ with 60 acoustic registration stops. From September to June, concerts take place at 12.30 pm on Wednesdays, and you can listen to for free.

#02

ANDALUSIA

"AL ANDALUZ" -THE LAND OF LIGHT, SO THE ARABS CALL, THE SOUTHERN PART OF SPAIN IS IN FACT AT THE CROSSROADS OF TWO CONTINENTS AND TWO SEAS. THE VERY SPECIAL LIGHT IN THIS REGION CAN NOT BE FOUND ANYWHERE ELSE IN THE WORLD, AND ITS CLARITY INSPIRES VISITORS TIME AND TIME AGAIN. ANDALUSIA IS ALSO A BLAZE OF COLORS. WHITE VILLAGES STAND OUT AGAINST A BRIGHT BLUE SKY, ORANGE, RED, YELLOW AND BLUE AZULEJOS EMBELLISHED HOUSE WALLS, BENCHES, PARKS OR EVEN ENTIRE SQUARES. PALACES IN GOLD COMPETE WITH THE LIGHT OF THE SUN, AND THOSE WHO LEAVE THE CITIES BEHIND DISCOVER GREEN LANDSCAPES, BEAUTIFUL FORESTS OR BIZARRE ROCK FORMATIONS. THE EVENTFUL HISTORY OF THE SOUTHERNMOST PART OF SPAIN CAN BE DISCOVERED JUST AS COLORFULLY. ALMOST EVERY CHRISTIAN CHURCH IS BUILT ON THE FOUNDATIONS OF A FORMER MOSQUE, MUSLIM ELEMENTS ARE INTEGRATED INTO THE HOUSES OF WORSHIP. BLUE-GOLDEN DOMES, RICHLY DECORATED WITH ARABIC ORNAMENTS, RISE UP IN THE MIDST OF ANGULAR TOWERS AND HOLY FIGURES.

Left: If you are traveling by car, you should not miss the opportunity to get to know the mountains of Andalusia with their pretty white villages. The historic centre of Frigiliana still retains its original Moorish structure with steep streets, low passageways and narrow staircases.

Right: The magnificent Plaza de España was designed in 1929 for the "Iberoamerican Exhibition" in Seville.

○ SEVILLE

The city on the river Guadalquivír. The best way to get to know this beautiful place is on a carriage ride to see the intense colors of the bougainvilleas rising up against old walls and façades, with the scent of flowers and fruits floating constantly above the enchanting city. No wonder that this atmosphere has always inspired writers and composers. Seville, the capital of Andalusia, connects historic districts, the Barrios, with lively modernity and bustling streets.

○ CATHEDRAL SANTA MARÍA DE LA SEDE

The cathedral is an imposing example of Gothic architecture. It is based on a rectangular plan and has five naves, all spanned by ribbed vaults and chapels on all sides. Altars, Madonna figures, crucifixes, sarcophagi of important personalities in the history of Seville, various relics and huge paintings demonstrate an immense wealth of art treasures.

○ GIRALDA

The Giralda is an impressive relic from the Islamic period, the former minaret of the mosque is now the bell tower of the cathedral. It was completed in 1198, built from stone blocks of the city's former Roman buildings. Its approximately 100 metres high tower consists of bricks, which were once brought to Andalusia by the Arabs. Islamic architecture can also be found on the windows, the typical striking horseshoe arches.

○ ALCAZAR

Puerta del León, the "Lion Gate", is the entrance to this magnificent palace of former Arab rulers. The path leads through the Patio del León into the heart of the Alcázar. A high crenellated wall surrounds the huge residence, which the subsequent Christian Kings repeatedly redesigned according to new styles. The highlight of the complex is the Mudejar Palace.

○ ARCHIVO GENERAL DE INDIAS

Here the history of the country is stored in a building that is a historical testimony of the Renaissance period in itself. The Archivo shelters miles and miles of important documents about colonisation and the discovery of America.

WHY VISIT IN SPRING? NOT ONLY THE PLEASANT WEATHER MAKES ANDALUSIA THE IDEAL DESTINATION IN SPRING FOR THOSE WHO CAN HARDLY WAIT FOR THE SUN.
EXPERIENCE CLOSE UP RELIGIOUS TRADITIONS, WITHOUT EVEN GOING TO CHURCH, IN ANDALUSIA DURING SEMANA SANTA. EVERYWHERE PROCESSIONS TAKE PLACE ON THE STREETS. AT THE BEGINNING OF MAY, EVERYTHING IN JEREZ REVOLVES AROUND OUR NOBLE FOUR-LEGGED FRIENDS AS THE ANNUAL FERIA DEL CABALLO HORSE FAIR TAKES PLACE. FOR THE INHABITANTS OF CÓRDOBA, IN TURN, ONLY ONE THING MATTERS IN THE SPRING: THE COMPETITON FOR THE MOST BEAUTIFUL PATIO. THE FLOWER-FILLED COURTYARDS ARE THEN ACCESSIBLE TO VISITORS.

○ CORDÓBA

The Arab heritage is unmistakable in the city. Even in the mentality of the inhabitants, who love colourful houses and bright vivid flowers. Iron railings protect the decorated patios from unwelcome visitors, but not from the admiring glances of passers-by. Cordoba is nicknamed "The City of Caliphs", which dates back to the heyday when the city was the metropolis of Moorish Spain for more than two centuries.

○ MEZQUITA

During the reign of Arab time, a famous mosque with its eleven naves and numerous pillars, the "Mezquita", was built, which offered space for over 10,000 people. When the Christians conquered Córdoba in 1236, the venerable mosque was consecrated as a Christian church.

○ GRANADA

Certainly a sigh of grief escaped him: Boabdil, the last ruler of a Moorish empire on the Iberian peninsula, had to hand over his city to the Christian king Ferdinand in 1492, and leave his kingdom forever. On a hill in front of the city, he looked back at the

Above: Andalusia owes its famous buildings like the Mezquita in Córdoba to the period of Arab predominance.

Left: Insights into the typical courtyards of Cordóba at a Patio Festival in spring.

Alhambra, beyond which rises the snow-covered Sierra Nevada. Even today, the panorama has lost none of its fascinating beauty.

○ ALHAMBRA

It overlooks Granada on a spur of the Sierra Nevada like a palace of the Arabian Nights. Through colonnades, you pass gardens with fountains, the royal baths and, no doubt a highlight of the complex, the Harem, the "forbidden" and private chambers of the Sultan.

GOING OUT

Sevilla: Casa Anselma // The Flamenco bar in the Triana quarter conveys a folksy atmosphere in the smallest of spaces. Flamenco and Sevillanas are still authentic here and it has not yet degenerated into a mere tourist spectacle.

// Calle Pagés del Corro, 49

Sevilla: Casa Robles // The long-established restaurant is one of the most famous names in the restaurant scene in Seville. Serves classics of Spanish cuisine, seafood and rich Andalusian specialties.
// www.casa-robles.com

Bei Sevilla: El Bulli // The restaurant El Bulli belongs to Ferran Adriá, the Spanish master of culinary art, who, among other things invented the molecular gastronomy in his restaurant on the Costa Brava and gained international fame. **// www.elbullihotel.com**

Córdoba: Casa Pepe de la Judería // For tapas, the bar on the ground floor or in the cosy patio are ideal, the restaurant is located on the first floor.
// restaurantecasapepedelajuderia.com

Right: The Alhambra of Granada: 23 Sultans of the Nasrid race have been involved with this highlight of all Spanish-Arabian buildings to date. The now defiant and elegant castle of Granada lies at the feet of the city - the Sierra Nevada forms its heavenly backdrop.

○ JEREZ DE LA FRONTERA

Some people associate the name Jerez de la Frontera with sherry, the city's most prominent product, and others with horses. Jerez gained world fame as the place sherry originated, as the English call it. Its grapes thrive on the white, calcareous soils of the area. Among horse lovers, the horses bred in Jerez, which are presented in the Royal Riding School, have an excellent reputation.

○ CÁDIZ

Behind the strait of Gibraltar, the gateway to the Mediterranean, it feels like another world: the wave-swept Atlantic coast with its miles of white sandy beaches are known for its strong winds, the sea is a surfing paradise - but only for the experienced, as the currents can be dangerous. Cádiz is called the city of light, because the sun conjures a special glow on the houses.

○ RONDA

Almost dizzying, Ronda lies on a rocky plateau at an altitude of 750 meters. It is characterised by its steep rock walls to the sides. From a distance, Ronda is a spectacular scenario. In 1913, Rainer Maria Rilke described his impression of the White Village, which divides the 100 to 180 meter deep Tajo Gorge in the Old and New Towns as a "city piled high on two masses of rock".

SHOPPING

○ EL POSTIGO IN SEVILLA

A stroll through the covered market provides a good overview of Andalusian handicrafts - including leather goods, textiles and original products made from olive wood.

WHERE TO STAY

Sevilla: Hotel Alfonso XIII // Built in 1929, this traditional hotel in the heart of Seville is a dream in Neo-Mudejar-style. It breathes the flair of a grand hotel, and the exterior decor transports guests to the past days in the Moorish city.
// www.hotel-alfonsoxiii-sevilla.com

Sevilla: Hotel Doña Maria // Named after a famous Sevillian, this hotel is located in the Santa Cruz district, only a stone's throw from the famous cathedral.
//en.hdmaria.com

Córdoba: Hotel Macia Alfaros // The hotel is located on the old Roman town wall and is only about ten minutes walk from the Mezquita and Judería. The designers have put a lot of emphasis on mood decor, which gives a little of the flair and ambience of the old Al Andaluz.
// www.maciaalfaros.com/en

○ ARTE CORDOBÉS IN CÓRDOBA

A good place for traditional Cordoba silverware. The selection ranges from small sculptures to finely processed silver and gold jewelery.

○ ALCAICERÍA IN GRANADA

Small alleys between the cathedral and Calle Reyes Católicos convey a bazaar like atmosphere. Here once lay the market of silk and jewelery traders, today the offer of souvenir shops is designed clearly to the taste of tourists.

○ HECHO EN CÁDIZ IN CÁDIZ

A successful example of how regional products can be successfully marketed. The excellent offer ranges from food, ham and cheese specialties to ceramics and braided articles from natural fibers.

DAYTRIPS

○ PARQUE NACIONAL SIERRA NEVADA

The "snow-capped mountains" south-east of Granada offer many excellent opportunities to experience nature and sporting activities both in summer and winter.

○ GIBRALTAR

When ancient seafarers sighted the Rock of Gibraltar, they believed they had reached the end of the world. From time immemorial, the Upper Rock nature reserve is home to the famous Barbary macaques of Gibraltar. The British Prime Minister Churchill himself is said to have placed them under protection so that their number would never be less than 24. The best views are from the Europa Point lighthouse on the southern tip or from the summit, which can be reached by cable car.

NOT TO BE MISSED

TAPAS, TAPAS, TAPAS

Don't miss out on feasting on tapas in one of the countless bars. Good starting point is in Seville El Rinconcillo in the Calle Gerona. The oldest bar in Seville was founded in 1670. The interior is a gem, the tapas are typically Andalusian and simply delicious. This means you might have to queue for a while.

HAVING A FEAST AT THE CONFITERÍA LA CAMPANA IN SEVILLA

Here you will find the famous Yemas Sevillanas - regional sweets made from a mixture of egg yolk and sugar, and many other sweet temptations.

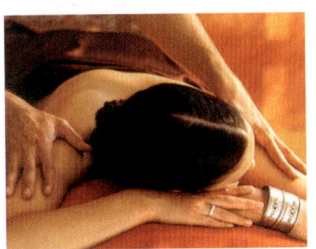

RELAXING AT THE HAMAM BAÑOS ARABES IN GRANADA

A soothing experience as well as a key to understanding the Moorish lifestyle and joie de vivre. Massages and aromatherapy according to individual tastes are also offered here.

SKIING IN THE MORNING, ENJOYING THE BEACH IN THE AFTERNOON

Spend the day in deep snow with your skis or snowboards and dip your feet in the Mediterranean sea in the evening - where else can you do that in Europe? The Sierra Nevada, with its 120 slopes, is not only the highest ski resort in Europe, but also an attraction with its high amount of sunshine hours. And last but not least, the panorama with a view over the Mediterranean is definitely worth a trip.

CELEBRATING LIFE IN SEVILLE

When the local women put on their best flamenco dresses and the men demonstrate their old gentlemanly manners, the Seville the Feria de Abril takes place. For a week, the folk festival is all about exuberant celebrations, colourful dances and traditions such as bullfights.

#03 BASEL

THE "GOLDEN GATE OF HELVETIA", AS THE FORMER EPISCOPAL CITY ON THE RHINE WAS ONCE CALLED, ASSERTS ITSELF AS THE ECONOMIC AND CULTURAL CENTRE OF A REGION THROUGH WHICH THREE NATIONAL BORDERS RUN. FROM SOUTH BADEN AND ALSACE, TENS OF THOUSANDS CROSS THE BORDER ARRIVING IN BASEL ON A DAILY BASIS, A CITY WHICH IS NOT ONLY OFFERING JOBS BUT ALSO A VERY ATTRACTIVE CULTURAL PROGRAM AND A REPUTATION AS A TRADE FAIR AND CONGRESS LOCATION. ONLY A FEW CITIES IN SWITZERLAND CAN LOOK BACK ON A MORE OUTSTANDING HUMANISTIC TRADITION THAN BASEL. IT WAS HERE IN 1460 THAT THE FIRST UNIVERSITY ON SWISS SOIL OPENED ITS DOORS, AND BASEL IS ALSO THE OLDEST PRINTING PRESS CITY IN THE COUNTRY. IN ADDITION TO THE OLD TOWN, THE BANKS OF THE RHINE WITH ITS CAFÉS AND RESTAURANTS ARE INVITING FOR A STROLL.

Above: The Basel Fasnet has its own tradition, which starts on Monday after Ash Wednesday.

Left and right: the Rhine flows through Basel and shapes life in the city. Walkers and sunset worshipers can be found along its shores, with swimmers and rowers romping on it during the summer months. The backdrop is characterised by the towers of the Basler Münster.

○ MÜNSTER

The former bishop's church, clearly visible from afar due to the two different towers, rises above the banks of the Rhine with its ornamented roof. The building, which has seen five centuries (1019-1500), combines two main styles: Romanesque and Gothic. Famous are the statues of St. George (1372) and Martin (1340) on the facade, the "Wheel of Fortuna" with its figures symbolising the ups and downs of fortune, and the Romanesque sculptural ensemble of the Galluspforte (around 1180), make it one of the most important of its kind in Switzerland.

○ KUNSTMUSEUM BASEL

It is one of the most internationally renowned museums and comprises 4,000 paintings, sculptures, installations and videos as well as 300,000 drawings and prints from seven centuries. This is a must visit museum for all lovers of art and design.

○ OLD TOWN

Historic gates, venerable magnificent buildings, nostalgic marketplaces, and all this on the idyllic banks of the Rhine: the best way to discover the attractions of the old town is on foot.

WHY VISIT IN SPRING?

THE "DREY SCHEGENSCHE DÄÄG", AS LOCALS LIKE TO CALL THE FASNET, COULD BE A GOOD ANSWER. WHEN ASH WEDNESDAY MARKS THE END OF THE SWABIAN-ALEMANNIC CARNIVAL CELEBRATIONS IN BASEL, THE COUNTDOWN FOR PROBABLY THE BIGGEST FOLK FESTIVAL IN SWITZERLAND BEGINS.DATING BACK TO THE 19TH CENTURY IN ITS PRESENT FORM, BUT THE BASEL FASNACHT DOES NOT HAVE MUCH IN COMMON WITH THE GERMAN CARNIVAL CELEBRATIONS.

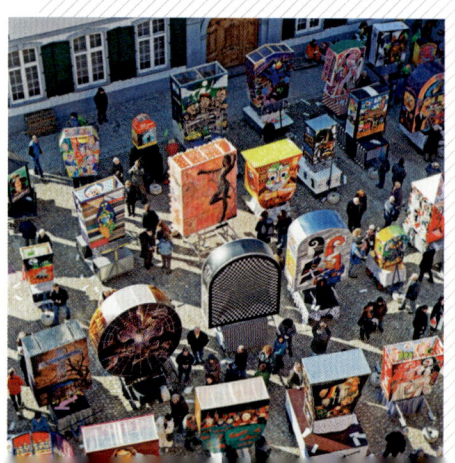

Left: Drummers and piccolo players make their way through the city at Fasnet with their fantastic masks.

At the top: The construction of the city hall began in 1504, dominating the market square with its red sandstone.

Above: The Merian Gardens are the city's recreational destination. Parts of them originated already in the early 18th century.

Right: The Spalentor was part of the once mighty inner Basel city wall.

○ MARKET SQUARE WITH CITY HALL

The most striking building at Basel market square is also its most important. The building made from bright red sandstone is the city hall. Weekly markets are held on the forecourt, where Swiss delicacies can be sampled.

○ TINGUELY FOUNTAIN

Where formerly Basel's Municipal Theater could be found, the extraordinary fountain of the artist Jean Tinguely was built in 1977. Ten moving water sculptures playfully interact here in a pool of water and are one of Basel's most popular landmarks.

○ KUNSTHALLE BASEL

The Kunsthalle is an institution in the city. Built in the second half of the 19th century, today it is a place for artistic works and exhibitions by local and international artists of the contemporary avant-garde.

○ CITY GATES

The Spalentor is the most imposing of the three still preserved Basel city gates. If you look closer, you will find a variety of figures such as 15th century console figures: a Madonna and two prophets. The St. Alban Gate was restored to its original state after a renovation, including its heavy piles. The massive wooden barrier was lowered in case of danger, blocking access to the city. The third gate is the 14th century St. John's Gate.

○ MERIAN GARDENS

Who would have thought that Switzerland could be so rich in flowers? In this area, kitchen gardens and agriculture combine with an English garden, several collection gardens and the Villa Merian to form a remarkable recreational area.

○ ROCHE TOWER

At 178 metres, this is the tallest tower in all of Switzerland. This office building of the Swiss pharmaceutical company Hoffmann-La Roche is proudly presented by locals as the city's most modern landmark.

GOING OUT

Zum Gifthüttli // Enjoy a rustic and traditional meal in the Gifthüttli. However, the restaurant made a name for itself for the numerous variations of Cordon Bleu, from classic to creative stuffing with shoulder cuts of ham and apple chutney.

// www.gifthuettli.ch

Cheval Blanc // Haute cuisine in Basel can be found in the restaurant Cheval Blanc. Exquisite specialties from Peter Knogl are served with a good glass of wine, mainly from the French cuisine, but internationally inspired.

// www.lestroisrois.com/en/restaurants/ cheval-blanc

Bar Rouge // Here it is the view that takes your breath away. After all, Bar Rouge is located on the roof of the tallest building in the city, the Messeturm. In honor of its name, it shines in its red light every evening.

// www.barrouge.ch

SHOPPING

○ MARKETHALL BASEL

Original Swiss cheese and chocolate or maybe you prefer luxurious oysters? In the ambience of this market hall, you will find everything under one roof. A little tip for all parents, there is even a small children's market hall in which the little ones can play.
// www.altemarkthalle.ch

WHERE TO STAY

Nomad // The designer Nomad Hotel offers more than just stylishly furnished rooms, including free bike rental it's ideal for a speedier city exploration tour.
// **www.nomad.ch**

Les Trois Rois // Traditional and luxurious, Les Trois Rois is the symbol of a Grand Hotel in Basel. Attention to detail meets five-star hospitality, which leaves no wishes unfulfilled.
// **www.lestroisrois.com/en/hotel**

Hotel Euler // If you are looking for a centrally located hotel for your weekend trip, that is easily accessible to all Basel's sights, you should stay at the Hotel Euler. Located directly at the main station, the most interesting sights and shopping destinations are only a stone's throw away.
// **www.hoteleuler.ch**

○ SHOPPING STREET FREIE STRASSE

The Swiss are known for their watches. But also for their love for anything luxurious. Both are combined on this exclusive shopping mile. Top-class fashion boutiques, jewellers, shops for home decoration, but also fine restaurants, bars and confectionery. If you are looking for something exclusive, you are in the right spot.

○ SHOPPING AROUND THE SPALENBERG

Here, consumption meets culture, the narrow streets and historic buildings of the Spalenberg accommodate today small fashion stores, as well as numerous art galleries and souvenir shops.

○ STÜCKI SHOPPINGCENTER

You can stroll and shop in two shopping areas in this mall. In addition, numerous restaurants, cafés and bars invite you to take a break. And the little ones are not left out either: In addition to regular craft events, there is also a children's play area.
// www.stuecki-shopping.ch

DAYTRIPS

○ VITRA DESIGN MUSEUM IN WEILAMRHEIN

This world-leading design museum offers visitors so much to see that a whole day trip should be definitely planned. From the outside, the futuristic building by the American architect, Frank O. Gehry, will amaze fans of modern design. The curved construction is extraordinary and took three years to build. Inside, the museum hosts two to three exhibitions each year on historical and current developments in design.

○ RHEINFALL WATERFALL

With a height of 23 metres and a width of 150 metres, it is considered the largest waterfall in Europe. A day trip here is certainly worthwhile because of the adjacent untouched landscape, which just invites for a walk.

NOT TO BE MISSED

TASTING AUTHENTIC FOOD IN THE LÄCKERLI-HUUS

It is well known that the Swiss love chocolate. But the fact that they also excellently understand the baking trade shows in Basel. The Basel Läckerli is a ginger-bread-like pastry that tastes delicious and makes for a great souvenir.

CRUISE ALONG THE RHINE ON A "FÄHRI"

On these nostalgic ships, you not only get a great new view of Basel's shore side, but you will also discover some architectural highlights, which will only stimulate a more intensive exploration of the city.

A VISIT TO THE FONDATION BEYELER

In this art museum in Riehen, visitors can expect to see numerous masterpieces. From Monet, Cézanne and Van Gogh through Picasso, Matisse and Klee to Giacometti, Warhol and Bacon, the most diverse artistic genres can be admired here.

FLOAT DOWN THE RHINE

The Rhine shapes the image of the city and invites all visitors to let themselves be carried away by its idyll. Swimming in the Rhine is also becoming increasingly popular. You can just drift down the river slowly with the current, your clothes safely packed in waterproof bags, which the city of Basel makes available.

EXPERIENCE CULTURE FOR FREE

In Basel, the first Sunday of each month is called Happy Day. On this day, many museums open their doors for free, including the Art Museum and the Natural History Museum. A day that bargain hunters and the culture hungry should remember.

#04   CINQUE TERRE

THE REGION NORTH OF PORTOVENERE WITH ITS "FIVE PLACES" ("CINQUE TERRE") - MONTEROSSO; VERNAZZA; CORNIGLIA; MANAROLA; AND, RIOMAGGIORE - AS WELL AS THE ISLANDS PALMARIA, TINO AND TINETTO, ARE ONE OF THE MOST CHARMING COASTLINES OF THE RIVIERA. THE "CINQUE TERRE" CLING SPECTACULARLY TO THE ROCKS AND BAYS OF THE LIGURIAN CLIFFS BETWEEN LEVANTO AND PORTOVENERE. UNTIL TODAY, THERE IS NO ROAD CONNECTION BETWEEN THEM ALONG THE COAST, PEOPLE EARLIER MASTERED THE ROUGH TERRAIN ONLY USING FOOTPATHS AND STAIRS.

Left: The church of Santa Margherita d'Antiochia dominates the silhouette of the fishing village of Vernazza. It dates from the year 1318 and has a special feature with the east-facing entrance.

Upper right: Riomaggiore is the easternmost town of the Cinque Terre. Due to its exposed position on one of the rock tongues, ships and boats are the most used means of transport.

Bottom right: The old town of Monterosso is located on the hill San Cristoforo. You should spend some time in this place, even just to admire the colourful streets.

○ RIOMAGGIORE

Riomaggiore is perhaps the most visually attractive of the Cinque Terre hamlets. Right and left of a tiny bay, where there is a ramp for the fishing boats, the town looms above. The boats themselves lie on the edge of the lane, which extends from the harbor to the rear on dry land, because the port, if you like to call it that, is far too small to accommodate them all. The façades are painted in Mediterranean colours, but mostly weathered. You can hardly find a more romantic place than the Cinque Terre with their many small restaurants and bars and the very numerous apartments.

○ CORNIGLIA

Corniglia is a dream. It lies on the edge of a steep cliff facing the sea, on a rocky outcrop 100 meters high, and is surrounded by expansive vineyards. The village is the smallest, but at the same time the highest of the Cinque Terre. An insider tip for a spectacular view of the Riviera is the large terrace behind the Cappella dei Flagellanti di Santa Caterina. The chapel is located in the main square and was built in the 18th century. Corniglia is the only place in the Cinque Terre that does not have its own port. Arriving by car is very difficult, so you better take the train or walk to Corniglia.

○ MONTEROSSO AL MARE

Monterosso al Mare has several unique selling points despite its equally charming neighboring villages. It has the only real sandy beach of the Cinque Terre, also, the village is separated by a rock protruding into the sea in two parts. A 100-metre-long pedestrian tunnel leads through the rock, the Torre Aurora watchtower can be found here. Visually still a little more exciting, however, is the Statua del Gigante on the western side of the bay. The 14-me-

tre-high colossus, representing the God of the Sea, Neptune, that is said to protect the fishermen. The 170-ton figure looks to the beach and the sea with its head bent forward. It was designed in 1910 by the architect Francesco Levacher and carved out of stone by the sculptor Arrio Minerbi. After damage in the Second World War, it was rebuilt in a slightly different form.

○ MANAROLA

Manarola is probably the oldest of the five villages. One does not know for certain, but the foundation

stone of the church of San Lorenzo bears the date of the year 1160. It is also interesting, however, that the cultivation of wine in Manarola must have a long tradition. Even ancient Roman scriptures pointed to the Sciacchetra, which was pressed here and is still cultivated in terraced fields. The houses of the former artists' village seem to be glued to each other and superimposed on the hillside in crazy interlacing. If you have time, make a detour to the small pilgrimage church of Nostra Signora della Salute in Volastra.

○ VERNAZZA

The place looks as if it had been poured into the mountains. Like a stronghold, a cliff rises above the sea and shields itself behind a natural harbour. A stream flows directly into the Mediterranean and supplies fresh water. With such perfect conditions, it is no wonder that the history of Vernazza can be traced back to the year 1080. At that time, the town acted as a port for the Genoese fleet. Again and again pirates arrived, so the population began to build stronger walls and fortresses. The Castle Doria, at the top of the village, is more than 1,000 years old and has been constantly expanded and extended. Impressive!

Top left: As in most places of the Cinque Terre, fishing is the main source of income in Manarola. However, the roaring surf makes a direct mooring impossible. The fishing boats must therefore be pulled up on winches in a rather spectacular way.

Bottom left: In the harbor of Vernazza, the lights of the evening illumination are reflected in the water.

GOING OUT

Riomaggiore: Ristorante Dau Cila // Cinque Terre is known for limes, olives, pesto and seafood. You can feast on all the specialties in the Ristorante Dau Cila and enjoy fine wine from the in-house wine cellar.

// **www.ristorantedaucila.com**

WHERE TO STAY

Monterosso: Hotel Porto Roca // Wake up to the view of the deep blue sea at Hotel Porto Roca. Located on the outskirts of Monterosso al Mare, it is, above all, a place to admire nature in peace and transquility.
// **www.portoroca.it**

La Spezia: Hotel Firenze e Continentale // The hotel is located not directly in the National Park, but in La Spezia. Due to the good train connection and the central location in the city, the Cinque Terre are only a few minutes away.
// **www.hotelfirenzecontinentale.it**

NOT TO BE MISSED

HIKING ON THE PATH OF LOVE

Kiss on the famous Via dell'Amore, the "Path of Love" between Manarola and Riomaggiore - provided it is opened to tourists again. It is a walkway with extremely romantic sunsets, which unfortunately was closed due to landslides in 2012. The reopening is expected soon. You can find more information about the path either at Manarola or Riomaggiore.

VISITING A WINE TERRACE

From the Muretti a secco, so called dry walls, the agricultural terraces in the Cinque Terre offer an impressive sight. Created over generations, next to wine, olives and vegetables were grown on them. From the path above and between Corniglia and Volastra, you can admire the scenary particularly well.

IMPROVING YOUR CULINARY SKILLS

If you would like to say that you can really cook like an Italian, you should not miss the opportunity to attend one of the cooking classes during your visit to Cinque Terre. Especially popular are the courses where you learn to make traditional pesto yourself. Also, learning about the regional olive oil is an added culinary education.

CELEBRATING LIFE THE ITALIAN WAY

It is well known that the Italians do not miss an opportunity to party – if you visit at the right time, you should definitely party with them. In the spring, for example, you can watch the processions on Labor Day, or the Liberation Day on April 25th. The month of May in Monterosso turns the city yellow when the "Festa di Limone" ("Festival of Lemons") starts. The whole village is then adorned with the fruits. Do not miss the culinary specialties, especially the Torta al limone, and the Limoncino.

ENJOYING THE VIEW AT THE "PUNTA MESCO"

You can reach Punta Mesco by hiking trails from Monterosso. The special feature of this vantage point is the view of all five villages of the Cinque Terre, arranged one after the other. Spectacular!

#05   CORNWALL

THE SOUTH WEST OF THE UK'S MAIN ISLAND HAS A WEALTH OF TOURIST ATTRACTIONS TO OFFER - HISTORIC TOWNS AND CHARMING SEASIDE RESORTS; MYSTERIOUS STONE CIRCLES AND MAJESTIC CATHEDRALS, TO NAME BUT A FEW. IN ADDITION, YOU WILL EXPERIENCE A VARIETY OF LANDSCAPES - FELLS, HEATHS, THE FERTILE GARDEN OF ENGLAND. BEAUTIFUL FISHING VILLAGES SUCH AS CAWSAND AND KINGSAND; THE TIDAL ISLAND OF ST. MICHAEL'S MOUNT; WIDE SANDY BEACHES AT ST LOY; PORTHCURNO; AND "LAND'S END". IN THE TRUE SENSE OF THE WORD, IT IS THE END OF THE ISLAND AND ENGLAND'S MOST WESTERN POINT WITH STEEP, UP TO 50 METRES HIGH CLIFFS. THE POPULAR SEASIDE RESORT OF NEWQUAY IS KNOWN FOR ITS WIDE SANDY BEACHES AND HIGH ATLANTIC WAVES AS THE SURFER'S DORADO; AND, ST. IVES IS THE QUINTESSENTIAL ENGLISH COASTAL TOWN.

Above: Probably because of its close resemblance to Mont Saint-Michel, the island in front of Penzance was named after the French original - the legend of the appearance of St. Michael was probably invented later, also based on the French model.

Left: One-eyed Nelson, a grey seal, was a frequent visitor to Looes Harbor and an entertainer for everyone for over 25 years. After his death in 2003, a bronze monument was erected in his honour.

○ LOOE

With the Victorian ideal to spend a vacation at the sea, Looe has become more and more a tourist town with many hotels, bed & breakfast and leisure facilities. The beach at Tailland Bay - not far away - is considered the "playground" of Plymouth.

○ NEWQUAY

The fishing village once specialised in sardines that were exported to the Mediterranean. In the 19th century it became the most important port on the northwest coast of Cornwall - mainly for coal and kaolin. Thanks to the railway connection, tourist development soon set in, making the city one of the most important centres in the region for more than 100 years. A whole series of smaller beaches, protected by mighty rocky outcrops, invite both big and small visitors to bathe. Especially Fistral Beach, this is a mecca for windsurfers and surfers who meet here for their annual competitions.

○ ST. MICHAEL'S MOUNT

In front of the city of St. Michael's Bay, the old castle of St. Michael's Mount sits proudly on a granite island. Legend has it that the Archangel Michael appeared in front of fishermen in 495 AD on the rock above the sea. The rugged island west of Cornwall was henceforth called St. Michael's Mount, and a church was built thereon. The former Benedictine monastery passed into the possession of the Crown in 1535, and was converted into a fortress. Historians date the monastery back to the 8th century. At that time, Celtic monks erected a monastery on Mont-Saint-Michel in Brittany, which looked remarkably like its counterpart in Cornwall. At low tide, the bay can be crossed on foot, otherwise you can reach the castle by boats during high tide. For a spectacular view over the "Penwith Peninsula", it is best to rock climb, however it is 70-metre-high.

WHY VISIT IN SPRING?

THE MILD CLIMATE MAKES SPRING-TIME IDEAL FOR HIKING, AND THE PLACES IN CORNWALL ARE NOT AS CROWDED AS THEY TEND TO BE IN SUMMER. EVEN THE SUN, WHICH IS STILL LOW, CONJURES UP WONDER-FULLY WARM LIGHTING MOODS. AL-THOUGH, THE MAIN ATTRACTION FOR A TRIP AT THIS TIME OF YEAR IS THE COLOURFUL FLORAL SPLENDOR - FROM MAGNOLIAS TO BLUBELLS - WHICH SEEMS TO INVADE THE ENTIRE REGION.

Top left: Bluebells, English bells, are typical spring flowers.
Bottom left: Beach caranations light up with the colours of the sky and look down on the Bedruthan Steps.
At the top: Porthmeor Beach in St. Ives.
Above: Land's End is a symbolic place: the most western end of the British mainland.

Right: Mussels are common on the menu in many Cornish restaurants - no wonder they can be found here in huge numbers just off the coast.

○ BEDRUTHAN STEPS

In a bay between Newquay and Padstow, five mighty boulders are picturesquely situated on the beach, as if thrown by supernatural forces. Early on, they inspired the imagination of the travelers, who eventually turned them into the stepping stones of the mythological giant Bedruthan. However, their formation is based solely on the leaching of the softer rock layers.

○ PENZANCE

The largest city of Cornwall is Penzance, however with just 21,000 inhabitants. It is a good starting point for a wonderful 35-kilometre drive across the Penwith Peninsula to Land's End. The area is also called the "Cornish Riviera" because of its mild climate. The town center is the old quarter between Chapel Street and Market Jew Street, where you can still bask in the atmosphere of the long-forgotten seafaring season.

○ ST. IVES

Today, Cornwall is mainly associated with beaches and beach holidays - tourism is also the principal source of income for the artist town of St. Ives, in which William Turner already praised the magnificent light. Grey houses made of granite characterise this former fishing village with one of the most beautiful beaches in Cornwall. Fascinated by light and landscape, painters and sculptors have come to St. Ives since the last century. Meanwhile, the Tate Gallery has opened a museum high above the northern Porthmeor Beach, where you can admire the works of the artists of St. Ives.

○ LAND'S END

The westernmost point of England is dominated by an open heath and moorland, which is virtually dotted with archaeological sites - tombs from the Iron Age and Bronze Age; Stone Circles; Celtic Crosses; and entire villages from the time before the birth of Christ testify to the millennia-old settlement history. The waves of the Atlantic were constantly crashing against the mighty rocks which the Romans named "Belerion" (Seat of the storms). The tip of Britain's main island is now dominated by a much-visited theme park dedicated to the history of Cornwall.

GOING OUT

Newquay: The Boathouse // Seafood is a must in Cornwall! The Boathouse in Newquay satisfies not only with excellent quality of the delicacies from fresh fish and seafood, but also with the perfect location right on the harbour and the maritime ambience.

// www.the-boathouse-newquay.co.uk

Carbis Bay: The Bean Inn // Vegetarians and vegans should not be stopped from travelling to Cornwall by the ubiquitous seafood specialties, because restaurants like the Bean Inn in Carbis Bay (near St. Ives) are devoted entirely to fish and meatless delights.

// www.thebeaninn.co.uk

Penzance: Victoria Inn // Noble and traditional, one of the oldest inns in Cornwall. Seasonal ingredients and regional recipes are combined with stylish decor and a well stocked bar. Do not miss out on the desserts.

// www.victoriainn-penzance.co.uk

SHOPPING

○ HELSTON FARMERS' MARKET

More local is barely possible: Farmers' markets can be found throughout Cornwall, one of the largest food-based markets is held on the first Saturday of each month in Helston.

// www.helstonfarmersmarket.co.uk

○ DRAKE CIRCUS SHOPPING CENTER

Located in downtown Plymouth, Drake Circus is a classic shopping centre with a wide variety of shops, restaurants and cafés.

// www.drakecircus.com

○ EAST LOOE

Looe does not offer big shopping malls, but there are small streets with lovingly run local shops, which make it wonderful to stroll. Especially in East Looe, you will find gift shops, antique shops and quaint boutiques.

○ GALERIES IN ST. IVES

Art lovers should not miss St. Ives. You will find galleries displaying a wide variety of works of art and offering them for sale everywhere, from classic oil paintings to modern sculptures or handcrafted ceramics.

// www.stives-cornwall.co.uk

WHERE TO STAY

Newquay: The Scarlet // Modern, luxurious and located directly on the sea, the Scarlet is ideal for those who have discerning taste and value relaxation in stunning pool and Day Spa area.

// www.scarlethotel.co.uk

Penzance: Artist Residence // Individuality is key at the Artist Residence. The rooms have been designed from a variety of artists and you will find unique rooms with hand-painted walls, vintage furniture and modern photographs.

// www.artistresidence.co.uk/ our-hotels/cornwall

Padstow: St. Petroc's Hotel // Those who like it idyllic should consider a classic bed and breakfast accommodation. St. Petroc's in Padstow combines English authenticity and comfort.

//www.rickstein.com/stay/ st-petrocs-hotel

DAYTRIPS

○ ISLES OF SCILLY

Forty kilometres off the coast to the southwest are the 140 Scilly Isles, which can be reached by ferry from Penzance. The approximately 2,000 inhabitants, who mainly live from tourism and flowers export, are spread over five inhabited islands. The main source of income used to be fishing, today it is tourism. On foot or by bike, explore the islands through their rugged granite rocks, white sand beaches and turquoise bays. In the mild climate, palm trees and exotic plants thrive, a collection of typical Scilly flora can be found in the Abbey Garden of Tresco. Halfway between Land's End and these islands are said to be the English Atlantis, the lost land of Lyonesse as mentioned in the Arthurian legend - but it has not been found so far. Though, there are a number of wrecks to admire.

NOT TO BE MISSED

VISITING EDEN PROJECT

These huge geodesic domes can be seen from afar. The spectacular Eden Project at Bodelva was completed on a 14-acre site in a disused kaolin pit. In two gigantic greenhouses, gardeners created two climate zones - the tropical rainforest zone, and the Mediterranean zone. The houses are densely covered with plants of these regions, so that a natural ecosystem could develop.

FOLLOWING IN KING ARTHUR'S FOOTSTEPS

The legendary ruins on Tintagel Head are considered the birthplace of King Arthur. Behind the small town of Tintagel, a path leads over the cliffs to a craggy green rocky outcrop in the Atlantic, which can be reached via steep stairs.

PASTIES, PASTRIES AND PIES

The British are not exactly famous for their bread, but they are known for their pastry. Pastries can be made from shortcrust, puff pastry or choux, and filled with both sweet and savory ingredients. For typical British pies, the filling plays the main role. The dough is usually unsweetened, but very fatty. Fruit- such as apples, blueberries, cherries or rhubarb - or nut and syrup mixtures are often added before the baking process. The most famous pasty comes from Cornwall. A Cornish pasty is a crescent-shaped pie pastry stuffed with beef, potatoes, onions and turnips.

BATHING IN THE JUBILEE POOL

In 1935, Penzance opened an impressive Art Deco outdoor swimming pool. In the form of a triangle, you can swim in the seawater, regardless of tides and protected from waves and currents.

#06   CÔTE D'AZUR

"THE BLUE COAST" IS WHAT THE FRENCH CALL THE MOSTLY ROCKY COASTLINE BETWEEN THE MASSIF DE L'ESTÉREL AND THE MARITIME ALPS. BUT OF COURSE, CÔTE D'AZUR IS NOT JUST A NAME OF A GEOGRAPHICAL REGION. RATHER, IT COMBINES VARIOUS LIFESTYLES: GLITZ AND GLAMOR, STARS AND STARLETS, BEACHES AND NIGHTLIFE, HUGE SHIPS IN THE HARBOURS AND VILLAS OVERLOOKING THE SEA. IN FACT, AFTER THE FIRST CANNES FILM FESTIVAL OF 1946, THE INTERNATIONAL JETSET OF THIS DREAMSCAPE SUCCESSIVELY SEIZED THE SURROUNDING AREA. AS A RESULT, FISHING VILLAGES SUCH AS SAINT-TROPEZ QUICKLY BECAME EXCLUSIVE HOLIDAY RESORTS. THE CHARMING ANTIBES STILL GIVES AN IDEA OF WHAT THE REGION USED TO BE LIKE. THE RICH AND THE BEAUTIFUL HAVE NOT WITHDRAWN COMPLETELY FROM THE "CÔTE", BUT NOWADAYS MOST PEOPLE WILL FEEL LESS ESTRANGED HERE.

Above: The "Club 55" is the most famous beach restaurant on the Côte d'Azur. It is located at the Pampelonne of Saint-Tropez.

Left: Around 1870, rich English people discovered the beneficial effects of the mild climate of the Côte d'Azur. Villas and sumptuous Belle Epoque hotels are reminiscent in Menton since the heyday of the British winter residences between the Alps and the sea.

○ SAINT-TROPEZ

Ever since Roger Vadim first directed the film "And God Created Woman" starring Brigitte Bardot in 1956, the once-dreamy fishing village has become a sophisticated seaside resort. Saint-Tropez is globally known as a playground for the rich and famous. Like no other place on the Côte d'Azur, it embodies the dream of the "sweet life." The summer is spent at the marina, where luxury yachts lie close to each other. The sinfully expensive bars and clubs are well visited, the old town streets full of day visitors. Despite this hype, Saint-Tropez has still remained a picturesque little coastal town.

○ CITADEL

With its hexagonal floor plan, the citadel could easily be mistaken for a military facility from the air. The Citadel of Saint-Tropez dates from the late 16th century and is one of the main attractions outside the centre. A beautiful footpath leads up the hill,

lined with Eucalyptus and Laurel trees.

○ PAMPELONNE

If there is a beach that perfectly represents Saint-Tropez, then it is probably this one. At least since the year 1956, when the young Brigitte Bardot starred in the film "And God Created Woman" with Curd Jürgens. The beach Pampelonne was the main film location and is still one of the most beautiful in the area - and the most popular. Here you can find the "Club 55", one of the most famous beach bars on the coast.

○ CANNES

The Celts and the Romans settled on the Golfe de la Napoule, but it was not until the 19th century that the bay became an attractive destination for the English and their construction of beautiful villas, hotels and the "Boulevard La Croisette" began. The old town of Le Suquet rises above the old port on Mont Chevalier. The summit features an 11th-century

WHY VISIT IN SPRING?

TO NOT SPEND CARNIVAL IN THE COLD AND DRIZZLE. IF YOU GO TO NICE FOR THE MARDI GRAS FESTIVAL IN FEBRUARY, YOU WILL BE LUCKY ENOUGH TO BE ABLE TO CELEBRATE WITH SUNSHINE AND OVER 14 DEGREES. THE BIGGEST WINTER EVENT ON THE CÔTE D'AZUR IS THE VERY LAST FESTIVAL BEFORE SHROVE TUESDAY AND THE - AT LEAST IN EARLIER TIMES - ABSTINENT TIME WITH LITTLE FOOD OR ALCOHOL. MORE THAN 1,000 INTERNATIONAL MUSICIANS AND DANCERS ARRIVE DURING THE TWO WEEKS, WHILE MAKEUP ARTISTS CREATE COSTUMES OF FEATHERS, RHINESTONES AND SEQUINS FOR THE GRAND PARADES THAT RUN THROUGH THE STREETS. IN MENTON, A FEW WEEKS LATER, THE LEMON FESTIVAL IS CELEBRATED. FOR TWO WEEKS, THE EVENT ATTRACTS HUNDREDS OF THOUSANDS OF VISITORS.

watchtower and the nearby Musée de la Castre. From the observation deck behind the gothic church of Notre-Dame-de-l'Espérance you will have a magnificent view of the entire bay.

○ BOULEVARD DE LA CROISETTE

An Englishman, Lord Brougham, brought the European nobility to the Croisette in 1834, with the building of the sophisticated Carlton Hotel with its white sugar baker's façade. Apart from well-known luxury hotels, the famous promenade is also home to a multitude of boutiques with names such as Prada, Gucci, Chanel, Louis Vuitton, as well as exquisite restaurants. The street is also known for the "Palais des Festivals et des Congrès", or better known in short as the "Cannes Film Festival" - the annual film festival is held, during which Hollywood stars, film directors, the rich and beautiful get together in one place here. However, this is a place where life can be enjoyed all year long.

○ ANTIBES

Especially interesting is the pretty, winding old town of Antibes and the cathedral with its Baroque façade from the 17th century. Its transept and choir date

Above: The port of Cannes. The city is known for its annual film festival; the rich and famous of the world meet on the Boulevard de la Croisette.

Left: Parade during the Mardi Gras in Nice.

back to the 12th century. Just next to the cathedral stands the massive construction of the former Grimaldi Castle with a 17th century fortified tower. A truly magnificent sight.

○ JUAN-LES-PINS

A small pine grove once gave this place its name. The Duke of Albany had the idea in the late 19th century. A few years later, a US millionaire, Frank Jay Gould, discovered the place and had a summer casino built here. This new attraction and the beautiful beaches quickly attracted wealthy and beautiful people, and so Marlene Dietrich, Josephine Baker, Charly Chaplin, Pablo Picasso, Klaus Mann and Coco Chanel all came to the small town that is now part of Antibes.

GOING OUT

Saint-Tropez: Club 55 // This bar is one of the classic clubs of Saint-Tropez. A bit out of the way, it has the character of a beach bar, but at the highest level, here you can sit on designer chairs under the gnarled trees, drinking and dining, and people watching.

// www.club55.fr

Nizza: JAN // In Nice, the JAN is the address known for top class culinary. Here, every dish is a unique composition, the could rightly be "a feast for the eyes". The chef is a native South African and combines recipes from his homeland with local ingredients.

// www.restaurantjan.com

Antibes: L'Oursin // Seafood and fish in all variations, a sunny terrace and maritime decor. L'Oursin looks and feels like a typical Mediterranean fish restaurant. Especially recommended here are the fresh oysters.

// www.restaurant-oursin.fr

Right: View of the old town of Antibes. The tower of the Picasso Museum rising high to the skyline.

○ NIZZA

The "secret" capital of the Côte d'Azur, and actual capital of the region Alpes-Maritimes is beautifully located on the Maritime Bay (Baie des Anges). Nizza is surrounded by the foothills of the Alps, and is a place of contrasts. While the beautiful boulevards try to keep the memories of the Belle Époque alive, parts of the old town still feel like they belong to an Italian village.

○ PROMENADE DES ANGLAIS

The flagship and landmark of Nice is the Promenade des Anglais directly on the sea. Rich British citizens chose Nice as their retirement home in the mid-19th century, hence the name "Promenade of the English". Today, there are numerous restaurants, cafés and, of course, hotels with sea views on the 8-kilometer long beach boulevard.

○ OLDTOWN

The old town presents itself as an extremely lively district, which not only boasts numerous Baroque buildings, but also a colorful gastronomic scene and diverse shopping opportunities. Countless of small shops, market stalls and restaurants lure with culinary delicacies in the quaint streets of the quarter.

○ ART MUSEUMS

It would be a mistake to visit Nice and ignore the noteworthy art museums. Even the façade of the Musée d'Art Moderne et d'Art Contemporain, the

Museum of Modern Art, is spectacular. The Yves Bayard-designed building was opened in 1990. The painters Chagall and Matisse are also honored here. The Musée Marc Chagall houses paintings, sketches, sculptures and glass windows by the artist. The Musée Matisse is based in a converted villa with 68 oil paintings and sculptural works. The Musée des Arts Asiatiques presents a different kind of art with a number of collectibles from Asia and also organises tea ceremonies and even dance events.

SHOPPING

○ CAGNES SUR MER: POLYGONE RIVIERA

The recently constructed centre is ideally suited for an expansive shopping day. Located in Cagnes sur Mer, between Antibes and Nice, it brings together more than 100 different shops, restaurants and cafés in the open air. // www.polygone-riviera.fr

○ PERFUME STORES IN GRASSE

Patrick Süskind's novel "The Perfume" made the village famous, and attracts connoisseurs of fine fragrences. Fragonard, Molinard and Galimard are the three most well known perfumeries in the area.

○ CANNES: RUE D'ANTIBES

Designer boutiques, international brands line up on Rue d'Antibes. A typical, vibrant shopping street, in which everyone will find something. For the pleasure of the palate, a visit to the chocolateries "Maiffret", or "Chez Bruno" is worthwhile for authentic delights.

○ SAINT-TROPEZ: PLACE DES LICES

The real provencal lifestyle. The market on the Place des Lices in Saint-Tropez takes place every Tuesday and Saturday, and offers local specialties, tunics, jewelery and much more. In addition, locals meet for a game of boules here.

WHERE TO STAY

Saint-Tropez: Hotel Le Byblos // The hotel complex, with its 5-star standard, is not only a popular place to sleep, but also a very good destination for going out with its Caves du Roy. Very exclusive.
// www.byblos.com

Nizza: Negresco // One of the most traditional hotels on the Côte d'Azur, and it has already accommodated many famous people in a bed under the dome created by Gustave Eiffel. The luxurious charm of the Belle Epoque is well preserved, but you will find other styles in some of the rooms.
// www.hotel-negresco-nice.com

Cannes: Five Seas Hotel // Centrally located, the Five Seas Hotel is a suitable base for short breaks. In the evening you can relax from spending the day in the city, in the sauna or the good restaurant on the roof overlooking the old town.
// www.fiveseashotel.com

NOT TO BE MISSED

MUSÉE DE L'ANNONCIADE IN SAINT-TROPEZ

The building once served as a sacred chapel. The painter Paul Signac went through a great period of creativity in the city, leaving many works to be shown to people here and now. They had first been exhibited in the town hall, but soon needed more space and the church became a museum. At first, only the upper floor was used, but soon the showroom conquered the whole house. Today, the museum shows mainly 19th and 20th century art, created on the Côte d'Azur or by painters who worked there.

STROLLING ALONG THE COUS SALEYA OF NIZZA

The heart of old Nice is the Cours Saleya, an elongated square where a flower market takes place every day, except Mondays. In the south, the Cours Saleya is lined with a series of flat roof houses, which are now joined by nice little restaurants, boutiques and galleries.

ROMANTIC SUNSETS AT THE CASTLE OF NIZZA

The Colline du Château in Nice is the ideal spot for a romantic picnic, where you can enjoy the view over the Mediterranean sea and the sparkling roofs of the city, delight in the setting sun and just let your mind wander. The vantage point can be reached either by a short hike or with a free of charge elevator.

PLAGE DES CANEBIERS

The beach of the Canebiers is just a few steps from the Villa La Madrague, where Brigitte Bardot resides to this day and once lived her love story with Gunter Sachs. If you want to follow in their footsteps, this beach is a must.

#07   DUBLIN

DUBLIN IS IN EVERY RESPECT THE CENTRE OF THE REPUBLIC OF IRELAND: POLITICALLY, ECONOMICALLY AND CULTURALLY. THE CELTIC SETTLEMENT, WHICH WAS OFFICIALLY FOUNDED BY THE VIKINGS IN THE 9TH CENTURY, BECAME POPULAR IN THE EARLY 18TH CENTURY WHEN IT WAS REORGANISED AT THE BEHEST OF A MEDIEVAL SETTLEMENT INTO A GENEROUS GEORGIAN TOWN. SOON AFTER THE INDEPENDENCE OF THE IRISH FREE STATE FROM GREAT BRITAIN (1922), DUBLIN BECAME THE CAPITAL. TODAY, EVERY EIGHTH INHABITANT OF THE COUNTRY LIVES IN THIS CITY.

Above: The road from O'Connell Street to O'Connell Bridge is the hub of downtown Dublin. The 70-metre-long, and almost as wide bridge, was built at the end of the 18th century.

Left: Temple Bar is not just the name of a trendy pub, but of a neighbourhood that stretches from the south of Liffey to Dame Street.

○ GENERAL POST OFFICE

The Classic Post Office building on O'Connell Street was the setting for one of the most important events in Irish history. On Easter Monday in 1916, Irish rebels occupied the post office for a week until it was stormed by British troops. Today, in this national monument day-to-day postal matters are dealt with as usual.

○ O'CONNELL BRIDGE

Many bridges connect the southern part to the northern part of the city via the Liffey, but the most magnificent is the 50-metre-wide, busy, three-arched O'Connell Bridge from the late 18th century. Street vendors sell a variety of items, and from here you have a nice view over the bustling O'Connell Street and across the river.

○ TEMPLE BAR

The Temple Bar district is the epitome of Dublin's wild night life. During the day, the small district is almost tranquil. At night, however, the pubs and clubs are teeming with life. More sophisticated is the Irish Film Institute on Eustace Street with its film library, bookstore and restaurant, as well as the Saturday farmers' market at Meeting House Square.

○ DUBLIN CASTLE

Dublin Castle is a huge complex of different styles and has been the symbol of the widely hated English domination for centuries. The Vikings erected a fort there in 841, and the Anglo-Normans expanded it several centuries later until in the 13th century it was converted into a castle. During the British domination, the building served as the headquarters of the English Viceroy in Ireland, as well as the headquarters of the police, and even as a prison. Today however there are regular public banquets.

○ CHRIST CHURCH CATHEDRAL

The Christ Church Cathedral is probably one of the oldest churches in Dublin and was originally founded by the Vikings. In its present version, however, it was not completed until the 1870s. In addition to the magnificent interior, the crypt with its coffins and tombs, which belongs to the oldest part of the church, are very much worth seeing.

WHY VISIT IN SPRING?

WHEREVER YOU SEE AN "IRISH SHAM-ROCK", ST. PATRICK'S DAY IS CELEBRATED WITH GREEN BEER AND A LOT OF FUN. THE MOST AUTHENTIC WAY TO CELEBRATE THE IRISH PATRON SAINT'S DAY IS IN THE CAPITAL DUBLIN. AT THIS FESTIVAL - THE MOTHER OF ALL IRISH FESTIVALS - HUNDREDS OF THOUSANDS GATHER IN THE STREETS AND VENUES OF THE CITY CENTRE TO "HONOUR" THE SAINT WHO IS SAID TO HAVE DRIVEN THE SNAKES OUT OF THE COUNTRY. STREET THEATERS, A PARTY MEADOW AND A MUSIC FESTIVAL ARE ON OFFER, AND THE FAMOUS ST. PATRICK'S STREET PARADE ON 17 MARCH IS THE HIGHLIGHT. IT STARTS AT NOON ON PARNELL SQUARE AND THEN MOVES DOWN O'CONELL STREET, ACROSS COLLEGE GREEN TO THE MATCHING DESTINATION, ST. PATRICK'S CATHEDRAL.

○ CHESTER BEATTY LIBRARY
The mighty Dublin Castle complex also includes this great library. The collection consists of books, manuscripts, papyrus scrolls, miniatures and ornamental objects, which the founder Alfred Chester Beatty collected mainly in the Orient, but also in Europe.

○ ST. PATRICK'S CATHEDRAL
The cathedral (12th century) is the largest church in Dublin and is said to stand on the oldest Christian grounds. The sprawling interior of the church is rich with tombs, including that of Jonathan Swift, who was Dean of St. Patrick's Cathedral from 1713 to 1745, and Turlough O'Carolan, the last Irish bard and famous harpist.

○ ST. STEPHEN'S GREEN
Built in 1664, the park is a veritable oasis in one of Dublin's busiest shopping districts. In addition to the duck pond and cosy corners, there are also numerous monuments to famous Dubliners, other personalities and events of history. The rectangular park is surrounded by some beautiful buildings from the 18th and 19th centuries.

○ TRINITY COLLEGE
The university was founded in 1592 by order of the British Queen Elizabeth I. One of the oldest buildings on the expansive grounds is the Old Library (1732) with the Long Room, 64 metres long, the

Above: Closely connected to St. Patrick's Cathedral is the author Jonathan Swift, especially known as the author of "Gulliver's Travels", who is very well incorporated into world literature. Jonathan Swift, who worked here as a dean from 1713 was also buried here. "Here lies the body of Jonathan Swift ..." is the epitaph written by himself (in Latin), where wild indignation can not tear his heart further.

On the left: On 17 March, all of Dublin becomes a green flush of color when inhabitants and spectators adorn themselves with shamrocks during the St. Patrick's Day parade.

Above: At Ireland's "Alma Mater," Trinity College, intellectuals such as the theologian and philosopher George Berkeley, poet Oscar Wilde, and Nobel Laureate Samuel Beckett studied. The University Library (pictured: the Long Room) contains many bibliophile treasures, including the "Book of Kells".

GOING OUT

Chapter One // Dublin's most established and finest restaurant in the basement of the Writers Museum, with its French-inspired cuisine, is still one of the city's top restaurant.
// **www.chapteronerestaurant.com**

Whelan's // A beautiful, old-fashioned pub, great for a pint, but also one of the best venues for top-notch live bands and soloists.
// **www.whelanslive.com**

The Cobblestone // The old pub still portrays a bit of the past and offers the best opportunity to experience traditional Irish live music almost every night.
// **cobblestonepub.ie**

Bewley's Grafton Street Café // Every visitor should at least once try a cup of tea and something sweet in the traditional Bewley's Oriental Café.
// **www.bewleys.com**

longest library room in Europe. The biggest treasure is the "Book of Kells", a richly illustrated manuscript crafted by around 800 monks at Iona.

○ BANK OF IRELAND

The building, opposite Trinity College, was completed in 1739 as the first European building built specifically for a parliament. Shortly afterwards, in 1801, the Irish National Parliament was dissolved. A few years later, the Bank of Ireland, which has been in the building since, acquired the Palladian structure. The ticket office was once the lobby of the Lower House of Parliament.

○ DOCKLANDS

Why should it be different in Dublin than in other port cities? Eventually the harbour became too small for modern ships and the district became one of the city's eyesores. But as in London, that was just the salvation of many old buildings - and at the same time the chance to create a brand new, modern urban hub right in the centre of the city. Living and work near the water became hip. Glass, concrete and steel palaces emerged, as well as a convention centre and a concert hall.

SHOPPING

○ **GRAFTON STREET**

Grafton Street is one of Dublin's most expensive and bustling shopping streets. The big names of chain stores and department stores have their branches in the pedestrian zone. Street musicians entertain the passers-by in summer and cafés offer relaxing breaks from the shopping tour.

○ **HENRY STREET & MOORE STREET**

Henry Street, just off the General Post Office, is the main shopping street on the north side of Dublin. Department stores and shopping centres lure here next to small shops. The small side street Moore Street is famous for its traditional street market.

○ **POWERSCOURT TOWNHOUSE CENTRE**

The shopping centre is housed in a beautiful 18th-century city palace. Fashion shops are in the spotlight (including the Design Center, which is a leader in Irish fashion), but also antiques, fine gift items and jewelry.

// www.powerscourtcentre.com

DAY TRIPS

○ **BEND OF THE BOYNE**

Before you arrive in Dublin, we recommend a stop in the Boyne Valley near Slane with its outstanding neolithic passage tombs. The 3200 BC Grave at Newgrange remained untouched until 1960. A 19-metre-long corridor leads to the six-metre high burial chamber with three side chambers.

○ **POWERSCOURT ESTATE GARDENS**

Directly in front of the southern gates of Dublin, there is a park with Italian and Japanese gardens, natural areas and artificial lakes.

Left: Whether during the day or in the evening, often a stroll along Grafton Street ends in one of the traditional pubs or in one of the sidewalk cafés, of which there are many to choose from.

WHERE TO STAY

The Clarence Hotel // Located on the edge of the Temple Bar district, this hotel dates back to the 19th century and was an accomodation without much ado. Then two members of the pop group U2, Bono and The Edge, bought it and transformed it into a cool hotel and a popular bar for the posher crowd.

// theclarence.ie

The Shelbourne // The most beautiful hotel in the city with a great history (the Irish constitution was drafted here in 1922) and with a prime location on Dublin's prettiest park offers high-class ambiance, while still retaining its historic style.

// www.marriott.com

Pembroke Townhouse // A well-kept Bed and Breakfast is hidden behind an impressive Georgian-style façade in the beautiful Ballsbridge neighborhood.

// www.pembroketownhouse.ie

NOT TO BE MISSED

VISITING MOLLY MALONE

At the junction of Grafton Street and Suffolk Street stands the bronze statue of "Molly Malone", created by Jean Rynhart in 1987 - the millennium anniversary of the city. James Yorkston wrote a song in the early 1880s about this beautiful, late-dead fishmonger (which in reality never existed). The song became one of the most famous Irish folk songs and is today the unofficial anthem of the city of Dublin.

FEASTING AT THE "QUEEN OF TARTS"

This tiny café is located on a side street off Dame Street and is a true oasis. In the morning you can have breakfast there, at noon there is an extensive range of bistro offerings from salads to sandwiches or small hot dishes. The best, however, are the cakes and tarts.

PARTICIPATING IN A PUB CRAWL

A musical pub crawl tour leads through music pubs around Temple Bar. Two musicians accompany the group, play traditional Irish music and talk about the origin and development of the old pieces. Likewise, the Literary Pub Crawl takes place: the tour leads through the literary pubs of Dublin with recitations, stories and drinks, as befits the drink-happy Dublin literati.

VISITING KILMAINHAM GOAL PRISON

The 18th century building is one of the largest former prisons in Europe and now a museum. The list of former detainees reads like the Who's Who of the Irish Resistance. The tiny cells will still have you shivering today.

VISITING ONE OF THE MANY MARKETS

Every Saturday, the large Meeting House Square in the heart of the Temple Bar District turns into one of Dublin's most beautiful markets. If you are in the mood for fresh vegetables and juicy fruits or if you want to try some of the culinary delicacies offered at the many stands, then this is the place for you. Fresh food is also being traded (Mo-Sa) on the traditional Moore Street Market and, throughout the week, in the George Street Arcade - a late 19th century covered market with a beautiful red brick facade. At the motley Cow's Lane Designer Market (Sa) you can find "funky urban streetwear" from young fashion designers and all sorts of arts and crafts.

#08   HAMBURG

IF YOU THINK OF HAMBURG, YOU WILL PROBABLY FIRST THINK OF THE HARBOR, THE ELBE AND THE ALSTER. MAYBE YOU THINK OF THE "MICHEL", THE FAMOUS FISH MARKET, THE NOBLE ELBCHAUSSEE AND THE LEGENDARY REEPERBAHN. BUT THE CITY OF MANY BRIDGES AND MILLIONAIRES OFFERS MUCH MORE. IT IS A VIBRANT BUSINESS METROPOLIS, AN INTERNATIONAL TRADING CENTRE AND A MULTIFACETED CULTURAL AND MEDIA CITY. IN THE COURSE OF THE CENTURIES, THE "GATEWAY TO THE WORLD", WHICH IN ITS MORE THAN A THOUSAND-YEAR HISTORY HAS NOT BEEN SPARED MAJOR BLOWS OF FATE, HAS CHANGED AGAIN AND AGAIN YET STILL REMAINED TRUE TO ITS TRADITION IN THE HANSEATIC WAY. DESPITE THEIR OBSESSION FOR UNDERSTATEMENT, THE SONS AND DAUGHTERS OF HAMMONIA ARE SELF-CONFIDENT, COSMOPOLITAN AND TOLERANT - NOT A CONTRADICTION IN THE METROPOLIS ON THE ELBE, BUT A PROMISE.

Left: Hamburg is a port city. Since the first containers were unloaded in the Port of Hamburg in the 1960s, the image of the port has changed fundamentally. With billions invested, new storage space was created and the technology to unload and load the ships was built.

Right: View over the Binnenalster on the Jungfernstieg.

○ JUNGFERNSTIEG

The sophisticated boulevard is one of the city's most popular promenades. Whether in the traditional Alsterhaus or in the established flagship stores of renowned fashion labels - shopping enthusiasts will find what they are looking for. From the Jungfernstieg steam boats also depart for a cruise of the Binnen and outer Alster.

○ CITY HALL

For the 1897 completed construction of the seat of citizenship and senate of the Free and Hanseatic City of Hamburg any Hanseatic restraint was thrown overboard. The building comprises a total of 647 rooms; the tower is 112 metres high; and the façade is decorated with elaborate sculptures, including some representation of German Emperors.

○ MÖNCKEBERGSTRASSE

The shopping street between the town hall and the main station, also known as "Mö", is characterised by department stores and branches of large retail chains. Occasional cultural events such as concerts and film screenings as well as a Christmas Market take place on the Gerhart-Hauptmann-Platz.

○ KUNSTHALLE

The architecturally relatively simple Kunsthalle is one of the best-known art collections in Germany. European art with a focus on German Romanticism is presented chronologically here. The Galerie der Gegenwart (the "Gallery of Contemporary Art") was established in 1997 as a new exhibition space for contemporary art in the Hamburger Kunsthalle.

○ MUSEUM FÜR KUNST UND GEWERBE

From the collection of antiquities to Islamic art and Art Nouveau to modern - the MKG, as a leading centre for art, crafts and design, offers a journey through all eras of human creativity. In addition to book art, the highlights of the museum include collections of musical instruments and items of clothing.

○ DEICHTORHALLEN

Exhibitions on contemporary art are held today in the two halls where markets used to take place. The bookstore for contemporary art is one of the best-sorted of its kind in Hamburg.

○ CHILEHAUS

The ten-storey office building in the Kontorhausviertel is a unique example of the Hamburg Clinker architecture of the 1920s. Its acute-angled floor plan is reminiscent of the bow of a ship.

○ DEICHSTRASSE

The Dyke Road (Deichstrasse) on Nikolaifleet is lined

WHY VISIT IN SPRING?

THE CITIZENS OF HAMBURG ARE SOMETIMES CONSIDERED A BIT STIFF AND RESERVED. BUT NOT MUCH IS NOTICEABLE AT THE ANNUAL "HARBOUR BIRTHDAY" AT THE BEGINNING OF MAY. THE EVENT GOES BACK TO THE CHARTER OF EMPEROR FREDERICK BARBAROSSA, WHO GUARANTEED THE HAMBURGERS THE PRIVILEGE OF FREE BOAT NAVIGATION ON THE LOWER ELBE ON MAY 7, 1189. ALTHOUGH THE DATE IS HISTORICALLY INCORRECT AND THE LATER ATTACHED DEED TURNED OUT TO BE A FORGERY. NEVERTHELESS, THERE IS STILL A HUGE CELEBRATION - SINCE 1977, EVEN WITH A LOT OF HUSTLE AND BUSTLE ON WATER, ON LAND AND IN THE AIR. HIGHLIGHTS ARE THE RUN-IN PARADE OF THE BIG AND SMALL TRADITIONAL AND MUSEUM SHIPS, THE TUG BALLET TO WALTZ SOUNDS, THE DRAGON BOAT RACE ON THE ELBE AND THE FIREWORKS OVER THE HARBOUR.

Left: A highlight of the Hanseatic holiday calendar is the harbour birthday on a weekend in early May.

At the top: The moated castle in the Speicherstadt sits enthroned on a peninsula between the canals.

Above: An eye-catcher in the lavish interior of St. Michaelis is the 20-metre-high marble altar.

Right: The façade of the Elbphilharmonie consists of 1,100 individually curved, iridescent glass panes. In the old warehouse, the parking garage, another concert hall, cafés, bars and restaurants are housed. In the gap between the old brick base and the glass structure, there is also a plaza at a height of 37 metres that is accessible to all visitors and has a panoramic view of the city centre, the harbour city and port.

with the oldest surviving merchant houses in the city, some buildings are from the 18th century. The small passages between the narrow houses to the water are known as "Fleetgänge".

○ ST. MICHAELIS ("MICHEL")

The most famous church in the city is one of the most beautiful baroque churches in northern Germany. The church tower, called "Michel" by the citizens of Hamburg, is 132 metres high and is the landmark of the Hanseatic city. The bell tower is famous, on weekdays at 10 am and 9 pm, and, on Sundays at 12 pm a chorale is blown in all four directions.

○ SPEICHERSTADT AND HAFENCITY

The harbour is the living heart of the Elbe metropolis. Here the past and the future meet. The Speicherstadt with its imposing brick buildings was built at the end of the 19th century for the storage of duty-free goods from all over the world. Right next to it, Hamburg's new quarter with a magnificent view of ships and quay facilities is growing, the HafenCity, one of the largest urban projects in Europe.

○ ELBPHILHARMONIE

Hamburg's spectacular new landmark. In 2004, the Senate commissioned the renowned Swiss architecture firm Herzog & de Meuron with plans for the Elbphilharmonie, the foundation stone was laid three years later. On the pedestal of the historic Kaispeicher, a curved glass structure rises up to a height of 110 metres. Inside it houses two concert halls.

○ JETTIES

Every visitor to the city will come to the jetties to smell the fresh sea air or just to eat a fish sandwich with a view of the harbour. The 688-metre-long pier is busy all year around. At the jetties, the harbour cruises start and end. The 205 metres long terminal building was built from 1907 to 1909 and has been a listed building in German cultural heritage since 2003.

○ OLD ELBTUNNEL

At the western end of the jetties, the 426 metres long Old Elbe Tunnel crosses the Norderelbe. Unlike cars, pedestrians and cyclists can use the tunnel that opened in 1911, free of charge and with no time limit.

GOING OUT

Deichgraf // The traditional restaurant offers its guests Hanseatic fish dishes such as plaice, eel or sole and red fruit jelly for dessert.

// www.deichgraf-hamburg.de

Himmlisches Café // Nowhere else in the city can you find coffee and cake as close to the sky as in the 84 metre high tower café. The fantastic views of the city centre and the Alster are unbeatable.

// www.jacobus.de

Oberhafenkantine // The crookedly built little house from 1925 is the last of the once over 20 "Kaffeeklappen" that existed in the Port of Hamburg. Today, you will find fantastic cuisine in a rustic ambience.

// www.oberhafenkantine-hamburg.de

Haifischbar // Authentic dishes such as Labskaus and Matjes are the hallmark here. The traditional restaurant is hardly larger than a living room.

// Große Elbstraße 128

○ REEPERBAHN

This 930 metres long street in the heart of the entertainment district of St. Pauli is certainly one of the best known in Germany. Bars, entertainment venues and cultural sites line the Reeperbahn on both sides. It owes its name to the Reepschläger, who turned ships rope here until the end of the 19th century.

SHOPPING

WHERE TO STAY

Cap San Diego // Where could you reside more stylishly in Hamburg than on board a ship in the harbour? On the former South America ferry, the nine passenger cabins have been restored for overnight stays.

// www.capsandiego.de

East Design Hotel // Multiple award-winning conversion of a historic iron foundry. Not only a hotel, but also a popular meeting place for the hip scene with its imaginative organic interior design of the restaurant, bar and lounge.

// www.east-hamburg.de

Empire Riverside Hotel // Since 2007, it is a new eye-catcher above the jetties of St. Pauli. The 20-storey hotel tower by David Chipperfield in the style of the 30s is completely covered with bronze plates on the outside.

// www.empire-riverside.de

○ NIVEA-HAUS

In this shop on Jungfernstieg you can not only buy the famous Nivea Creams & Co., but also be pampered with massages.

○ ALSTERHAUS DELICACIES

The highlight in the historic department store is the gourmet department. Caviar, confiserie and cheeses are available in many small specialty shops.

// www.alsterhaus.de

○ BONSCHELADEN

Bonbons or sweets are called Bonsche in Hamburg. They are handmade in the Friedensallee in Ottensen.

○ STILWERK

In a culturally heritage listed brick building on the banks of the Elbe on 11,000 square metres you can get everything related to furnishing.

// stilwerk.com/de/hamburg

○ FLEAMARKETS

Whether antique or flea markets - the Hanseatic city has something for everyone. For example, the Flohmarkt in der Fabrik, a market in an old factory in Altona, the Markt der Völker in the Ethnographic Museum. Or, once a month the Sternbrücken Nachtflohmarkt, a flea market held at night.

DAYTRIPS

○ EISERNER KANZLER IN THE SACHSENWALD

Bismarck was given the forest by Emperor Wilhelm I. In Friedrichsruh, a museum reminds visitors of him. Worth visiting are the mausoleum and butterfly garden.

○ DAS ALTE LAND

A detour is not only worthwhile during the flowering season. Many old farms, lakes and windmills and the town of Stade impress all year round.

NOT TO BE MISSED

DROPPING BY THE AUCTION HALL AFTER THE FISH MARKET

The party starts at the fish market on Sunday morning. Then the crowds flock to the fish auction hall. You sit on long benches for brunch or dance to the music of live bands to well-known songs, including many oldies. Of course, a visit to the market barkers on the fish market is worthwile beforehand. Every Sunday until 9.30 am you can find fish, fruits and plants on Grosse Elbstrasse. Best of all, at the end of the day, traders loudly sell their goods to people at rock bottom prices.

BEING AMAZED AT THE MINIATURE WONDERLAND

Not only railroad fans feel comfortable in this world of superlatives, more than 700 wagons of the largest digitally controlled model railroad in the world travel through reconstructed landscapes down to the smallest detail, such as the Grand Canyon or the Swiss Alps. Among the highlights of this scene is the replica of Las Vegas.

DIALOGUE IN THE DARK

Blind people lead visitors through a world of darkness. In this world of sounds, textures and fragrances, there is nothing to see, but a lot to discover - a new experience for seeing people to experience a culture without sight.

CATCHING A HARBOUR FERRY

The inexpensive alternative to the commercial providers of harbour cruises. The Hamburg Transport Association also operates a route network on the Elbe. On lines 61, 62, 64, 73, and 75 anyone can put together an individual tour of the harbour - for the price of a simple subway ticket.

EATING A TRADITIONAL FISH SANDWICH

Fish sandwiches are classic North German snacks. Of course, you can buy them with matjes, crab or fishcakes at the fish market or bridge 10 at the jetties. All while listening to the roar of the ships!

#09   COPENHAGEN

A RELAXED ATMOSPHERE AND HAPPY PEOPLE - THAT'S COPENHAGEN. HOW COULD IT BE OTHERWISE, WHEN THE FAMOUS LITTLE MERMAID FROM THE FLOODS GREETS VISITORS AND EVEN THE ROYAL FAMILY MAINTAINS A CAREFREE LIFESTYLE! THE DANISH CAPITAL HAS A LARGE AND VARIED CULTURAL OFFERING, AND THE NIGHTLIFE AND ENTERTAINMENT DISTRICTS ARE WORLD FAMOUS. ESPECIALLY WHEN THE SUN IS SHINING, LIFE TAKES PLACE ON THE STREETS, IN THE PARKS, AND NOT LEAST, ON THE WATER. THE HISTORIC CENTRE, BORDERED TO THE WEST AND NORTH BY WATER, THE COPENHAGEN LAKES, AND BORDERING THE HARBOUR TO THE EAST, BOASTS AN ENSEMBLE OF MAGNIFICENT RENAISSANCE AND CLASSICIST BUILDINGS. THE CITY FLOURISHED ON THE BANKS OF THE ORESUND DURING THE LATE MIDDLE AGES, AND DEVELOPED FROM A TRADE CENTRE TO BECOME THE CAPITAL OF DENMARK IN 1443.

Above: Colorful houses are lined up at Nyhavn (New Harbour). Where once a significant harbour arm was, today you will find the most important entertainment district of Copenhagen.

Left: The sculptor Bertel Thorvaldsen dedicated an interesting museum to his hometown.

Right: Strøget is not only the best known, but also the oldest pedestrian street in Denmark.

○ STRØGET

Copenhagen's famous pedestrian zone stretches over five streets from the Town Hall Square to Kongens

Nytorv, the Royal market. A stroll through the promenade is a must for every visitor, because there is something to see and admire at every turn. Strøget is lined by magnificent, high Renaissance buildings. Interesting shops, cafés and restaurants are everywhere, and street musicians are also performing for free. You will find some of the museums and sacred buildings en route.

○ TOWN HALL SQUARE

Of course, the eye-catching feature of the sprawling Town Hall Square is the town hall itself, built between 1892 and 1905, which was modeled after its counterpart in Siena, Italy. If you turn from the Town Hall Square into the Frederiksberggade, after a few minutes you will reach Gammeltorv - one of the most beautiful squares in the city and a meeting place for young people.

WHY VISIT IN SPRING?

AT PENTECOST, THE OTHERWISE RATHER COOL COPENHAGEN TURNS INTO ONE BIG LIVELY CARNIVAL CELEBRATION. THE CARNIVAL LURES WITH A SOUTH AMERICAN FLAIR, PAIRED WITH DANISH TRADITIONS. IN PARADES, ARTISTS STROLL THROUGH THE CITY. IN THE EVENING, CONCERTS ARE HELD IN THE PEDESTRIAN ZONE.

○ LATINERKVATERET

North of the square is the "Latin Quarter" with the main building of the University built in the 1830s, the St. Petri Kirche and the Liebfrauenkirche. Although most of the university buildings have moved in the meantime, the former student district has retained its charm.

○ TIVOLI

The amusement park, located behind the Town Hall Square, is probably the most famous landmark of the Danish capital, next to the Little Mermaid. For more than 170 years, dozens of carousels and other rides, jugglers and acrobats have been enticing visitors to Tivoli. Several times a week concerts take place.

○ SLOTSHOLMEN

On this island located on the Inderhavn and separated on three sides by a narrow channel from the rest of the city, lies the political heart of Denmark. Here you will find Christiansborg Palace - the seat of the Danish Parliament, the Government and the Supreme Court.

○ THE LITTLE MERMAID

Cruise ships calling at Langelinie Pier, but also crowds of tourists walking ashore, pass by Copenhagen's landmark. Since 1913, the statue of only 125 centimetres sits on its boulder on the waterfront promenade and looks lost at the sea. It is named after a fairy tale by Hans Christian Andersen and was created by the sculptor Edvard Eriksen on behalf of the patron Jacob Christian Jacobson.

○ NYHAVN

The canal north of the city centre connects Nytorv with the harbour and is one of the tourist attractions of the Danish capital. Worth seeing are the colourful old office building fronts in the north of Nyhavn. Since the 1980s, a lively pub and restaurant scene has developed here.

○ THE CASTLE OF AMALIENBORG

Halfway between Nyhavn and the cruise pier Langelinie is Amalienborg Palace - the residence of the Danish Queen. The ensemble of four palaces grouped around an octagonal square is praised worldwide as an extraordinary Rococo complex. A visit is not only a must for fans of the royal family.

Top left: Colourful and full of South American glamour, the Copenhagen Carnival.

Lower left: rather melancholic, the symbol of Copenhagen appears to be: the little mermaid by Edvard Eriksen, yearning at the harbour entrance waiting for her prince.

○ CHRISTIANSHAVN

The district on the island of Amager is one of the most quaint areas of Copenhagen. It was built under King Christian IV from 1619 on the model of Amsterdam and equipped with a channel system.

GOING OUT

Frederiks Have // A bright, friendly restaurant that constantly reinterprets Nordic cuisine. Especially good are the wines. The Frederiks Have is located in the Frederiksberg district.

// www.frederikshave.dk

Det lille Apotek // Copenhagen's oldest restaurant is proud of its tradition. Hans Christian Andersen is said to have been a frequent guest in the house not far from the Frauenkirche. Today, meals are cooked according to original recipes, at noon and in the evening.

// www.detlilleapotek.dk

1105 // The cocktail bar is not easy to find, but comes highly recommended to spend the evening in a cosy atmosphere with the supposedly best drinks in the city.

// www.cocktailkompagniet.dk

Since it was spared devastation, many parts of the historic buildings are preserved. Christianshavn became known around the world for the free city Christiania, founded in 1970 by hippies, in which alternative ways of life and concepts should be developed and tested. Christiania is still a quaint pocket of 1970's flower-power era.

○ NATIONAL MUSEUM

Housed in the Rococo Palace, the National Museum's collection reflects the history of Danish culture from the Bronze Age to the 20th century, the centrepiece is the famous Trundholm Sun Chariot.

SHOPPING

○ **AMAGERTORV**

This place is the mecca of Danish design, especially as here the stores are all so close together. Moreover, the Amagertorv is a good starting point for a shopping trip on the Strøget.

○ **HOUSE OF AMBER**

Amber is popular again. In the House of Amber, Copenhagen alone has three branches, one can find classic and modern jewelry creations here. The Ravhuset in Nyhavn also houses a museum presenting the world's largest amber.

// www.houseofamber.com

○ **ILLUMS BOLIGHUS**

A special department store for designer articles. Here, from furniture and kitchen equipment, you can find decorative items, from lamps to mirrors, from carpets to wallpapers. In addition, you can dress yourself and equip yourself with accessories. Cosmetics can be found here as well.

// www.illumsbolighus.com

○ **MAGASIN DU NORD**

This traditional department store still conveys the elegance and a bit of the elitism that surrounded the wealthy citizens at the beginning of the 19th century. Already from the outside it is an eye-catcher. As far as interior design and product range are concerned, Magasin has made the leap into the modern age.

// www.magasin.dk

○ **FLEAMARKETS IN COPENHAGEN**

You have not properly visited Copenhagen, if you did not visit a flea market. A well-known "Loppemarked", as it is known here, takes place every Saturday morning at Israel's Plads between May and November. Here you will find knick-knacks and antiques. If the weather is bad, you can visit the sheds, where there is a covered flea market almost every weekend.

Left: The designer shopping centre Illums Bolighus lives up to what is sold here: The sales rooms are dominated by simple Nordic design.

WHERE TO STAY

Ibsens Hotel // Urban and yet chic, but above all very central. The sights are within walking distance and this makes the Ibsen ideal for those who do not like to start their day of sightseeing with long journeys.

// www.arthurhotels.dk/ibsens-hotel

Hotel Bertrams // This hotel pays close attention to sustainability, from organic ingredients at breakfast to clever waste management. Apart from that, it will win you over with the cozy lounge and garden with the first rays of spring sunshine.

// www.guldsmedenhotels.com/ bertrams

Hotel Alexandra // Danish lifestyle of the 50s and 60s awaits individualists at the Hotel Alexandra. The designer hotel looks like a museum with the pieces of furniture by Arne Jacobsen and Co. - a museum, however, in which one may live.

// www.hotelalexandra.dk

NOT TO BE MISSED

VISITING THE OPEN FOYER AT THE OPERA

The controversial building - the patron, of the Maersk family, decided every detail himself instead of including the city in the layout plans - is located directly opposite Amalienborg Palace. Guided tours are offered daily (around 14 euros). Three hours before a performance, the foyer can be viewed for free.

EATING A TRADITIONAL DANISH HOTDOG AT A PØLSEVOGN

The sausage in a bread roll with mustard, ketchup, remoulade, fried onions and cucumber slices belongs to Denmark as red wine belongs to France. Try DØP at the Round Tower or at the Heiliggeistkirche, or at Mortens Pølser, Stubbeløbsgade - directly from the butcher.

STROLLING THROUGH THE BOTANICAL GARDEN

Since 1874 the Botanical Garden has been the green lungs in the centre of the city. Be sure to visit the old palm house and climb the spiral staircase! Afterwards enjoy delicacies from the Citroën van on the terrace.

A TOUR OF CHRISTIANIA IN SPRING

This district on a former military site is called a "Free Town". In fact, the residents organise many things themselves, which are otherwise usually regulated or provided by the city administration. They also make their own laws. Photography is strictly prohibited here. Anyone who violates this must be prepared to be treated in a rather unpleasant manner. You can explore the grounds on your own or dine in the café, but for safety's sake you should join with a guide.

ADMIRING EXHIBITIONS IN THE DANSK DESIGN CENTRE AND THE DESIGN MUSEUM

Danish designs are famous. In the museum you can view them and also buy some. At the Design Centre, DDC for short, Danish and international people from the creative scene meet to exchange views.

#10

LONDON

LONDON IS A CAPITAL AND RESIDENTIAL CITY, THE BRITISH SEAT OF GOVERNMENT, AN INTERNATIONAL FINANCIAL CAPITAL, AND A COSMOPOLITAN CITY IN THE TRUEST SENSE OF THE WORD. UNTIL HALF A CENTURY AGO, LONDON WAS THE CENTRE OF A GIGANTIC EMPIRE, THE BRITISH EMPIRE, AND IT IS STILL CLEARLY VISIBLE TODAY. THE CITY OF LONDON - THE HISTORIC HEART OF THE METROPOLIS - IS A CITY WITHIN THE CITY, EMERGED FROM THE ROMAN LONDINIUM AND STILL HAS ITS OWN ADMINISTRATION. FOR ALMOST 1,000 YEARS, TRADING HAS HAPPENED HERE AND TRANSACTIONS OF IMMENSE AMOUNTS OF MONEY HAVE AND STILL ARE BEING MADE HERE.

Above: The upper pedestrian crossing of the Tower Bridge is part of a permanent exhibition about its history and construction design.

Left: The St Paul's Cathedral, a grandiose creation of Christopher Wrens, with its 110-meter-high dome was built from 1675 to 1711, after the predecessor was destroyed in 1666 at the Great Fire of London.

○ TOWER BRIDGE

Opened in 1894, the Tower Bridge is not only one of London's landmarks, but also a testimony to the engineering of the time. By the mid-19th century, the London East End was so densely populated that a bridge became necessary. The solution was a combined folding and suspension bridge. Steam engines started the hydraulics, which could open the bridge within a few minutes, today, this is done with electricity. In both towers there is an exhibition on the history of the building. The glazed pedestrian crossing high above the actual bridge offers a stunning view over London.

○ TOWER OF LONDON

On the eastern edge of the city, the massive complex with the long name "Her Majesty's Royal Palace and Fortress The Tower of London" watches over the Thames. Until the 17th century, the tower was a royal residence, a prison until the 20th century, and until today a royal treasury, in which the crown jewels have been presented to the public for more than 300 years.

○ ST. PAUL'S CATHEDRAL

The magnificent dome of St. Paul's Cathedral stands proudly and prominently in the midst of the financial palaces of the city. For 1,400 years there has been a Christian church on Ludgate Hill in the city. The present English-Baroque St. Paul's Cathedral is already the fifth version and without question the most magnificent one.

○ WESTMINSTER ABBEY

Unique is this church, officially called "Collegiate Church of St. Peter", not only for its magnificent architecture, but above all, for its meaningful symbolism. Since William the Conqueror, with all but a few exceptions, all monarchs of England have been crowned in this church - traditionally by the Archbishop of Canterbury - and many have found their final resting place here as well. The tombs of other historical personalities, including writers, artists and politicians, can be found here.

WHY VISIT IN SPRING?

THERE ARE TWO REASONS FOR A VISIT IN THE SPRING. ON THE ONE HAND THERE IS THE CHELSEA FLOWER SHOW: IN THE LAST WEEK OF MAY, THE GROUNDS OF THE ROYAL HOSPITAL ARE TRANSFORMED INTO A GARDEN OF ARTWORKS, IN WHICH GARDENERS COMPETE FOR AWARDS. ON THE OTHER HAND, THERE IS THE LONDON MARATHON – IT IS NOT JUST A RACE, BUT AN INSPIRING WAVE OF HUMANITY. MANY OF THE MORE THAN 35,000 PARTICIPANTS START OUT NOT TO BREAK RECORDS, BUT TO TAKE ON THE CHALLENGE, AND SOME ARE EVEN SPONSORED FOR CHARITY. THE LONDON MARATHON IS ALSO THE LARGEST ONE-DAY CHARITY EVENT IN THE WORLD, AND THEREFORE ALMOST LIKE A CARNIVAL. FROM GARISH NEON VESTS TO HUGE RHINOCEROS COSTUMES, EVERYTHING CAN BE SEEN HERE.

○ WESTMINSTER PALACE

The Neo-Gothic façade of Westminster Palace with its characteristic towers, including the bell tower with the Big Ben, gives the impression that it has been mirrored in the Thames since the Middle Ages. In fact, since the 11th century, there has been a seat of power on this site. However, the current building, along with Westminster Abbey, a UNESCO World Heritage Site, was not built until the mid-19th century.

○ TRAFALGAR SQUARE

In Trafalgar Square, the entire history of the former British Empire seems to be concentrated, reflecting the presence of the country in all its facets. The square in the heart of the West End was named after one of the most important battles of the English against Napoleon.

○ NATIONAL GALLERY

The National Art Gallery on Trafalgar Square is a building that actually resembles a Greek temple. The focus is on Italian masters and works by Dutch painters.

○ PICCADILLY CIRCUS

The Piccadilly Circus is home to five busy streets, including Haymarket, Shaftesbury Avenue and Regent Street. The sprawling square is therefore an entrée to the London entertainment districts of the West End, Soho and major shopping streets. Because of the cen-

tral and convenient location on the busy Piccadilly Line, it has therefore always been a popular tourist meeting place.

○ BUCKINGHAM PALACE

Buckingham Palace is the official residence of the English royal family, but only on weekdays and outside the summer holidays. The palace can therefore not officially be visited - except in the months of August and September, when 19 of its rooms are open to the public. Worth seeing, however, is definitely the "Changing of the Guard" at the gates of the palace.

GOING OUT

Geales // Fish and chips are a famous symbol of English cuisine. In this restaurant, the traditional dish is served in its finest form.
// www.geales.com/

The Tipperary // Irish pubs can be found around the world, but this was the first one outside of Ireland - founded by Dublin brewers back in 1700 - and features Guinness and original Victorian interiors.

Fabric // The famous club is one of the best in London. The best gigs and parties are held here every weekend in its large rooms. But plan for long waiting times at the entrance.
// www.fabriclondon.com

Freud // In this cellar bar, you will be spoiled with delicious cocktails. And it was in this house that Sigmund Freud found his first refuge in London.
// freud.eu/cafe-bars

○ THE SHARD

This "skyscraper" towers 310 metres high and is the new landmark in Southwark. In July 2012, the building was inaugurated, in February 2013 the viewing terrace was opened to the public.

○ VICTORIA AND ALBERT MUSEUM

Not a house at which you can just take a quick look, because it has no less than 145 individual galleries with over four million objects! A museum of literally everything, a smorgasbord of artefacts from all over the world of the erstwhile British Empire.

○ NATURAL HISTORY MUSEUM

The natural history museum resembles a sacred building. In its four areas you can see dinosaurs, the consequences of earthquakes and understand the influence of mankind on nature.

○ HYDE PARK

The green lungs of the city is one of the royal parks. At anytime you can attend concerts or hold a lecture at the Speakers' Corner - as long as the Queen and the royal family are not mentioned.

Far left: In addition to sporting ambitions, many are also inspired by a good cause for running the London Marathon.

Left: The equestrian statue of Richard the Lionheart watches over the palace façade of Westminster Palace.

Right: The Prince Albert Memorial on the southern edge of Kensington Gardens is the epitome of Victorian art, with rich figureheads and ornamental opulence.

SHOPPING

○ **CAMDEN PASSAGE ANTIQUES MARKET**
A wealth of small shops and markets offering antiques of all kinds. On Thursday and Friday a book market takes place, on Sunday farmers sell organic vegetables.

○ **HARRODS**
Harrods is not only famous for designer fashion or the food department, but also for the two memorials for Lady Di and Dodi Al-Fayed.
// www.harrods.com

○ **FORTNUM & MASON**
For over 300 years now, you can buy tea at Fortnum & Mason, as well as specialties and delicacies of all kinds.
// www.fortnumandmason.com/

○ **HARVEY NICHOLS**
The posh district of Kensington cannot be missing a superfine department store. Harvey Nicks offers the finest designer goods.
// www.harveynichols.com

○ **CAMDEN MARKET**
Every day, the markets in Camden Town await their visitors. More than 100 shops present clothing, gifts and unusual items.

○ **PORTOBELLO ROAD MARKET**
Every Friday and Saturday, there is a flea market on Portobello Road, many stands are there the whole week. The focus is on beautiful antiques.
// www.portobelloroad.co.uk

○ **LIBERTY**
More of a Tudor castle than a department store, it is a feast for the eyes during a shopping spree. The furnishing section offers only the very best from designer cutlery, luxurious fabrics, fine porcelain and Vitra furniture.
// www.libertylondon.com

Left: Fine restaurants and five-star hotels line the expensive Brompton Road in the fine district of Knights Bridge. However, the highlight is Harrods, probably the most famous department store in the world.

WHERE TO STAY

Threadneedles // A jewel of a hotel housed in a former 19th century bank. The lobby is spectacular, crowned by a dome of hand-painted glass. The 70 spacious rooms all offer 5-star luxury.
// www.hotelthreadneedles.co.uk

Mad Hatter // The old-fashioned 19th century facade hides a small, modern hotel with all the comforts not far from the Tate Modern and Shakespeare's Globe.
// www.madhatterhotel.co.uk

London Bridge Hotel // Following the concept of the Southwark hotel on the south bank of the River Thames, near the southern end of London Bridge, this property enjoys a blend of traditional comfort and modern technology.
// www.londonbridgehotel.com

NOT TO BE MISSED

A RIDE ON THE LONDON EYE

The London Eye, a ferris wheel between County Hall and Southbank Centre, opened in 1999 and has since become a highlight of the metropolis. At 135 metres, it is the largest ferris wheel in Europe. During the operating times, it rotates continuously, but slowly - taking about 30 minutes to complete one round, so there is plenty of time to take in the vistas of London.

TEA TIME AT THE RITZ

Very classy and typically British, try the "Tea at The Ritz": A cup of tea with milk, in addition to scones and clotted cream - what can be more British. The noblest variant takes place with much splendor in the Palm Court of the hotel Ritz. Make a reservation or try The Savoy or The Dorchester instead!

EXPERIENCE SHAKESPEARE'S WORKS FIRSTHAND

The Globe Theater, next to the Tate Gallery is a replica of the original Globe, in which Shakespeare was part of the ensemble. This in no way detracts from the pleasure of a Shakespearean performance.

STROLLING ALONG COVENT GARDEN

Covent Garden has been a centre of popular entertainment since the 17th century. It started with the big market, which today still attracts countless shoppers. But soon there were all sorts of entertainment facilities and traveling artists. The old Covent Garden Market, now Covent Garden Piazza, is a glass-roofed building with an overwhelming selection of boutiques and cafés, while in the open street performers entertain passers-by.

PARTICIPATING IN A LITERARY LONDON WALK

London is home to many authors and the scene of numerous books. Thematic tours allow you to get to know the city from a very specific perspective. For example, on the Charles Dickens Tour, or following the footsteps of Sherlock Holmes.

#11 MADRID

WITH OVER THREE MILLION INHABITANTS, MADRID IS ONE OF EUROPE'S MAJOR CITIES. THE CENTRE OF THE CITY IS THE LIVELY PLAZA MAYOR. THE CAFÉS OF THE GRAN VIA ARE MEETING PLACES OF THE INTELLECTUALS. MADRID'S MUSEUMS ARE AMONG THE MOST BEAUTIFUL IN THE WORLD, SUCH AS THE PRADO WITH THE GRANDIOSE COLLECTION OF ANCIENT MASTERS, THE CENTRO DE REINA SOFIA FOR 20TH CENTURY ART AND THE MUSEO TYSSEN-BORNEMISZA WITH ITS IMPRESSIONISTS AND SURREALISTS. FOR A REST, PARQUE DEL RETIRO INVITES YOU TO SHOP AND STROLL DOWN CALLE SERRANO, THE MOST EXCITING BULLFIGHTS TAKE PLACE IN THE PLAZA DE TOROS, AND THE BEST FOOTBALL PLAYERS PLAY FOR REAL MADRID. MADRID IS A MODERN AND LIVELY CITY, WELCOMING TO VISITORS AND A PARADISE FOR THE MADRILEÑOS.

Above: A monument thrones over the city, visible from almost everywhere, the Palacio Real rises high above the Rio Manzanares.

Left: The Madrilenes pay homage to their city with the adage "de Madrid al cielo" - after Madrid, only the sky is more beautiful. This expresses their attitude to life. Here, emphasis is placed on good food, fashion and design.

○ PUERTA DEL SOL

This is the liveliest place in the city. In the heart of Madrid, people flock from the metro station "Sol" past their landmark, the statue of the bear nibbling on the madroño ("strawberry tree"), to their offices or at the counters of the shops. Puerta del Sol is considered the centre of Madrid. In front of the Casa de Correos (post office) which is the centre of the entire Spanish road network, the 0 kilometre mark.

○ MUSEO DEL PRADO

One of the largest and most important art museums in the world is right here. The Prado is best known for its extensive collection of old Spanish masters such as Goya and Velázquez. The museum alone has 4,800 oil paintings from the 12th to the 19th century. Around 140 works by Goya can be found here. In addition, there are 8,200 drawings and 900 sculptures.

○ PALACIO REAL

On Christmas Eve 1734, a catastrophe struck the royal castle, when a fire broke out on the 24th December. When, the fire alarm bells rung, they were mistaken to be the Christmas bells. Philip V planned a new building, which was in no way inferior to the huge royal palaces of Europe, such as Versailles. He commissioned the Italian architect Filippo Juvara, and his pupil Giovanni Battisti Sacchetti continued the project. The building, with more than 2,000 rooms, was so monumental that construction lasted 17 years.

○ JARDINES DE SABATINI

In the 1930s, the magnificent Neo-Classical Sabatini Gardens were built on the north side of the palace. Its geometric shapes and decorative style make it a real visitor magnet.

○ PLAZA MAYOR

This square is impressive with its size alone, 129 metres long and 94 metres wide is the Plaza May-

WHY VISIT IN SPRING?

SPRING IS SIMPLY THE BEST TIME FOR A CITY TRIP TO MADRID. IT IS WARM ENOUGH TO ESCAPE THE WINTER, BUT NOT AS (SOMETIMES UNBEARABLY) HOT AS IN SUMMER. IN ADDITION, COUNTLESS FESTIVALS SUCH AS THE BANKIA FLAMENCO FESTIVAL TAKE PLACE AT THIS TIME, AND IN MANY PLACES IN THE CITY THE TRADITIONAL SPANISH DANCE IS PRACTICED.

or. It is considered one of the first markets of the city, but above all as the centre of the "Madrid de los Austrias", the House of Habsburg of Madrid, and is surrounded by magnificent buildings with arcades.

○ CENTRO DE ARTE REINA SOFÍA

The Prado belongs to the Old Masters, modern art has had its own museum in Madrid since 1986. The Centro de Arte Reina Sofía, with its collection of works of art from the 19th century until today seamlessly connects to the works shown in the Prado. On three floors you can find works by the most important artists of the past two centuries: Dalí, Miró, Picasso or Juan Gris. The spectrum ranges from Surrealism to Cubism to Pop Art.

○ PARQUE DEL RETIRO

The name says it all: rest and relaxation are what visitors will find in this extensive green area. Particularly worth seeing is the statue of Lucifer and the rose garden.

Above: On September 10, 1992, the modern art museum Centro de Arte Reina Sofia was officially inaugurated. In addition to the collection of paintings the library of the museum is worth seeing.

Left: Flamenco has been known in Spain since the 16th century. The hoarse voice of the singer, the characteristic chords of the guitar and the rhythm of the castanets are the basic elements of flamenco. Much of the dance is based on improvisation.

Right: The splendid Plaza de Cibeles is embedded in a group of striking structures, such as the Palacio de Comunicaciones (main post office), which reminisces of a church with its historical monumental style.

○ TEATRO REAL

From the front, it looks quite square, but then the Royal Theater surprises with a hexagonal floor plan that looks a little like a modified kite. Queen Isabella II consecrated the theatre in 1850. Soon, however, reconstruction work began again in 1925, the building got new façades, and in the 1960s, the building turned into a concert hall, and later even into a weapons warehouse. But since 1997 it only serves as a theatre.

○ MUSEO THYSSEN-BORNEMISZA

The golden triangle of art at the end of the Paseo del Prado also includes the second largest private art collection in the world. In the converted noble palace Villahermosa, the visitor walks through 68 rooms full of art treasures from the 13th to the 20th century. Especially the modern paintings complement the offerings from the Prado. Highlights include the collection of Flemish and Dutch paintings from the 17th century and impressionist oil paintings.

○ PLAZA DE CIBELES

This statue gets kisses from world stars: When the footballers of Real Madrid celebrate, they lead their triumphal procession to the Cibeles Fountain. Then they wrap the shoulders of the Greek goddess Cybele in their flags. No easy task, because after all, the fountain and statue measure a total of eight metres. The water feature from 1782 is one of the city's landmarks.

○ REAL JARDÍN BOTÁNICO

In the 18th century one of the most important botanical gardens in the world grew in Madrid. The Real Jardín Botánico was created by King Charles III because the old garden at Manzaranesfluss was too small. From the entire Iberian Peninsula and many parts of Europe, medicinal plants were rooted here, as the garden originally served as a royal court pharmacy.

○ ESTACIÓN DE ATOCHA

This station is at the same time a palm garden. While travelers wait for their local and long-distance connections, they can walk in the magnificent hall between tropical plants.

GOING OUT

Bodega de Candeli // Located in the district of Chamberí, the restaurant offers market-fresh produce as well as excellent fish and meat, together with award winning wines.
// restaurantecandeli.com/bodega

Vinícola Mentridana // The Bohemian scene of Lavapiés stays here. The atmosphere is casual to chic. The wine list is quite impressive, and served with all sorts of local delicacies.

Las Cuevas de Luis Candelas // Suckling pig ("cochinillo"), tripe ("callos a la madrileña") and stew ("cocido de puchero") are the specialties in this traditional restaurant on the Plaza Mayor.
// www.lascuevasdeluiscandelas.com

Pajarita // Located in the heart of Madrid, this tapas bar offers modern fusion cuisine. Accompanied by good music and great cocktails, this spot promises a perfect evening.
// www.barpajarita.com

SHOPPING

○ **GRAN VÍA**

On this bustling shopping street Gran Vía, one boutique is next to the other. Anyone who can break away from the shop windows for a moment should take a look at the impressive, sometimes pompously designed historic buildings.

○ **CALLE DE PRECIADOS**

The "Street of Treasures" is a lively shopping street in the city centre. Shopping malls, big chain stores and smaller shops provide everything your heart desires.

○ **MERCADO DE SAN MIGUEL**

The market hall is over 100 years old. If you stroll between the iron pillars, you can see at several stalls how rich Spain's culinary diversity is. Here you come to shop, to stroll, but also for the tapas in the evening.

// www.mercadodesanmiguel.es

GOING OUT

○ **TOLEDO**

What a diverse history: Romans, Visigoths, Moors - they all ruled here until King Alfonso VI Toledo made it the capital of Castile. Traces of the past can be found in many corners of the city, its medieval town centre is preserved to this day and is now a UNESCO World Heritage Site.

○ **SEGOVIA**

Also a city with a long tradition, whose historical centre tells an exciting story. In the middle of it all is the famous aqueduct (now a UNESCO World Heritage Site), the late-Gothic cathedral in the centre of the old town, and the impressive Alcázar Castle.

Left: The market hall San Miguel is today the only one of its kind in the city, and a meeting place for a little bit of lobster, olives or ham in between. If that's too expensive for you, just sit down in one of the street bars.

WHERE TO STAY

The Principal // This luxury hotel impresses with its central location and offers high standards of comfort, wellness and breathtaking views over Madrid from its own rooftop terrace.

// www.theprincipalmadridhotel.com

Roome Mate Óscar // With clear colours and modern furniture, a tribute to the avant-garde! Add to that are free Wi-Fi, a rooftop bar and great attention to service - what more do you expect from a designer hotel?

// www.room-matehotels.com/
en/oscar

La Pepa Chic Bed & Breakfast // Here functionality is key and the name says it all because the Pepa Chic offers what you need for a weekend trip, a bed and breakfast. Without a lot of bells and whistles - but that does not mean good service is not included.

// www.lapepa-bnb.com

NOT TO BE MISSED

RUMMAGING AT EL RASTRO

The most famous flea market in Spain starts at dawn on Sundays, when the merchants set up their stalls selling clothes, vases, antiques and kitchen utensils. El Rastro is the city's largest flea market, stretching between Plaza de Cascorro, Ribera de Curtidores and Tirso de Molina. The traditions of this old market dates back to the 15th century when tanners and butchers peddled their wares here. Today, more than 3,000 stalls provide a colourful mix of old porcelain, uniforms and caps, picture frames, CDs and of course books.

ENJOYING CHURROS

If you believe the locals, the Churros tastes the best in the Chocolatería San Gínes. Here, the fried biscuit is produced and consumed around the clock. Also the dipping chocolate is particularly delicious here.

LAS VENTAS MUSEUM OF TRADITIONAL BULLFIGHTING

Bullfighting has been a tradition in Spain for centuries. In Madrid, they still take place today in Las Ventas, but for some years now, the pressure from politicians and animal rights activists has caused a sharp decline in visitor numbers. Anyone who wants to get an idea of the controversy can experience the arena on a guided tour from the point of view of the main actors and then learn more about the impressive history of the Tauromaquia at the museum.

EXPERIENCING THE NIGHTLIFE IN HUERTAS

Madrid's nightlife is legendary - and every night the saying goes that this city never sleeps. Celebrations are loud, bustling and international on Calle Huerta and in the surrounding streets.

ENJOY A BREATHTAKING VIEW OVER MADRID

One of the best views of Madrid is from the roof top terrace of the Circulo de las Bellas Artes, and afterwards you should treat yourself to a visit in the café on the ground floor.

#12 MAJORCA

MAJORCA IS THE LARGEST ISLAND OF THE BALEARIC ISLANDS AND PERHAPS THE MOST BEAUTIFUL OF THE ENTIRE MEDITERRANEAN. MILES OF WHITE SANDY BEACHES, THE TURQUOISE BLUE SEA, THE SPECTACULAR ROCK FORMATIONS OF THE SERRA DE TRAMUNTANA, THE LARGELY RURAL LANDSCAPE OF THE ISLAND WITH SMALL DREAMY VILLAGES LIKE FORNALUTX, OR ALARÓ AND THE LIVELY ATMOSPHERE OF THE CAPITAL PALMA MAKE THE ISLAND WITH ITS MILD MEDITERRANEAN CLIMATE VERY ATTRACTIVE FOR VISITORS. IF YOU ARE CURIOUS ENOUGH AND LEAVE THE STRONGHOLDS OF TOURISM, YOU CAN DISCOVER THE REAL MAJORCA EVERYWHERE: IN THE HIDDEN CREEKS WITH THEIR FISHERMEN'S HUTS, IN THE FARMERS' MARKETS OF THE MOUNTAIN VILLAGES, IN THE LOCAL BARS OR IN THE CAPITAL'S AVANT-GARDE ART CAFÉS.

Left: At the core, the idyllic mountain village of Valldemossa with its nested stone houses in front of an impressive mountain backdrop remains comparatively unimpressed by the stream of visitors.

Right: The spacious courtyard of the Castell de Bellver is surrounded by impressive two-storey rows of arcades.

○ PALMA DE MAJORCA

Palma, the shining pearl of the Mediterranean, has many faces: the bustling metropolis, which rarely sleeps, with trendy nightclubs, excellent restaurants, elegant and hip boutiques. The old town with tropical-floral Art Nouveau façades and restored noble palaces, in whose courtyards time seems to stand still, with the cathedral La Seu, which guards it like a baby. The city of art with generous museums and names like Miró, Dalí, Tàpies, Saura or Barceló. And not least miles of beaches and countless pubs, bars and cafés in every price range.

○ CATHEDRALE

Sa Seu - "seat of the bishop" - the Majorcans call the Cathedral of St. Mary of Palma. In 1230, shortly after the reconquest of the Moors, King Jaume I. laid the foundation stone for a church. From 1306, the actual construction of the cathedral began, which should also serve as a mausoleum for the Majorcans royal family. The round window was built in 1370, which was only glazed in 1599 and is still one of the most beautiful rosettes in the world today.

○ PALACES

Palma has more than 100 city palaces, which are barely visible from the outside, magical courtyards are hidden behind shielding walls and thick wooden doors. Today, some are split into smart condos, others are converted into hotels, art galleries and boutiques. The romantic courtyards are blocked only by gates, and around Corpus Christi area most are open to visitors.

○ PLAÇA DEL MERCAT

On the Plaça del Mercat, where the market is held today, goods were offered for sale since the time of the Moors. Particularly striking are two houses in the flawless style of Modernism, the magnificent Gran Hotel is opposite Can Casasayas, both buildings were designed by Franscisco Roca Sima. One, known as Pensió La Menorquina, dates from 1908, the other was built in 1909.

○ CASTELL DEL BELLVER

Bellver Castle makes a striking silhouette on the skyline of Palma. The castle, located above the Es Terreno district, was commissioned by King Jaume I. shortly after the conquest of the island. It was only completed in 1309 by the court architect Pere Salvà, who also led the conversion of the Almudaina Palace.

○ DEIÀ

In the picturesque artist village of Deià, many non-residents have settled down over the years. Bou-tiques, small galleries and numerous restaurants fit seamlessly into the rural flair of the pastel-colour-ed stone houses of Deià. A few kilometres from the village centre lies the small pebble cove, Cala de Deià. It is framed by Aleppo pines and fishermen's huts.

○ NATURAL PARC S'ALBUFERA

The swampy nature park in the north is the most important wetland in the Balearic Islands. In a world of its own, you can watch over 200 species of birds and, with luck, discover amphibians.

○ CAPDEPERA

In Capdepera you can still experience the original Majorca. Overlooked by many, this place is quite in-teresting with its ancient charm. A cultural-histori-cal attraction is the former city wall of Capdepera with its triangular plan. To the side of it, there is a small watchtower whose square pedestal is proba-bly one of the last witnesses of the Arabian archi-tecture.

○ CAP DE FORMENTOR

The Cape of the Formentor peninsula in the ex-treme north can be reached from Pollença via a narrow serpentine road. At the end of an approx-imately 15-kilometre drive, past pine trees and holm oak-covered, steep rocky slopes, you finally reach the bright white lighthouse. From its platform, you have the northwest and northeast coast in view, and on a clear day, you can see all the way to Menorca.

○ THE VALLEY OF SÓLLER

The fertile valley at the foot of the Tramuntana moun-tains is best visited by train. The views along the way are breathtaking. After you can enjoy the magical atmosphere of the valley of Sóller.

○ FORNALUTX

Orange trees instead of beach promenades, quaint taverns instead of fast food restaurants. Fornalutx has been repeatedly voted the most beautiful village in Spain. The valley is surrounded by huge rocks.

Left: For visitors who want to take home souvenirs from the almond blossom event, the museum shop of Sa Granja and other well-stocked souvenir shops are recommended. They stock the perfume and eau de toilette of the brand "Flor d'Ametler" - the scented water is based on the almond blossoms that have been grown here since the 1930s.

○ SANTUARI DE LLUC

The Lluc Monastery in the Serra de Tramuntana is considered the spiritual centre of the island. Only a few monks live there, but the Brothers of the Order of the Sacred Heart also welcome visitors overnight to the former cells - especially when the traditional pilgrims arrives on the first Saturday in August. The object of worship is the black Madonna holding her child in her arms on an altar behind the basilica.

○ COVES DEL DRAC

In the "Dragon Caves" on the east coast, you can admire one of the largest underground lakes in the world. Unforgettable classical concert followed by the natural light effects from the sunrise.

Above right: Archaeological finds prove that the caves of the Coves del Drac were inhabited about 3,000 years ago.

Bottom right: The 14 km long, serpentine asphalt road down to Sa Calobra is a true work of art by the Italian engineer, Antonio Paretti, who was commissioned to build the road in 1932.

GOING OUT

Palma: La Boveda // La Boveda is the ultimate tapas bar in Palma. Although the prices are quite high, the kitchen is excellent and authentic. At noon and in the evening, tourists, local Majorcans and often celebrities meet here.
// www.restaurantelaboveda.com

Algaida: Hostal d'Algaida // Here Majorcan home cooking comes to the table. Especially delicious is bread with olive oil, pa amb oli. This can be eaten as a main course with home-made sausage.

Fornalutx: Ca'n Antuna // The restaurant is known far beyond the Tramuntana - even the king comes here sometimes. Here you can eat the best roasted suckling pig of the island, in addition you can enjoy the wonderful view of the pretty village and the surrounding mountains.

○ POLLENÇA

This pretty village is located in a valley in the north of the island. Worth seeing is this historic old town. The community also has beautiful sandy beaches and cliffs.

○ SA CALOBRA

You can reach this dreamy place only from the water, or over the 14-kilometre long serpentine roads, which are a masterpiece of the Italian engineer, Antonio Paretti.

○ VALLDEMOSSA

Valldemossa is visited by half a million tourists every year, most of them following in the footsteps of Frédéric Chopin and George Sand. But confining Valldemossa only to the Carthusian monastery would be rather one-sided. For example, there is also the cultural centre Costa Nord, an initiative from the actor Michael Douglas with information about the natural enviroment of the Serra de Tramuntana, and regular cultural events.

Left: Kitchen accessories made of olive wood are a popular souvenir from the island. At the Rastro, a flea market in Palma, for example, you can buy themin good quality.

SHOPPING

○ ENJABONARTE IN PALMA

The soaps, shower gels and shampoos from Enjabonarte are something very special. You can buy them here in all colours and scents - the soaps can also be bought very cheaply per gram in blocks.

// enjabonarte.es

○ RIALTO LIVING IN PALMA

This is one of the most beautiful shops in Palma and one of the most unusual of all. Housed in an old cinema, the Swedish owners offer selected items from cashmere scarfs to fine silk cloth. Also, furniture, dishes, stuffed toy animals, and even scented stationery can be found here.

// rialtoliving.com

○ FLEA MARKET IN PALMA

Every Saturday morning, the Avinguda Gabriel Alomar i Villalonga becomes a hub for kitsch and curiosity.

○ ARTESANÍA EUGENIO IN SÓLLER

If you are lucky, you will meet the master of wood-carving art at work. Beautiful olive wood bowls, salad servers and other olive wood items can be purchased directly from him.

○ POTTERY FROM PÒRTOL

Not far from Palma, Pòrtol is located on a hill. The place has made a name for itself with its beautiful clay potterywork.

WHERE TO STAY

Palma: Hotel Born // Dark curved wood, noble furniture typical for the island - the small Hotel Born exudes the elegance of a bygone era.

//www.hotelborn.com/en/

Palma: Hotel Portixol // For those who like small, comfortable and stylish properties, this 24-room hotel ticks all the boxes. It is located in the old fishing port of Portixol, about one kilometre east of the old town. It has a first class restaurant and a bar with a terrace.

// www.portixol.com

Deià: Hotel Belmond La Residencia // In the romantic artist village of Deià, the former mansion thrones over the olive groves and gardens. If you just want to relax, you will find a variety of offerings, ranging from a rich spa program to participation in the olive harvest, to dining in the restaurant El Olivo, one of the best restaurants on the island.

// www.belmond.com

NOT TO BE MISSED

THE SUNSET AT THE TALAIA D'ALBERCUTX

Above the Mediterranean Sea sits a watchtower at an altitude of 380 metres. There is barely a more impressive view of the Formentor peninsula and the Majorcan coast than from this location.

EATING ENSAÏMADA AT THE CA NA JUANITA BAKERY IN ALARÓ

This cute place offers quaint accommodation and pretty shops. Best of all, the bakery, which is more than 100 years old, and makes the crunchiest "ensaïmadas", lard-baked yeast slices.

DIVING IN FRONT OF THE ILLA DE CABRERA

The smallest inhabited island of the Balearic Islands leads an existence away from tourism. We recommend a day trip by boat with a dive and visit to the Blue Grotto.

EATING ALMOND CAKE AT THE XOCO LATERÍA

In the Xocolatería Ca'n Joan de S'aigo in Palma, the chocolate is so thick that you can actually spoon it. And for those who like it even sweeter, we recommend the authentic almond cake Gató.

VISITING AN OLIVE OIL MILL

The valley of Sóller is famous for its olives. In the past, the oil obtained was a major source of income. The 16th century mill Can Det is worth a visit.

#13 PRAGUE

HERE SHE WOULD RATHER BE ABLE TO PAINT THAN WRITE, AS THE ROMANTIC CAROLINE DE LA MOTTE FOUQUÉ ONCE SAID. THERE IS A POINT AT THIS HEIGHT FROM WHERE THE VIEW BECOMES ALMOST INTOXICATING, SINKING INTO THE FULLNESS OF THE GREATEST POSSIBLE WEALTH. IMMEDIATELY BELOW THE SLOPE THE VLTAVA, ABOVE IT SITS THE ROYAL PRAGUE! THIS CITY WAS INDESCRIBABLE, PERHAPS INCOMPARABLE, AND THAT IS PRECISELY WHAT FASCINATED VISITORS AT ALL TIMES. THE "GOLDEN PRAGUE" WITH ITS HISTORIC CENTRE PROTECTED AS A UNESCO WORLD HERITAGE SITE, THAT HAS CHANGED THROUGHOUT ITS HISTORY AND HAS ALWAYS REMAINED THE SAME - IT IS, INDEED, "INCOMPARABLE". AND IF, MORE THAN TWO DECADES AFTER THE "VELVET REVOLUTION", EVERYTHING CONTINUES TO CHANGE, THE WORDS OF THE POETS STILL APPLY HERE: "ALL OF PRAHA IS A GOLDEN NET OF POEMS", WROTE DETLEV VON LILIENCRON.

Left: For centuries, the "Golden City" has been an important spiritual-cultural centre characterised by a uniquely beautiful urban ensemble.

Right: The St. George's Basilica dates back to around 915. After several fires, the visible part seen today was built in the 12th century.

○ CASTLE OF PRAGUE

Not only visually, the castle located on the "Hradschin" hill overlooking Prague has dominated the city for over 1,000 years; today, it is still the political centre of the country. From the early 12th century to the second half of the 16th century, the three-storey old Royal Palace served as a residence for the respective rulers. The showpiece is the Vladislav Hall, built in 1493-1503. Due to its enormous dimensions - 62 metres long, 16 metres wide, 13 metres high - not only could markets be held in it, but even equestrian games and tournaments can take place here.

○ MONASTERY ST. GEORGE

One would not initially suspect viewing the Baroque façade from around the year 1670, that the two-towered St. George's Basilica on the north side of the Georg's square is the oldest surviving church building in the area of the Prague Castle. But if you walk through the entrance way, a three-aisled building opens-up, the Romanesque character of which was largely restored during renovations. The church was donated around the year 920 by Prince Vratislav I.

○ GOLDEN LANE

Legend has it that alchemists tried to make gold here. In fact, it was just a poor settlement with tiny houses - Franz Kafka lived in one of them - which are now souvenir shops.

○ SAINT VITUS CATHEDRAL

The St. Vitus Cathedral stands for the glorious history of the Kingdom of Bohemia, and is the coronation church of 30 rulers. Herzog Wenzel in the year 925 built a round chapel where it stands today, in honour of the early Christian martyr, Vitus (Veit). Wenzel, later also sainted, ascended to be the patron Saint of Bohemia, his grave in the chapel he himself founded became a place of pilgrimage. In 1344, the foundation stone was laid for the Gothic cathedral, the construction of which was completed after many interruptions in 1929. The building captivates with its rich artistic design as well as its over-sized dimensions, with an outside length of 124 metres, this is the largest church in Prague.

○ MONASTERY STRAHOV

The Premonstratensian monastery is open for visitors - a stunning library, a picture gallery and a wondeful chamber with many archaeological findings.

○ MALA STRANA

The Malá Strana, also known as the Lesser Town, is the district below the castle and the castle hill Hradschin. A walk through the district with its countless

magnificent palaces seems like a journey into another time. The centre of the Mala Strana is the Town Square, which is lined with important buildings.

○ ST. NICHOLAS CHURCH
The monumentality of St. Nicholas, the largest Baroque church in Prague, is also explained by the fact that the church was built in the 17th and 18th centuries at the time of the Counter Reformation and Re-Catholization of the Bohemian lands: the power and splendor of the architecture should also symbolise the triumph of the christian orthodoxe doctrine over the deviant doctrines of the Protestants.

○ CHARLES BRIDGE
The first stone bridge in Prague, the Judith bridge built in the 12th century, originally crossed the Vltava. After breaking during a flood in 1342, a replacement was needed, as a firm connection across the river was vital to the city. However, the construction of the new bridge first began in 1357 with the laying of the foundation stone by Emperor Charles IV and was completed after about 50 years. Here the Coronation processions of the Bohemian kings were led.

○ OLD TOWN SQUARE
After an extension to the Vltava around the year 1900, today already around 9,000 square metres, this large old town ring had already developed in the 11th/12th century as a central marketplace of merchants. But they were also home to the pillory and blood courts, and throughout history, the square has many times been the scene of cruel, often bloody events.

○ OLD TOWN CITY HALL AND CLOCK
A visit to this Gothic town hall is certainly worthwhile, particulary for the astronomical clock from the 15th century. Every hour figures of the twelve apostles appear to the sound of the bells.

○ CHURCH OF OUR LADY TÝN
After St. Vitus Cathedral, the Týn Church is the most significant religious building in Prague. Although the three-aisled basilica is not directly located on the east side of the Old Town Square, but being slightly offset, by the upstream Teyn Parish School, it still dominates the appearance of the square as otherwise only challenged by the town hall.

Left: Stars of the scene like cellist Alisa Weilerstein, or the London Philharmonic Orchestra conducted by Vladimir Jurowski, are also on the program in the "Prague Spring", as well as newcomers. The final climax is always a performance of Beethoven's Ninth Symphony.

GOING OUT

Klášterní pivovar // This monastery brewery was transformed in 2000 into a modern brewery. However, the founding of the brewery, St. Norbert, on the Strahov site dates back to the 13th century. In the brewhouse, you will find a more authentic tavern atmosphere than in the actual restaurant.

// **www.klasterni-pivovar.cz**

Café de Paris // In the 1920s, the Art Nouveau coffee house was a meeting place for artists and writers. Historic charm meets modern design today - you will still find a cultivated audience.

// **www.cafedeparis.cz/de**

U Maleho Glena Bar & Jazz Club // Not far from the Charles Bridge, night owls meet in this popular jazz and rock club. Mondays always has blues on the program, every evening a different live band performs. The bar is also very popular.

// **malyglen.cz**

○ **JEWISH QUARTER**

Not far from the centre is the Josefov. Unfortunately there is not much left of it, only some synagogues and the old cemetery with densely packed tombs. A tour of the district is still recommended.

○ **CLEMENTINUM**

In 1556, the Jesuits established a Catholic university in an empty monastery. With the support of other pro-catholic patrons, the Clementinum until 1726 was extended to the second largest building in Prague (after the castle) - a whole district had to relocate. In addition to living quarters for students and teachers, seminar and lecture halls, the Clementinum located near the banks of the Vltava River, also housed a theatre and a printing press, an observatory and, last but not least, several sacred buildings such as the Mirror Chapel. Today, you can find the Czech National Library here.

○ **WECESLAS SQUARE**

It is one of the largest squares in Europe and often the scene of political demonstrations. But it is also architecturally interesting, for example due to the facade of the Grand Hotel Europa.

○ **JOHN LENNON WALL**

It started with a portrait of John Lennon, whose music was banned in Czechoslovakia. It was followed by pictures and quotes on freedom, which today adorn the colourful wall.

○ DANCING HOUSE

The office building with gallery and restaurant consists of a glass and a concrete section, which nestle together. The style of the architect Frank O. Gehry is very visible.

SHOPPING

○ POHODLÍ

A small shop crammed with music from all over the world. A look inside is highly recommended.

// www.pohodli.com

○ KOTVA

The special feature of this five-storey department store lies in the ambience of a communist era.

// www.od-kotva.cz/en

○ MYSLBEK

Spectacular glass façade, inside brand and designer shops, and internatioal cuisine restaurants.

// www.ngmyslbek.cz/en/

○ MANUFAKTURA

Bohemian handicrafts are offered in the stores, as well as products made with local ingredients.

// www.manufaktura.cz/en/

DAYTRIPS

○ STALACTITE CAVES OF KONĐPRUSY

The stalactite caves were discovered just over 60 years ago, millions of years old rock, bats and an exposed coin counterfeiting workshop from the Middle Ages.

Left: Barely visable under layers of colour: John Lennon's portrait on the wall named after him.

WHERE TO STAY

Antik City // This elegant hotel is characterised by the aesthetics of the time under King Charles IV, who made Prague the architectural pearl of Central Europe. The house with the pretty façade is tucked away in a quiet little alley near the Wenceslas Square.

// www.antikcity.cz/en

Hotel Černý Slon // Just behind the Tyn Church and near the Old Town Square, the hotel "The black elephant" offers 16 tastefully furnished guest rooms, which hide behind a Gothic façade.

// www.hotelcernyslon.cz/en

Hotel Ametyst // This popular four-star boutique hotel sparkles like a gem with its award-winning cuisine, art gallery, sumptuous breakfast buffet, friendly service, yet a relaxed casual atmosphere.

// https://www.hotelametyst.com

NOT TO BE MISSED

SEARCHING FOR ART NOUVEAU

What was called Jugendstil in Berlin was called a secession in Prague, based on the Viennese variant. The most famous Czech representative of this new art form is the painter and graphic artist, Alfons Mucha. His touch can also be clearly seen in the Representation House, one of the prime examples of Art Nouveau in Prague. Many of Prague's buildings still bear the stamp of Art Nouveau. The Peterka house and the Hotel Central are influenced by the early stages. Also the main station, the Grand Hotel Europa as well as the Topic Publishing House are assigned clearly to the Jugendstil style.

BOOKING A BOAT TRIP AT NIGHT

Many of the attractions are located on the banks of the Vltava River, so a boat trip is the best way to see them. Especially beautiful when the skyline silhouette is illuminated. There are regular trips with dinner on board.

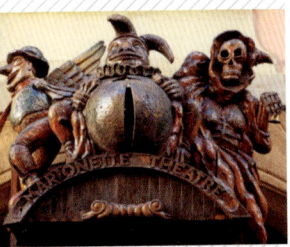

VISITING A PUPPET THEATRE

The puppet show on a big stage has a long tradition with its classical operas in Prague. Equipment and costumes can easily compete with a state theater. A puppet theater performance should be experienced by everyone who visits Prague.

BEING AT THE ASTRONOMICAL CLOCK AS THE HOUR IS FULL

The upper dial of the Astronomical Clock shows the orbit of the sun, the moon and time; the lower circle serves as a calendar. Every hour there is an apostle parade, and "Death" rings when he pulls the cord. Other characters move as the rooster flutters and the twelve apostles slide by in front of the open window, this was how Guillaume Apollinaire described the spectacle.

VISITING A PRAGUE COFFEE HOUSE

Some of them are no less splendid and elegant than the coffee houses found in Vienna. The visitors here are also often writers who are finishing parts of their novels. Art Nouveau tiles adorn the wall in the Café Imperial, mosaics cover the ceiling. In the old days, you could throw donuts at other guests for a small amount of money. But not today unfortunately!

#14 ROME

A WALK THROUGH THIS CITY WILL MAKE YOU FEEL THE PRESENCE OF THE MYTHICAL FOUNDER, ROMULUS, AS WELL AS THE EMPERORS OF THE ROMAN EMPIRE OR THE POPES WHO, DURING THE RENAISSANCE AND BAROQUE PERIODS, RESIDED IN THE CAPITAL OF CHRISTIANITY AS SECULAR RULERS. ROME SHOWS THE DEVELOPMENT OF EUROPEAN CULTURE LIKE NO OTHER PLACE. YET, THIS CITY HAS NOTHING MUSEAL ABOUT IT. IN THE SHADOW OF THE OLD MONUMENTS, LIFE PASSES IN A ROUSING "VITAL" WAY. THERE ARE RESTAURANTS, BARS, THEATRES AND LIVELY PLACES. IN THE NATURE OF THE ROMANS MERGE VIVACITY AND NONCHALANCE; THE ATMOSPHERE IS JOYFUL AND RELAXING, IT IS STIMULATING AND CAN CARRY YOU AWAY. OR, AS GOETHE SAID: "HERE THE CURRENT CARRIES YOU AWAY AS SOON AS YOU HAVE BOARDED THE BOAT".

Above: In Rome "one is carried away by the current as soon as one has boarded the boat" as said by Goethe. And the history is omnipresent. The numerous church domes testify to the power of the curia, and the many archaeological sites to the long and eventful history of the Eternal City.

Left: Rome, the city of pilgrims: St. Peter's Church is the most important church of Christianity.

○ COLOSSEUM

The Colosseum, built between 72 and 80 AD, takes its name from a colossal statue of Emperor Nero. Once it served as an amphitheatre for show fights by gladiators and animal hunters. It housed about 75,000 spectators, had awnings and a very exemplary system of entrances and exits.

○ FORUM ROMANUM

Here lays the centre of the city and the political centre of the Roman Empire. Temples and state buildings, such as the Curia for the Senate meetings, were supplemented by a triumphal arch, lecture platforms, halls for court and business transactions and taverns.

○ CAPITOL

The religious centre of ancient Rome with the Temple of Jupiter Optimus Maximus has a plaza designed by Michelangelo. The Palazzo Nuovo on the left, and the Conservatory Palace on the right, house the Capitoline collections. The famous equestrian statue of Emperor Marcus Aurelius in the centre is a copy.

○ SANT ANGELO BRIDGE AND CASTLE

The angels on the bridge carrying Christ's Passion tools were implemented by his disciples according to Bernini's designs. Castel Sant'Angelo, once the tomb of Roman emperors from Hadrian to Caracalla, is nowadays a museum.

○ ST. PETER'S BASILICA

The largest church in the world until 1989, and the centre of Catholic Christianity, but also a monument of art history. Built according to the plans of Bramante and Michelangelo in 1506 as a central building, extended by Maderno and Bernini and equipped with façade and a plaza, the building also contains a wealth of artworks inside, including the main works of Bernini and the Pietà Michelangelo. From the dome, you also have magnificent view of the city.

WHY VISIT IN SPRING?

ROME HAS REACHED A PROUD AGE - BUT THEY STILL KNOW HOW TO CELEBRATE HERE. THE CITY WAS FOUNDED ON APRIL 21, 753 BC. BY ROMULUS, ONE OF THE TWO ABANDONED SONS OF MARS, WHO WAS THEN NURSED BY A SHE-WOLF AND LATER KILLED HIS BROTHER REMUS. TODAY, THE CITY CELEBRATES ITS FOUNDING DAY EVERY YEAR WITH CONCERTS, FESTIVAL PARADES, HISTORICAL PERFORMANCES AND LOTS OF PEOPLE IN TOGAS. MANY OF THE ARCHAEOLOGICAL SITES AND MUSEUMS OFFER FREE ENTRY ON THIS DAY, BUT THE MAIN VENUE OF THE FESTIVITIES IS THE AVENTINE. IF YOU WANT TO HAVE A GOOD VIEW OF THE FIREWORKS, MAKE SURE YOU GO TO THE CAPITOL HILL ON TIME.

○ SANTA MARIA IN TRASTEVERE

Rome's oldest church of St. Mary is famous for its mosaics. The exterior mosaic on the façade depicts Mary between saints; in the interior of the apse mosaic she sits enthroned beside Christ. The scenes from her life are all interpretations by Pietro Cavallini (1291). It is a trendy district around the St. Marys church.

○ CAMPO DE' FIORI

Around the monument to Giordano Bruno, the Dominican monk who lost his way on the path to righteousness, who was burned here as a heretic in 1600, is one of the largest markets in Rome. The market is open in the mornings and in the evenings. You will find here a very colourful street life of Rome.

○ SPANISH STEPS

Over the hill Pincio with its beautiful view of Rome, past the Villa Medici with the French Academy and the Church of Santa Trinità dei Monti, you get to the "staircase of all stairs" - The Spanish Steps - that sweep like a river between the buildings. The life of the artist took place around the Piazza di Spagna below. From here, the luxury shopping streets around the Via Condotti open up.

○ FONTANA DI TREVI

This display fountain by Nicola Salvis is a main attractions for tourists. Fountain water is fed by an ancient aqueduct, it is an extravagant display, not just in its decoration, but also in its water features.

○ PANTHEON

Formerly a temple for all gods, today the building owes its good preservation to a conversion into a church. Originally built under Augustus, the Pantheon then got its famous round shape under Emperor Hadrian, with the dome symbolising the sky of the gods. The classic proportion of 1:1 in relation to the cylinder dome height (43 metres) gives the building its perfection.

○ PIAZZA NAVONA

The elongated oval space above the floor plan of an ancient stadium has three fountains, including the central Four Fountain with the Danube, Nile, Ganges and Rio de la Plata rivers, by Gianlorenzo Bernini. Behind it are the Baroque façades of the Church of Sant'Agnese in Agone and Palazzo Pamphili.

Left: Rome's birthday celebration starts with a large firework display every year. Especially beautiful is the view when seen from the Tiber.

○ SAN GIOVANNI IN LATERANO

The actual episcopal church of the Pope is the highest-ranking church of Catholic Christianity. It still preserves the early Christian structure of the Constantinian period in its walls, but its present form is based on a Baroque redesign by Francesco Borromini in the 19th century.

○ SANTA MARIA MAGGIORE

This pilgrim church goes back to a legend, according to which in August snow fell on a place on which gods church should be built. The Baroque period colonnades and mosaics on the high wall, and the triumphal arch in front of the choir area, date back to the construction period from the Year 432 onwards.

○ QUIRINAL PALACE

The palace, originally the papal summer residence, then the residence of the Italian kings, is today the seat of the Italian President. The square in front is decorated with an Egyptian obelisk and the group of Dioscuri Castor and Pollux from the thermal baths of Emperor Constantine.

GOING OUT

Sora Lella // For 65 years now, this family-run trattoria on the Tiber Island has been a Roman institution. The dishes are typically Roman, and the portions very generous. Be sure to try the meatballs in sauce, salad or soup.

// www.trattoriasoralella.it

Antico Caffè della Pace // Since 1891, the place decorated with antiques and painted interiors is a popular meeting place. In front of the ivy-covered house, you can treat yourself to a coffee or a drink.

// Via della Pace 3–7

Shari Vari // In the rooms of the formerly legendary supper club, you can first indulge your palate at the Ristorante and then celebrate with all your senses in the club. Decoration and furnishings are noble and extrovert.

// www.sharivari.it

Top right: In the Fountain della Barcaccia, in the Piazza di Spagna, Bernini placed a dilapidated piece of wood - a reminder of the Tiber flood in 1598, when this area could only be reached by boat.

Bottom right: Over the centuries, the construction of Santa Maria Maggiore has been repeatedly renovated and changed, so that you can nowadays read, almost as in a building guide, about the various art and architectural styles.

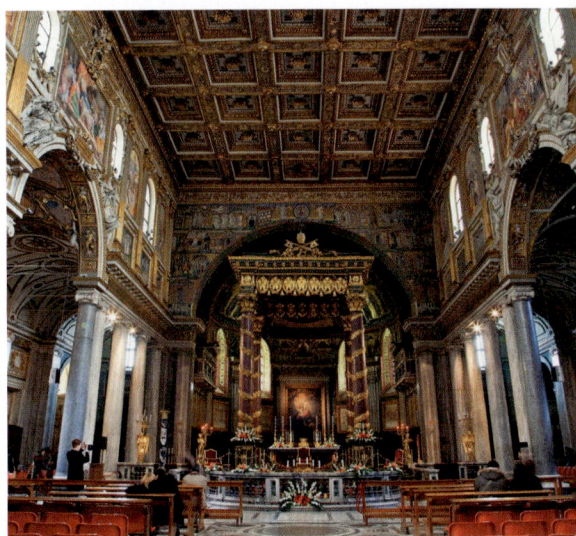

SHOPPING

○ L'ANTICA SALUMERIA

Cheese, olives, wine - a perfect combination. In Salumeria you will get all these ingredients with the finest quality, with a piece of pizza to go.

○ MERCATO DELL'UNITÀ

The market hall in the Prati district alone is worth a visit. The fresh food even more so. Just the variety of tomatoes will makes you speechless.

○ MERCATO VILLAGGIO OLIMPICO

In addition to food, you will also find jewelry, clothing and paraphernalia. A paradise to stroll around and discover.

○ GALLERIA ALBERTO SORDI

The chic gallery on Piazza Colonna offers a good mix of high-end designer goods and affordable products.
// www.galleriaalbertosordi.it

○ VIA CONDOTTI

With the Spanish Steps in view, the Via Condotti is the noble mile par excellence. Elegant Roman ladies and gentlemen stroll along here and delight in the displays of Armani, Gucci, Beltrami or Ferragamo.

DAYTRIPS

○ OSTIA & OSTIA ANTICA

In Rome's southwestern region of Ostia, 30 kilometres from the city itself, there is the open-air museum of Ostia Antica. Temples, a ruined city, multi-storey residential buildings and the cemetery are partially well preserved. You should also pack your bathing suit - here, the Romans like to relax on the beach of Ostia.

WHERE TO STAY

De Russie // An absolute top class hotel, just a few metres away from the Spanish Steps or Piazza del Popolo. The house has a recommendable gourmet restaurant, a spa facility worth visiting ,and a wonderfully landscaped garden.
// **www.roccofortehotels.com**

Farnese // A beautiful 17th century villa in the Prati district, within walking distance of the heart of the Vatican, houses this pleasantly quiet hotel.
//**www.hotelfarnese.com/en**

Richmond // Within a few steps you can reach large monuments and shopping streets. The hotel is owned by the Gnecco family, which offers impeccable service. It has a beautiful rooftop terrace to enjoy the wonderful view of the Imperial Forum during breakfast.
// **www.hotelrichmondrome.com**

NOT TO BE MISSED

BE COMPLETELY ASTOUNDED IN THE VATICAN MUSEUMS

On seven kilometres through 1,300 exhibition rooms - the Vatican Museums show what treasures the church has accumulated over the centuries. The Sistine Chapel is the centerpiece of the Vatican Museums. Wall and ceiling paintings are mainly by Michelangelo, but also Botticelli. In addition, you should absolutely visit the Raphael Rooms - living rooms that the artist designed in the Apostolic Palace.

ENJOYING AN ESPRESSO IN THE ANTICO CAFFÈ GRECO

At Antico Caffè Greco, you can enjoy coffee in an atmosphere that evokes bygone eras. Anyone who sips the little black one feels like one of the artists who would come and go here.

EXPERIENCING A SUNSET ON THE GIANICOLO

Its historical significance, its monuments and botanical treasures are forgotten when gazing from the hill over the city. You will not find a better view of the Vatican, ancient ruins and palazzi.

DINING ON THE ROMAN PIAZZAS

Life takes place outside in Rome. A good meal in one of the squares combines culinary delights with an elegant Roman version of people watching, ancient sites and the buzz of scooters.

THROWING MONEY IN THE TREVI FOUNTAIN AND MAKING A WISH

Anita Ekberg and Marcello Mastroianni bask in the fountains in the film "La Dolce Vita". But it is enough to just throw a coin and to make a wish for the good life.

#15 VALENCIA

THE CAPITAL OF THE AUTONOMOUS REGION OF THE SAME NAME LIES ON THE TURIA RIVER, AND IS ONE OF THE MOST IMPORTANT PORT CITIES ON THE MEDITERRANEAN SEA. VALENCIA IS ONE OF THE FEW LARGE SPANISH CITIES IN WHICH TRACES OF THE PAST, BEGINNING WITH THE ROMANS, HARMONIOUSLY MEET AVANT-GARDE BUILDINGS, SUCH AS THE IVAM ART MUSEUM OPENED IN 1989, OR THE PALAU DE LA MÚSICA. IN 1096, THE CITY WAS TAKEN FROM THE MOORS BY THE SPANISH NATIONAL HERO, EL CID. IN THE 15TH CENTURY, IT DEVELOPED INTO A STRONG TRADING POWER. VALENCIA'S OLD TOWN BOASTS A VARIETY OF ARCHITECTURAL TESTIMONIES FROM ALL PERIODS OF ITS EVENTFUL HISTORY. STARTING WITH THE RUINS OF THE ROMAN SETTLEMENT, WHICH TODAY ARE EXHIBITED TOGETHER WITH FINDINGS FROM MOORISH TIMES IN THE REMARKABLE ARCHAEOLOGICAL MUSEO DE LA ALMOINA; GOTHIC CHURCHES AND BAROQUE PALACES; TO THE BUILDINGS IN THE STYLE OF THE CATALAN MODERNISM HALL OF MERCADO CENTRAL - ALL THESE BUILDINGS MAKE VALENCIA A JEWEL AMONG EUROPE'S CITIES.

Above: Santiago Calatrava's designs for the Ciudad de las Artes y de las Ciencias are based on the organic design language of nature.

Left: The Valencia Silk Exchange symbolises the enormous wealth of this medieval trading centre. The hall was designed as a paradisiacal trading temple, in which the columns symbolise trees and the domes the firmament.

○ THE SILK EXCHANGE (LONJA DE LA SEDA)

Under the Catholic monarchs, Isabella of Castile and Ferdinand II, a long period of peace began for Valencia, during which the port city flourished and became an important trading centre. A particular building is significant among the secular buildings of that period and reflects the wealth of the city: the Lonja de la Seda. The entire complex of the Silk Exchange covers an area of 2,000 square metres, and faces the church of Santos Juanes and the Central Market. In 1483, the construction of the stock exchange begun under the architect, Pere Comte, who also created many other buildings in Valencia. In the late Gothic building, numerous elements from the early Renaissance time can be seen.

○ CATHEDRALE

In the centre of the old town is the "Cathedrale", whose origins go back to the 13th century, but which was rebuilt again and again in the centuries after that and therefore combines a variety of architectural styles. The landmark of Spain's third largest city is the octagonal bell tower of the cathedral, the Torre del Miguelete. In the chapter house, the most important treasure is on display, an agate goblet, which the legend claims is the Holy Grail. Nearby, the regional government is based in the Palau de la Generalitat (15th century).

○ CIUDAD DE LAS ARTES Y DE LAS CIENCI

The city not only impresses with its magnificent historic buildings, but has also attracted attention recently by

WHY VISIT IN SPRING?

BOISTEROUS AND ANARCHIC, "THE FALLAS" ARE EUROPE'S WILDEST SPRING PARTY. THESE DAYS, THE CITY IS FULL OF THE EPONYMOUS "FALLAS" - HUGE SCULPTURES, MADE FROM WOOD AND PAPIER MÂCHÉ, BY LOCAL ARTISTS. WHEN THE CITY AWAKENS AFTER THE NOCTURNAL PLANTÀ (CONSTRUCTION) ON THE MORNING OF MARCH 16, OVER 350 OF THESE FIGURES STAND ON THE STREETS. WHEN THE FALLAS ARE READY, IT STARTS: THEY CAN BE FOUND IN ALL DISTRICTS, AND YOU HAVE FOUR DAYS TO ATTEND EVENTS SUCH AS PAELLA-COOKING, OPEN-AIR CONCERTS AND BULLFIGHTS. THE FALLAS ARE KNOWN FOR THEIR FIREWORKS: EVERY DAY AT 2 PM, THE CITY SHAKES AT THE MASCLETÀS (FIVE MINUTES OF DEAFENING NOISE). AT MIDNIGHT ON THE 19TH OF MARCH (JOSEPH'S DAY), HOWEVER, THE BIGGEST SPECTACLE TAKES PLACE: THE FALLAS ALL GO UP IN FLAMES – MANY MONTHS' OF WORK FALL APART TURN TO RUBBLE AND ASHES IN SECONDS! THE FESTIVAL CONCLUDES WITH A PRESENTATION FOR THE BEST FALLA.

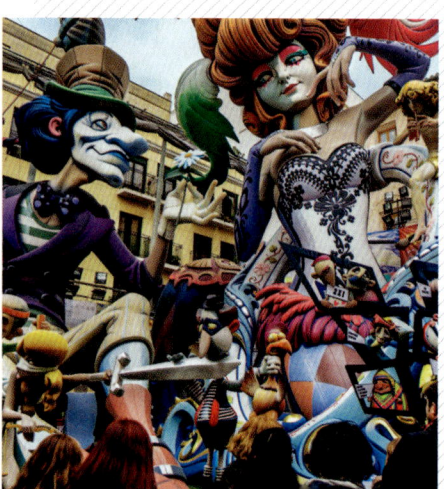

spectacular futuristic buildings, such as Norman Foster's Palacio de Congresos or the Ciudad de las Artes y las Ciencias by local architect Santiago Calatrava. The Ciudad includes a planetarium with IMAX cinema, a science museum, an opera and with the Oceanogràfic, the largest aquarium on the continent.

SHOPPING

○ MARKETS

Valencia is famous for its numerous markets, the most famous is certainly the elegant building of the Lonja. However, the largest market in the city is the Central Market (Mercado Central) - because of its clarity and brightness, as well as a well thought-out arrangement of the stands (thanks to the wide forecourt, the entire complex is considered a masterpiece of Modernism). From there, it is not far to the much visited market stalls on the Plaza Redond, the merchants are there throughout the day.

WHERE TO STAY

Hotel Hospes Palau de la Mar // Located in the city centre, the hotel performs a daring balancing act between the avant-garde and the 19th century. The result is a luxury city hotel with a twist.
// www.hospes.com

Hotel Caro // This design hotel is within easy reach of the cathedral, but located in a side street, whereby the usual city noise is not so bothersome. The rooms are individually and luxuriously designed.
// www.carohotel.com

Left: The annual Fallas offer a fascinating spectacle. At the traditional Spring Festival, hundreds, some very tall, ornately crafted papier mâché figures fill the streets from March 15 to 19.

NOT TO BE MISSED

STROLLING THROUGH THE BOTANICAL GARDEN

The Jardí Botànic is Spain's oldest botanical garden, founded in the 16th century and housed here since 1803. After decades of neglect, the park was beautifully restored. The lush greenery forms a heavenly oasis away from the noise and traffic of the big city. Around 3,000 different tree and plant species grow here.

SHOPPING ON THE COLOM

The Colom, actually Calle Colón, is the main shopping street of the city. The Mercat de Colom, which dates back to the Modernist era, was extensively restored to its old splendor. In the shopping centre you can buy great souvenirs. Nearby is a branch of El Corte Inglés, Spain's largest department store chain.

IMMERSE YOURSELF IN THE NIGHTLIFE AT EL CARME

In the Barrio del Carmen, also called El Carme, a quarter of the old town, things get wild in the evening. Nightclubs, bars and restaurants line up in the narrow, labyrinthine streets. Here beats the nocturnal pulse of the city.

EATING PAELLA FOR LUNCH

It is the national dish of Valencia, and that's why you should not miss out on trying it on a visit to the region. If you want be like the locals, you eat Paella for lunch, supposedly only tourists would eat the dish in the evening.

VISITING THE OCEANOGRÀFICO

It is the largest aquarium in Europe, and even the architecture of the building suggests that the Oceanogràfico is something special. Inside, you can marvel at marine life in a variety of habitats, as well as butterflies and crocodiles.

SUMMER

Summer brings with it the beguiling scent of lavender for Provence, adding a sea of violet flush of colour to the landscape.

#16 EDINBURGH

THIS SCOTTISH CAPITAL IS FASCINATING WITH ITS ARCHITECTURAL UNITY AND A VERY LIVELY CULTURAL LIFE - ESPECIALLY IN SUMMER DURING THE FAMOUS MUSIC AND THEATRE FESTIVAL. AS EARLY AS THE 18TH AND 19TH CENTURIES, EDINBURGH WAS THE CULTURAL CENTRE OF THE NORTH. FAMOUS AUTHORS LIKE ROBERT BURNS AND SIR WALTER SCOTT LIVED HERE. EDINBURGH HAS BEEN A UNESCO WORLD HERITAGE SITE SINCE 1995. PARTICULARLY NOTEWORTHY IS THE ARCHITECTURAL CONTRAST BETWEEN THE MEDIEVAL OLD TOWN AND THE 18TH CENTURY PRUDENTLY PLANNED NEW PART OF THE CITY IN GEORGIAN STYLE. THE FACT THAT THE OLD TOWN STILL GIVES RISE TO CREEPY AND EXCITING STORIES BECOMES UNDERSTANDABLE, ESPECIALLY DURING A STROLL THROUGH THE CITY AT NIGHT.

Above: On Calton Hill you can find the Dugald Stewart Monument in memory of the Scottish philosopher.

Left: A striking point of the Scottish capital Edinburgh's silhouette, next to the belfry of the Balmoral Hotel. The time displayed on the clock is not accurate. Since 1902 they have made sure that the clock runs a bit too fast. After all, the hostel was once a railroad hotel, and officials wanted passengers to be on time.

○ EDINBURGH CASTLE

Standing on Castle Rock, 100 metres above the city, the castle is undoubtedly the main tourist attraction of Edinburgh. As the residence of Scottish kings, it looks back on an eventful history. The oldest preserved building, St Margaret's Chapel, dates from the late 11th century. Until the unification of Scotland with England, after the Battle of Culloden in 1746, Edinburgh Castle was repeatedly besieged, destroyed and rebuilt. The fortress therefore includes buildings from almost every epoch of Scottish history.

○ OLD TOWN

Edinburgh's Old Town is separated from New Town by Princes Street. Tiny medieval streets are lost here amidst the unusually high, partly medieval houses. Steep, narrow and gloomy streets with coarse cobblestones hide nested backyards. During a walk, you often come across quaint pubs and cosy restaurants that are in some previously undiscovered corner. Literary inspiration stimulated the likes of Arthur Conan Doyle's Sherlock Holmes; Robert Louis Stevenson's Dr Jekyll and Mr Hyde; and, J.K. Rowling's Harry Potter series.

○ ROYAL MILE

The Royal Mile, the main artery of Edinburgh's Old Town, is crossed by steeply sloping and ascending narrow streets, backyards and passageways. The Closes, once considered a grubby, dangerous place and decried as a retreat for petty criminals. Today, the old walls are carefully restored and it is a tourist magnet. Of particular interest are the Old Fishmarket Close and Advocate's Close.

○ ST. GILES' CATHEDRAL

In the middle of the Royal Mile, between Victorian houses, you will find St. Giles' Cathedral, the mother church of the Scottish Presbyterianism - stocky

WHY VISIT IN SUMMER?

IN AUGUST ARTISTS FROM A VARIETY OF PLACES COME TOGETHER TO FORM A SUPERLATIVE: THE FAMOUS EDINBURGH FESTIVAL IS A COLLECTION OF DIVERSE FESTIVALS THAT ATTRACT AROUND 2 MILLION VISITORS EVERY YEAR. DURING THIS TIME, JUGGLERS CONQUER THE STREETS; THEATRE GROUPS STILL WORK THE LAST BACKYARD TO THE STAGE; MUSIC STARS PERFORM; CABARET; CIRCUS; OPERA; FILM; AND BALLET ARE OFFERED. AND OF COURSE, THERE ARE BAGPIPES EVERYWHERE. THE START OF THE LEGENDARY CULTURAL SUMMER IS AT THE END OF JULY, WHEN THE "BLUES AND JAZZ FESTIVAL" BEGINS, FOLLOWED BY THE "FRINGE FESTIVAL", WHICH HAS DEVELOPED AS AN ALTERNATIVE EVENT BEFORE THE ACTUAL "INTERNATIONAL FESTIVAL".

and without a proper church tower, but its open stone crown stands out from afar. Especially worth seeing inside is the Thistle Chapel. Lions, labradors, winged mythical creatures, clenched fists of the whole world under a rainbow - the diversity of the crests in the Thistle Chapel an amazement. The coat of arms that hangs there is the reigning knight of the Thistle Order, Scotland's highest knightly order.

○ PRINCES STREET GARDENS

In summer, Princes Street Gardens becomes Edinburgh's open-air living room. Cool drinks, ice cream and hot sausages are sold at numerous stalls, while bagpipers perform for sun worshipers. Concerts and performances at the Ross Open Air Theatre are quickly sold out.

○ NEW TOWN

Despite sinking political importance after the union with England in 1707, Edinburgh remained an important cultural centre. Towards the end of the 18th century, the Georgian New Town was built with the right-angled streets to the north. Along Princes Street there are a number of monuments worth seeing; It separates Edinburgh's Old Town from the New Town.

Above: An atmosphere of "Dr. Jekyll and Mr. Hyde overcomes the Old Town especially after sunset, like here on Cockburn Street.

Left: During the Fringe Festival, the Royal Mile transforms into an open-air theatre stage.

PRINCES STREET

It is arguably one of Edinburgh's most famous streets, offering the most spectacular views across Princes Street Gardens to the Castle. At its eastern end lies Calton Hill. Along the street there are several shops at either end of the price scale. In between, you can rest in numerous cafés and restaurants.

WAVERLEY STATION

Edinburgh Central Station is named after Scott's novella "Waverley" (1814). In terms of size, it is the second largest English railway station after London Waterloo. Built in Victorian style, the station was extended in the late 19th century.

ST. ANDREW SQUARE

Initially designed as a pure residential area, with a square and park in the 1772 newly built New Town, the St. Andrew Square with the posh George Street has transformed the eastern part of the financial district. The Melville Monument at St. Andrew's Gardens is the iconic landmark.

CALTON HILL

From here, you can first enjoy the "Crowns" of the city: Edinburgh Castle on its cliff, the top of the Scott Monument, and, to the left, the tower of the Balmoral Hotel. A perfect vantage point for visitors, the view extends over the whole city and even farther: westwards, you can see over Corstophine Hill to Cairnpapple Hill.

HOLYROOD PALACE

The official residence of the British royal family in Scotland is open for visits in the absence of the Royals. Although most visitors are interested in another resident of the palace: in Holyrood House, Maria Stuart resided between 1561 and 1567. Here she married Lord Darnley in a second marriage, and it was also here that she had to watch, as her private secretary and presumed lover, David Rizzio was stabbed in the back. In the northwest tower of the palace there is an exhibition with an assortment of memorabilia.

GOING OUT

The Kitchin // Located in the district of Leith, the restaurant presents itself with a simple Nordic-inspired interior. The food with the French influences, however, comes from a much different direction.

// www.thekitchin.com

Hendersons // Established in 1962, Hendersons has become an Edinburgh institution. There are four restaurants serving freshly prepared vegetarian and vegan dishes made from the best organic ingredients that are in season. Here you can start the day with vegan pancakes for breakfast and finish it with fine Greek spanakopita.

// www.hendersonsofedinburgh.co.uk

The Abbotsford Bar and Restaurant // One of the most traditional pubs in Edinburgh. Here you can enjoy whisky and ale in the roomy Victorian dark wood counter or calm down your hungry stomach in the upstairs restaurant.

// www.theabbotsford.com

Right: Princes Street Gardens is a beautiful park that overlooks the Old Town and the Castle. There are statues of important men, including Sir Walter Scott and David Livingstone, a flower clock and the Ross Fountain to admire.

○ ROYAL BOTANIC GARDEN

Called "The Botanics" by the locals, the Royal Botanic Garden Edinburgh (RBGE) is a scientific centre for the study of plants, their diversity and conservation, as well as a popular tourist attraction. Founded in 1670 as an actual garden to grow medicinal plants, today it occupies four sites across Scotland — Edinburgh, Dawyck, Logan and Benmore — each with its own specialised collection of medicinal plants.

WHERE TO STAY

Grassmarket Hotel // Offering many extras, the hotel attracts primarily guests who are looking for a city break and sightseeing. Takeaway lunches, the central location right next to Edinburgh Castle, and a magnetic city map that covers a full room wall are just three of its highlights.

// www.grassmarkethotel.co.uk

The Dunstane Houses // If you do not want to miss out on luxury when traveling or you have a taste for Neoclassical design, then it's worth checking in to the Victorian Dunstane Houses.

// www.thedunstane.com

Tigerlily Boutique Hotel // The Tigerlily is the address for all shopping queens and party animals. Stylish interiors, free entry into the club and bathrooms with an amazing selection of accessories that even extends to hair straighteners, in short: a bit of a VIP feeling in the middle of the city.

// www.tigerlilyedinburgh.co.uk

SHOPPING

○ GEORGE STREET

Designer shops line up here next to exquisite jewelry stores. Traditional British brands can be found on George Street as well as hip newcomers. For breaks in between, you can find a variety of cafés.

○ GRASSMARKET

Located in the historic Old Town, you can find souvenirs, leather goods and jewellery as well as some treasures in the antique bookstores. Every Saturday is also market day, and then you can haggle for fresh vegetables, fish and other delights.

○ WAVERLY MALL SHOPPING CENTRE

Formerly known as the Princes Mall Shopping Centre and located right by the train station, the well-arranged shopping centre is a hodgepodge of international brands and fast food chains, making it perfect for rainy days.

DAY TRIPS

○ LINLITHGOW PALACE

Linlithgow is around 25 kilometres from Edinburgh. In addition to the modern residential complexes are houses dating from the 16th century to admire. No wonder, because it is an old royal domicile. The most obvious witness of this era are the ruins of Linlithgow Palace. None other than Mary Queen of Scots was born here, better known as Maria Stuart.

○ FORTH BRIDGE

It has been a UNESCO World Heritage Site since 2015. The railway bridge over the mouth of the River Forth is still praised today as a marvel of technology and architecture.

NOT TO BE MISSED

VISIT THE SCOTCH WHISKY EXPERIENCE

The Gaelic Uisge Beatha once gave the whisky its name, because it means something like "water of life". If you want to experience the real history of Scotch whisky before the liquid gold flows into the glass, take a seat in the barrel and drive through the world of whisky in Edinburgh's Whisky Experience. Of course, there is whisky tasting at the end and you can even take your glass home as a souvenir.

ENJOY THE VIEW FROM THE SCOTT MONUMENT

The walk-in monument dedicated to Sir Walter Scott in 1846 is centrally located on Princes Street near Waverley Station. With its height at 61 metres, it towers over Princes Street Gardens. For a small fee, you can take the 287 steps leading up to the highest viewing platform.

STROLL THROUGH DEAN VILLAGE

A city trip can be more exciting than relaxing. If you need a break from the hustle and bustle of Edinburgh, just take a few steps away from the main shopping area of Princes Street, to the northwest, and you'll reach an oasis of village life: Dean Village. The settlement was built in the Middle Ages, when there were more than ten mills in the valley, which were driven by the waters of the river Leith.

VIEW A PLAY AT THE ROSS THEATRE

The open-air concert arena of West Princes Street Gardens in the New Town can accommodate up to 2,000 people. The venue impresses with its location of Edinburgh Castle as a magnificent backdrop, and the green and rolling hills of Edinburgh Castle Garden.

UNDERSTANDING THE WORLD IN "OUR DYNAMIC EARTH"

Located at the foot of Holyrood Road, near Parliament and Holyroodhouse Palace, the first thing that stands out is the huge white fabric roofs designed by architects Michael Hopkins and Partners, which stand in stark contrast to the towering Arthur's Seat that is just behind. Since 1999, geoscientific correlations have been presented in an interactive and easy-to-understand way for all ages, from the Big Bang theory to the formation of planets; the evolution of the Earth; the interrelation of geological forces; and, the impact of environmental influences on the climate, including the future.

#17 FLANDERS

FLAT LAND AND CANALS, DIKES AND WINDMILLS, MEDIEVAL HOUSES REFLECTED IN THE WATER - ALL THESE REPRESENT FLANDERS, PLUS, BUSTLING TOWNS WITH OLD MARKETS AND TOWN HALLS. THE NAME "FLANDERS" COMES FROM THE HISTORIC COUNTY ON THE NORTH SEA COAST WHICH HAD BECOME RICH THROUGH CLOTH MAKING AND LONG-DISTANCE TRADE. EVEN TODAY, YOU WILL FIND IMPRESSIVE EVIDENCE OF THE HIGHLY DEVELOPED FLEMISH CULTURE IN THE LATE MIDDLE AGES AND THE RENAISSANCE.

Above: The Belfry of Bruges was built in 1240. The spire was first built with a wooden tip, which burned down three times in succession. Since 1822, therefore, the tower has a neo-Gothic crown built of stone.

Left: Behind St. Bavo Cathedral of Ghent, the belfry towers high. These belfries, typical of Flanders, symbolise the strong self-confidence of bourgeois cities towards the feudal forces of the Middle Ages.

○ BRUGES

The profitable cloth trade between England and the continent ran over Bruges in the Middle Ages. With Jan van Eyck and Hans Memling, Bruges became, thanks to a generous patronage, an art and cultural city of the highest rank. The most luscious sheen unfolded, as in the 15th century, the standard bearers of the late Gothic court culture, the Dukes of Burgundy resided in their walls. The city is criss-crossed by numerous canals and streets with gabled houses. The domiciles of the patricians, the offices of the merchants, or the richly decorated town hall tell of their former splendor. Among the multitude of churches dominate in the charming and picturesque cityscape the Salvator and Liebfrauenkirche.

○ CASTLEYARD

Bruges' heart beats at Burgplatz, an ideal starting point for a sightseeing tour of the city. It is surrounded by spectacular buildings from the 12th to the 19th century.

○ TOWN HALL (STADHUIS)

Originally built in the 14th century as a prison, the elegant town hall with three turrets is the oldest secular building in Flanders. The murals with biblical motifs and the oak vaulted ceiling in the Gothic Hall are very impressive.

○ BELL TOWER

The Belfry dominates the marketplace, Bruges second most important area. The stock exchange had its seat here in the Middle Ages. There are 366 steps that lead upwards on a steep spiral staircase. From here, you can enjoy a fantastic panorama of the city.

○ GENT

Visitors unjustly spend much less time in the birthplace of Charles V than in the pretentious Antwerp or in the museum city of Bruges. The most important sights are located in the well-preserved historic centre between the Castle of the Counts and the slightly raised and visible from afar St. Bavo Cathe-

dral (14th century) with the famous "Ghent altar" of the Hubert brothers and Jan van Eyck (15th century) as the largest church treasury. Also worth a visit are the Cloth Hall, the Great Meat Hall, the Castle of Grafenburg, and the Town Hall, each has different character and style.

○ BELL TOWER OF BAVO CATHEDRAL

The Bell Tower towering 95 metres above the Bavo Cathedral was a symbol of the rising bourgeoisie in the 14th century. The Belfry houses the former municipal treasury. It is outfitted with 47 tower bells.

○ ANTWERP

Belgium's second-largest city is home to Europe's most important seaport after Rotterdam. Thanks to its favorable position, Antwerp developed into one of the leading commercial and financial centres as early as the late Middle Ages. The magnificent townhouses of the historic centre still bear witness to the wealth that Antwerp merchants generated during that period through the cloth trade.

○ GROTE MARKT

The Old Town not only boasts medieval monuments, but also Renaissance and Baroque gems. Its centrepiece is the Grote Markt, which is lined with magnificent guildhouses from the 16th and 17th centuries. Built between 1561 and 1565, the town hall on the west side is considered an outstanding example of Renaissance architecture.

○ CATHEDRALE ONZE LIEWE VROUW

The cathedral is a Gothic masterpiece and the largest church in Belgium with a tower 122 metres high. The three large paintings inside by Peter Paul Rubens are very impressive.

○ MUSEUMS

The Koninklijk Museum houses an excellent collection of Dutch art. Also worth seeing are the Rubens House (City Palace with Portico of the Painter), the Maritime Museum in the Steen Fortress, and the Plantin en Moretus Museum, a 16th century printing works, which is also a UNESCO World Heritage Site.

Top left: A popular music festival is the Tomorrowland Electronic Music Festival near Antwerp.

Bottom left: Town Hall and Brabos fountain on the Grote Markt in Antwerp. The bronze sculpture on the fountain shows the legendary city founder, Silvius Brabo.

○ BRUSSELS

Headquarters of the EU and many international organisations. The Belgian capital and residence city presents itself as a true cosmopolitan city. Great sights make it a tourist magnet. Gothic and Baroque as well as architectural styles of the 19th and 20th centuries have shaped the cityscape of Brussels. The historical development is also a great signpost for a city tour. You can start with the easily manageable Old Town around the Grand Place. Here, Brussels is elegant and sophisticated. The 19th century with its magnificent buildings, boulevards and parks is prevalent in the Old Town, which became the representative capital of the newly founded Kingdom in 1830.

GOING OUT

Antwerp: Marcel // A small but fine bistro restaurant. The menu is not very wide, but the food is exquisite. Especially in summer, you should not miss dining in the cosy terrace.

// www.restaurantmarcel.be

Brussels: Bonnefooi // The Bonnefooi is a magnet for the students of Brussels and for everyone who likes to discover new music. The bar not only serve drinks in a friendly atmosphere but later in the evening also transforms into a place for dancing, live music and performances by a variety of DJs and bands.

// www.bonnefooi.be

Gent: Simon Says // A young café that offers more than just coffee and cake. It is open for breakfast in the morning and offers light meals such as quiche or soup at lunchtime. Ideal for catching your breath during the sightseeing tour.

// www.simon-says.be

Right: The centre of the Grand Place of Brussels is the seven-storey town hall (on the left). It was housed next to the city magistrate until 1795 and the Estates Assembly of Brabant. The east wing dates from the early 15th century, the western one was added around 1450.

○ BRUSSELS' GROTE MARKT

The Grote Markt - or Grand Place - in Brussels is one of the most beautiful squares in the world with its unique ensemble of public and private buildings. Victor Hugo called the place "a true miracle". It measures only 110 metres in length and 68 metres in width, but the closely constructed buildings with guild houses around the town hall make it one of the most beautiful architectural complexes in Europe. The centre of the square is the seven-storey town hall.

○ ART NOUVEAU BUILDINGS BY VICTOR HORTA

Victor Horta (1861-1947) created a unique architectural ensemble of early Art Nouveau buildings in Europe with his city palaces and residential buildings in Brussels. The Tassel, Solvay, and van Eetvelde hotels, as well as the home and studio of the Belgian architect, are early examples of urban dwellings, in which he articulated the design principles of Art Nouveau in ever new variations.

○ ATOMIUM

One of the most insane buildings in the world was built on the occasion of the 1958 World Fair: The 102-meter-high Atomium, a symbol of the atomic age, became the symbol of Brussels. It represents a 165 billion-fold increase in the cell of an iron crystal and offers viewing platforms and restaurants at dizzying heights.

Left: The Ooidonk Castle, with its playful Flemish Renaissance style can easily be reached from Ghent.

SHOPPING

○ **BRUGES: WOLLESTRAAT**

Starting from the Grote Markt, the Wollestraat runs to Nepomucenusbrug. On the street, small shops, cafés and restaurants line up. Whether you go shopping or not, you should at least take a look at the architecture of the houses here, especially if you are in front of the number 9.

○ **ANTWERP: GROTE MARKT AND GROENPLAATS**

In the Old Town, there are many small shops selling everything imaginable. Specialties are of course the laces, and delicious chocolates - Burie, Korte Gasthuisstraat 3 - and the typical biscuits - same street no. 11 at Philips Biscuits.

○ **BRUSSELS: MARCHÉ DU MIDI**

Every Sunday in Brussels, the third largest market in Europe takes place, and it is not only the tourists that make it international. Products from all over the world are traded here, from spices to vegetables to leather and fabric goods. It can be a noisy at times, as the vendors try to outdo each other in the promotion of their goods.

DAYTRIPS

○ **WATER CASTLE OOIDONK**

15 kilometres away from Ghent lies the beautiful Water Castle Ooidonk between Deinze and Ghent, a complex from the 17th century. The name means "High Ground in the Marshes", which goes back to a word from the Lower Franconian language "hodonk".

○ **KNOKKE**

On a beautiful dune landscape near the Dutch border, Knokke-Heist, next to Ostend, is the most elegant Belguim Seaside Resort. The sandy beach is 12 kilometres long.

WHERE TO STAY

Antwerp: Hotel Julien // Close to the cathedral and other attractions, lies the Boutique Hotel Julien. A lounge, bar and its own spa area complete the offer.

// www. hotel-julien.com

Brussels: Hotel NH Bloom // The Bloom is a hip city hotel near the Botanical Gardens. A highlight is undoubtedly its own Waffelwagen, which makes the breakfast absolutely Belgian.

//www.nh-hotels.de/ hotelnh-brusels-bloom

Bruges: B&B Côté Canal // You do not have to look for romance in Bruges for long, especially not in this lovingly run Bed and Breakfast. If you enjoy fresh orange juice in the morning, surrounded by a green garden, overlooking the gently flowing canal Groenerei, you will want to spend the whole day here.

// www.bruges-bedandbreakfast.be

NOT TO BE MISSED

SPEND A SUMMER DAY IN JUBELPARK

The Jubelpark or Parc du Cinquantenaire in Brussels is a popular meeting place for locals. Especially in summer, you can get together under shady trees for a cosy picnic or take a long walk. But not only peace in nature can be found here, there are also museums to visit, and the park's magnificent triumphal arch. Locked for years from the public eye was the Pavilion of the Passions Humaines. The reason was that at this time the scandalous colossal marble bas-relief from Jef Lambeaux was inside the Temple.

A MINI EUROPE IN BRUSSELS

No one can visit all the sights of Europe in just one morning. Unless you come to the miniature park in Brussels. For the young and old, there is much to discover, participate in various attractions, and for the adults, there is a little political education on topics from the European Union.

PADDLING TOUR AT NIGHT

Whether Bruges or Brussels: The canal boat tour is highly recommended on any visit to the city. If that is too normal for you, do a stand-up paddling tour of Ghent at night. At night time, the medieval buildings are illuminated beautifully and you will not be disturbed.

GOURMET FOOD

Anyone who spends time in Flanders without ever having visited a confectionery shop misses out on something special here. The chocolates taste divine, and there are great variety and they are certainly not boring. With ingredients such as Tomato Chutney, Black Pepper or Lime, the chocolatiers make each one a work of art that melts in your mouth.

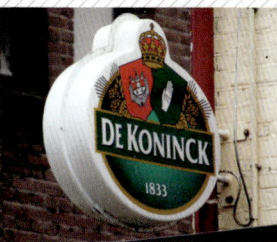

VISIT A BREWERY

Anyone who associates beer with Bavaria will be taught a lesson in Belgium. The variety is as enormous as are the number of breweries. Reason enough to watch the production, for example in the De Koninck Beer Experience Centre in Antwerp.

#18 HELSINKI

THE SEA GIVES FINLAND'S CAPITAL THAT SPECIAL FLAIR. LOCATED ON THE NORTHERN COAST OF THE GULF OF FINLAND, LARGE PARTS OF HELSINKI STRETCH OUT ON PENINSULAS AND OFFSHORE SKERRIES. EVEN IN THE CITY CENTRE, ON THE PENINSULA VIRONNIEMI, YOU CAN FEEL THE SEA DESPITE THE DENSE URBAN DEVELOPMENT EVERYWHERE. HELSINKI OWES ITS EXISTENCE TO THIS MARITIME LOCATION: THE KING OF SWEDEN, MASTER OF FINLAND UNTIL THE BEGINNING OF THE 19TH CENTURY, SENT SWEDISH SETTLERS HERE IN THE LATE MIDDLE AGES, TO CHALLENGE THE THRIVING HANSEATIC CITY OF REVAL (NOW TALLINN, THE CAPITAL OF ESTONIA). UNFORTUNATELY THE HELSINKI SETTLEMENT AT THAT TIME REMAINED INSIGNIFICANT DESPITE THE INTERVENTION. ONLY THE RUSSIAN TSAR, WHO CONQUERED FINLAND IN 1808, PROMOTED THE CITY AND MADE IT A STRONGHOLD OF CLASSICAL ARCHITECTURE.

Left: After Helsinki became the capital of the Russian Empire (1812), the Czar sent German Architect, Carl Ludwig Engel, to give the hitherto insignificant place a representative, contemporary facelift. He created the "Senatsplatz", one of the most beautiful classical squares in Europe, which is dominated by the widely visible dome.

Right: The Uspenski Cathedral, inaugurated in 1868, symbol of former Russian rule (1808-1917), is the largest Orthodox church in the west of Europe.

○ KAUPPATORI

A good starting point for a city exploration is the Kauppatori, the market place, located at the ferry terminal. Helsinki's main attractions are all close to each other and can be easily reached on foot. The Kauppatori is busy all year round - it is here that the locals buy fresh fruit and vegetables, fish and meat. The Market Hall located to the south of the Square from 1888 has been extensively restored. Even today, the stalls are still organized by guilds. A little way north of the Kauppatori is the impressive Senate Square, which was built in the early 19th century under Tsar Alexander I. The archetypal buildings that line this surrounding is a clear indicator of Helsinki's status as the new capital of Finland, which has belonged to the Tsarist Empire since 1809.

○ DOME

Visible from afar, the Senate Square is dominated by the Dome of the Cathedral. Like the other buildings in this area, it was designed by the Prussian Architect Carl Ludwig Engel, and is a major landmark of Helsinki. During the summer, concerts are held on the Senate Square. The Cathedral stairs and the Monument of Tsar Alexander II in the middle of the square are popular meeting places for young people.

○ USPENSKI CATHEDRALE

In the west of the Katajanokka peninsula, the 13 onion-shaped domes of the Uspenski Cathedral, inaugurated in 1868, tower into the sky. A visit to the Orthodox Church is a must for any Helsinki visitor.

○ TEMPPELIAUKION KIRKKO

At the end of the 1960s, in the Kamppi district, a unique church was built. The "Rock Church" is located in an open-topped cave, especially blasted for this purpose. The walls of the circular hall are "natural", and the roof is a dome structure made of glass and steel.

○ SUOMENLINNA

This mighty fortress at the harbour of Helsinki was built between 1748 and 1772 by the Swedes. Its purpose was to be a bastion against the Tsar's desire for expansion in the Baltic Sea region and controlled by the Russians after the end of the Swedish rule over Finland. The whole complex extends over several small islands and takes 20 minutes by ferry from Kauppatori; ideally you should plan half a day to visit the complex. Museums and galleries have been set up on the grounds and there are cafés and restaurants. In summer, Suomenlinna is

a popular destination. The fortress has been on the UNESCO World Heritage List since 1991.

○ MUSEUMS

Helsinki has an extensive museum landscape. If you are interested in the Art Nouveau inspired Finnish paintings from the beginning of the 20th century, you should not miss a visit to the National Gallery. The National Museum informs about the history of Finland and offers interesting Ethnological Exhibitions. Seurasaari Island has an open-air museum with typical farms from all over Finland.

SHOPPING

○ POHJOIESESPLANADI

From Kauppatori, Helsinki's most elegant commercial street leads west. It is lined with magnificent Art Nouveau buildings. The shops here offers expensive but truly exquisite items.

Top left: The one with the "medieval" door is the Finnish National Museum. Decorated with bay windows and round arches - all are architural characteristics of the Finnish national romanticism, in which elements of history and Art Nouveau mix.

Bottom left: Suomenlinna Fortress is a popular tourist destination. The extent of the structure is enormous and includes defensive walls and numerous buildings over several islands.

GOING OUT

Saaristo // A boat shuttle takes you to Klippan Island. The only house on this small island is the restaurant Saaristo. While you feast your way through the Finnish specialties from seafood to moose meat, a panoramic view of the city and its archipelago is on display right in front of you. Exclusively open only in summer.
// www.ravintolasaaristo.fi

WHERE TO STAY

Klaus K Hotel // A design hotel whose concept is on Finnish national tale. That may sound like an old-fashioned gallery, but the Klaus K presents itself in an unexpectedly modern way. However, it is more about colors and shapes, rather than function. **// www.klauskhotel.com**

F6 Hotel // The F6 team wanted to create a place where guests feel at home, and they really have achieved that. This includes not only a hotel dog named, Runar, that will greet you, but also a wonderful typical Finnish breakfast.

// www.hotelf6.fi

NOT TO BE MISSED

STROLL THROUGH KAMPPI

The district, which begins west of the main station and is still part of the city centre, is worth a visit not only because of its Art Nouveau buildings. Here, you can admire some outstanding examples of Modern Finnish architectures. The Finlandia-Talo, built in the 1970s, is a masterpiece by the famous architect, Alvar Aalto. It is used as a convention centre as well as a concert hall.

VISIT THE NATIONAL MUSEUM

Ten-thousand years of history - from the Stone Age to the present day - all come to life in the National Museum. The building alone, at the Mannerheimintie from 1910, is already a first-class cultural monument. In the entrance hallway, the ceiling frescoes created in 1928 attract everyone's attention. The painter Akseli Gallen Kallela has used motifs from the Finnish national epic "Kalevala" to make a work full of national pathos.

ENJOY A CUP OF COFFEE

The fact that the Finns love coffee is no secret. So, here in the capital you will find many cafés that not only grind the fresh coffee beans and brew this national drink, but actually celebrate the art of making and drinking it!

BE AMAZED BY THE VARIETY OF MODERN ART

Lovers of modern sculptures should not miss a visit to the Sibelius Monument, created in honour of the famous Finnish composer. The Eila Hiltunen Monument, made of steel tubes and dedicated to the city in 1967, reminds some observers of an organ, others of the Finnish forest.

CELEBRATE THE CITY'S BIRTHDAY

Every year, Helsinki celebrates its founding on June 12th. When the entire city throws a birthday party, it's a PARTY. That means live music, performances, theatre, free admission to many museums and, above all, an extravaganza parade and exuberant mood fill the streets and in the parks.

#19 KRAKOW

NOT EVEN THREE PERCENT OF GERMANS SPEND THEIR HOLIDAYS IN POLAND, ACCORDING TO THE LATEST SURVEY, ALTHOUGH CITIES LIKE KRAKOW HAVE SUCH A WEALTH OF HISTORY, ART AND CULTURE TO OFFER. KRAKOW WAS POLAND'S CAPITAL UNTIL 1596 AND THE CORONATION PLACE OF THE POLISH KINGS FROM THE 11TH TO THE 18TH CENTURY. SUCH IMPORTANCE IS VISIBLE AT THE WAWELHÜGEL WITH ITS ROYAL CASTLE AND CATHEDRAL. THE OLD TOWN WAS DESIGNED BY MASTER BUILDERS AND ARTISTS FROM ALL OVER EUROPE FROM THE 12TH TO THE 17TH CENTURY. ESTABLISHED IN THE 14TH CENTURY, THE UNIVERSITY, WHICH HAS A PRECIOUS GOTHIC CLOISTER, TAUGHT IMPORTANT PEOPLE OF THE MIDDLE AGES. THEY MADE KRAKOW A SPIRITUAL AND CULTURAL CENTRE OF EUROPE. THE RICH HISTORY OF THE CITY IS DISPLAYED THROUGH NUMEROUS GOTHIC, RENAISSANCE AND BAROQUE BUILDINGS, INCLUDING MANY CHURCHES AND MONASTERIES.

Above: Narrow but long, the Cloth Hall presents itself on Krakow's Market Square. It measures at least 108 metres in length, but is only 18 metres wide. The Cloth Hall is especially beautiful in the evening as the building shimmers in the bright lights.

Left: The landmark of Krakow is undoubtedly St. Mary's Church, with its differently shaped towers and beautiful interior design.

○ MAIN MARKET (RYNEK GŁÓWNY)

One of the largest medieval marketplaces in Europe is the Rynek Główny with its 200 × 200 metres square. In addition to the Market Halls, which are called Cloth Halls here, it is especially the Town Hall Tower that dominates the square. The associated building was demolished in 1820 due to its danger of collapsing. As a companion to the leaning Town Hall Tower, two churches mark the historic site. St. Adalbert's Church is considered the smallest church in Krakow.

○ CLOTH HALL

The Cloth Hall is a monumental reminder to the heyday of the city's cloth trade in the 16th and 17th centuries. The halls are built in the Renaissance style, after the original building burnt down in 1555. Not only the arcades and the barrel vault are special features, but also the decorative figures on the roof, which represent bad qualities such as drunkenness and envy. Inside the building today, there are numerous arts and crafts shops and a gallery on the upper floor.

○ MARIENKIRCHE

At the northeast corner of Krakow's Main Market Square, two asymmetrical towers of St. Mary's Church stand tall up to the sky. The church is part of Krakow's Old Town and is a World Heritage Site. The three-aisled Gothic basilica from the 13th to the 15th century reveals its true greatness only once you are inside: there are the vaults floating above the colourfully painted pillars, struts and arches of the central nave, dark blue night sky with golden stars, and especially the various coloured glass windows at the choir end. The altar of the Nuremberg master, Veit Stoß (c. 1447-1533), is one of the most revered and important carvings of late Gothic times with about 200 gilded figures up to 2.70 metres tall.

○ WAWEL HILL

A steep cliff high above the Vistula and close to the city was the perfect defence post. Until the early Middle Ages, evidence of castles could still be found here. One thousand years ago the Marienrotunde, one of the oldest buildings of the hill, was built here. Later, Polish Kings built the fortress, towers, arcades, and galleries - all carry architectural manuscripts from the Gothic to the Baroque era.

○ WAWEL CATHEDRALE

People say "you have not really been to Poland if you were not on the Wawel"; and the most important place of worship is the Wawel Cathedral. The three-aisled Gothic basilica with its 14th century brick facade is considered today a prime example of Krakow Gothic.

○ FRONLEICHNAMS CHURCH

King Casimir wanted to donate his own church to the newly founded City of Kazimierz. He had the Corpus Christi Church built in the 14th century. However, the construction period lasted until the middle of the 15th century, so the façade is still in late Gothic, but in the tower, many Baroque elements can be seen.

Left: Coronations, weddings, but also burials of the Royal Family took place for centuries in the Cathedral that sits on the Wawel Hill.

GOING OUT

Szara G // The restaurant is located directly on the marketplace in a historic setting; If you grab a table by the window, you will have a good view of the evening bustle on the square. The cooking is done with fresh and local ingredients and traditional Polish recipes, some of which are interpreted in a modern style.

// **www.szarages.com**

WHERE TO STAY

Hotel Metropolis // Modern and with vividly colourful, the Metropolis sets standards among the Design Hotels in Krakow.

// **www.metropolisdesign.pl**

Tango House // This Bed and Breakfast is located right in the Old Town, making it a good base for anyone wishing to explore Krakow on foot.

// **www.tangohouse.pl**

Hotel Copernicus // Historical meets a touch of luxury in Hotel Copernicus. The Heritage listed building consists of much stone and wood; the rooms combine this with subtle decoration. The Vault houses the hotel's pool and sauna.

// **www.copernicus.hotel.com.pl**

NOT TO BE MISSED

TASTE SOME TRADITION

Obwarzanek is an edible symbol of the city. The ring-shaped yeast pastry is often sprinkled with salt, poppy seeds or sesame seeds, and is pretty much sold on every street corner in the city. Traditional dishes also include the Pierogi, which are often referred to as Polish raviolis and are filled with various ingredients.

STROLL THROUGH THE MAIN PARK

Especially in summer, it is worthwhile to leave the hustle and bustle of the Old Town behind for a little while and take a leisurely stroll through Planty Park, which forms a ring around the Old Town. Monuments, flowerbeds and fountains line the shady paths. A good place for both a leisurely stroll or to just sit and relax.

VISIT THE JEWISH QUARTER

Hollywood director Steven Spielberg filmed some scenes from his famous film "Schindler's List" (1993) here. In fact, Oskar Schindler's factory was once located in this vicinity! Not least thanks to this film, the Jewish Quarter today attracts visitors and is being honoured once again, instead of being demolished and replaced by new buildings.

FOLLOW THE FOOTSTEPS OF THE KINGS

Feel like a king and at the same time seeing the most famous sights of the Old Town can be wonderfully combined in Krakow along the Royal Route. It begins at the Matejkoplatz and ends at the Wawelburg, marking the traditional route the Polish Kings took to their coronations. The route passes landmarks such as the Florianstor, the marketplace with the Cloth Hall, Town Hall with the St. Mary's Church, and the Peter and Paul Church.

KRAUKOW'S HISTORY UNDERGROUND

Directly below the main market you will find a museum that takes its visitors back to the medieval Kraukow. Here, you will find many fascinating discoveries from various excavations.

#20

LISBON

PORTUGAL'S CAPITAL LISBON SPANS OVER SEVEN HILLS ABOVE THE TAGUS. THE CITY IS FILLED WITH DISTINCT LIGHT AND BUZZES - THE EXOTIC FLAVOURS FROM PORTUGAL'S COLONIAL PAST. MANUELINE AND BAROQUE STYLES CELEBRATE THE SIZE OF THE FORMER NAVAL POWER ON THE FACADES OF CHURCHES AND PALACES. THE SLIGHTLY MORBID CHARM OF LISBON'S HISTORIC DISTRICT BLENDS WITH THE BOLD ELEGANCE OF MODERN ARCHITECTURE TO CREATE AN IRRESISTIBLE INVITATION TO DISCOVER THE "WHITE CITY" ON FOOT.

Above: From almost every point of the city, you can see the huge ancient fortress of the Castelo de São Jorge, perched high above the rooftops of Lisbon. The view from the Fortress Hill, which was already used before the Romans, is breathtaking.

Left: A romantic sight to see when the yellow wagens of the Tram 28 meander through the streets.

Right: Dense alleyways, small restaurants and flea markets - give Alfama a special atmosphere and charming characteristic.

○ ALFAMA

A labyrinth of narrow streets and alleys run from the banks of the Tejo Bay up to the Castelo de São Jorge. The poor used to live in the Alfama; today, this oldest part of Lisbon is a trendy neighborhood. The best way to explore this still original neighborhood is on foot.

○ CASTELO DE SÃO JORGE

The 12th century fortress was renovated a few years ago and is one of the most beautiful viewpoints in the city. Those who make the effort to climb to the top will be rewarded with a fantastic view of Lisbon.

○ ROSSIO

This Central Square is one of the largest and most important in Lisbon and serves as a meeting place for locals and tourists alike. The extravagant wave pattern on the floor should remind us of the sea. The Rossio (officially: Praça de Dom Pedro IV) was already established in the 16th century as a trading center. The goods shipped across the Atlantic and landed via the Tejo at the Praça do Comércio are all traded here.

○ PRAÇA DO COMÉRCIO

The impressive Trade Square is entered through a triumphant arch. A monumental equestrian statue of José I, King of Portugal from 1750 to 1777, seems to glitter under sunlight, opening up to the Tejo Bay. Apart from its geometrically structured expanse, which leaves plenty of room for cafés and restaurants, it is

WHY VISIT IN SUMMER?

ON THE 13TH OF JUNE, THE FEAST DAY OF ST. ANTHONY, THE PATRON SAINT OF LISBON, PORTUGAL'S CAPITAL GOES CRAZY ABOUT SARDINES. A CUSTOM DATING BACK TO THE 13TH CENTURY, WHEN THE CATHOLIC SAINT VISITED RIMINI IN ITALY. DISILLUSIONED AT THE LACK OF INTEREST IN HIS SERMONS, HE WENT TO THE SHORE TO CONFIDE TO THE FISH. SUDDENLY, FLOCKS OF FISH STUCK THEIR HEADS OUT OF THE WAVES AND BOWED. TODAY, IN HIS HONOR, THERE IS A PARADE ON THE AVENIDA DE LIBERDADE AND UNMARRIED GIRLS PERFORM DANCES TO IMPLORE ST. ANTHONY TO HELP THEM FIND A GOOD MAN.

in its history that makes this a special place: it is also known as the "Place to Receive" of Lisbon.

○ MUSEO NACIONAL DO AZULEJO

In the former Monastery of Madre de Deus, a museum is dedicated to an extraordinary exhibition piece: the typical Portuguese ceramic tile, the Azulejos.

○ CATEDRAL SÉ PATRIARCAL

The oldest church in Lisbon was built as early as the 12th century, and over the centuries, it has been repeatedly modified and expanded. This has resulted in an impressive and, above all, interesting mix of different architectural styles.

○ CONVENTO DE CARMO

The earthquake of 1755 also destroyed the Carmelite Monastery; the towering ruins are reminiscent of this catastrophe. Particularly lovely is a visit in the evening hours, when you can look out from the roofless nave into the beautiful clear starry sky.

○ ELEVADOR DE SANTA JUSTA

This architecturally impressive elevator, which has been connecting the Upper and Lower Towns for more than 100 years, is also a magnificent viewpoint over the city.

○ MUSEU CALOUSTE GULBENKIAN

This impressive museum, named after its founder, a wealthy English businessman and engineer of Armenian descent, showcases important works of

Above: In the 15th century, the Monastery Church was built, which today forms a magnificent setting for the Azulejos Museum.

Left: On the feast day of St. Anthony, around the 13th of June, sardines are grilled throughout the city.

art from Rembrandt, Rubens, Renoir, and several other artists from different periods.

○ MOSTEIRO DOS JERÓNIMOS

This imposing Monastery of the Hieronymites is built in the late Gothic style and is a "must see" place. The wealth and the heyday of Portugal as a seafaring nation are not only recorded in the history books, but also in the buildings and their architecture. In doing so, a very unique style was created, which exists only in Portugal called the "Manuelinik".

○ TORRE DE BELÉM

A UNESCO World Heritage Site. It tells stories of the former glory of seafaring days and wealth of the discovery for Portugal. Decorated with ornaments wrapped around the turrets like ropes, with anchors

and shells, the tower is strikingly a maritime monument. Dated from the mid-16th century, a period when Portugal was at the height of its maritime and commercial points. Built in 1521, the lighthouse at the mouth of the Tejom once functioned as a prison and as a customs station.

○ PADRÃO DOS DESCOBRIMENTOS

Mariners and explorers all influenced the history of Portugal and this monument built in 1960 on the banks of the Tagus River commemorates Magellan and many others.

○ PONTE 25 DE ABRIL

This impressive two-storey Suspension Bridge connects the districts of Almada and Alcântara. The bridge is more than 2 kilometres long.

○ OCEANÁRIO DE LISBOA

The second largest marine aquarium in the world is located on the Tagus River, at the former World Expo site. The centerepiece is an impressive aquarium that extends over two floors and allows visitors to immerse themselves in the fascinating sea world through huge glass windows.

○ JARDIM BOTÂNICO

A Garden of Eden in the middle of the city: the Botanical Garden. Amidst old, tropical trees and picturesque ponds, you can completely escape the hustle and bustle of the big city. It is absolutely peaceful here.

Right: The significant discovery of "Monument in Belém" evokes a proud history of Portuguese seafaring. A good 52 metres high, the concrete giant rises on the banks of the Tejo Bay. It depicts a ship that has immortalized 33 major Portuguese sailors, including Vasco da Gama, Pêro Escobar and Bartolomeu Dias. The bow of the concrete ship is adorned with the statue of Henry the Navigator, holding a caravel in his hand.

GOING OUT

Café A Brasileira // The A Brasileira, is an old-style café in Lisbon, perhaps the last of its kind but still in operation and it makes excellent tasting coffee. It is reassuring to see, in the midst of our fast-moving times, how long this cultural relic has maintained its dignity and elegance.

// Rua Garrett 120

Clube de Fado // The owner himself is a Fado guitarist. Here you can enjoy classical Fado, with a wonderful atmosphere among famous guests.

// www.clube-de-fado.com

Alma // Hard to find, but worth the search, is this gourmet restaurant with innovative, aesthetically sophisticated signature dishes characterized by the unusual. Entry is strictly only with reservation.

// www.almalisboa.pt

○ MUSEU DE FADO

Since 2011, the melancholic music style of the Fado belongs to the intangible world of cultural heritage. A great place to visit, particularly if you want to learn more about the history of this traditional music style.

SHOPPING

○ RUA GARRETT

Here it is not just the lovely cafés and many shops that are fascinating for a stroll, you will find one of the oldest bookstores in the world, the Aliança. The bookstore also boasts of being the most beautiful shop in Lisbon, whose Rococo interior is more than 100 years old.

○ MERCARDO DA RIBEIRA

The entrance of the Old Market Hall is an admired representative of years gone by. The west wing has been renovated, and you will find fast food as well as stands with the best traditional cuisine. Those putting together their favourite menu, should take a seat at one of the long tables in the middle, so you have easy access to all food stalls.

○ BAIXA

Baixa is the centre of Lisbon. Here you will find the traditional shopping street Rua Augusta. In addition to retail chains, many family-run businesses can be found here. Luxury boutiques can be found lined up in the Avenida de Liberdade.

○ EMBAIXADA

Not just any shopping centre, but probably the most fashionable mall in Portugal. Housed in a palace from the 19th century, fashionable shops, Portuguese designs and fine-dining restaurants, combine with the beautiful historical architecture, makes this place an opulent shopping experience.

// www.embaixadalx.pt

DAYTRIPS

○ SINTRA

Since Alfonso I re-conquered the town from the Moors in 1147, it has become a popular place to escape the heat of summer. In addition to the pleasant climate and picturesque location at the foot of the Sierra Sintra, there are many historic buildings and sites that will make a visit to this town worthwhile.

WHERE TO STAY

Lisbon Short Stay // Whether for a weekend for two, a trip with the family or friends, this place offers trendy accommodation that's perfect for everyone. The individual apartments can accommodate up to 7 people, and comes with a fully equipped kitchen.

// www.lisbonshortstay.com

Internacional Design Hotel // Perfectly located in the city centre, the hotel offers discerning guests four differently designed styles guest rooms - from Zen to Pop Art.

// www.idesignhotel.com

Santiago de Alfama // This luxurious city hotel is located in the district of the same name and has 19 suites, some with beautiful sea views. The restaurant is opened from early morning for breakfast until late at night supper.

//www.santiagodealfama.com/santiago-de-alfama

NOT TO BE MISSED

IMMERSE IN THE BAIRRO ALTO NIGHT LIFE

You know it is a good sign if the pub is full. Accordingly, the Bairro Alto is just teeming with fantastic bars, with night owls jostling in front of almost every door. And if there's no space inside, it's no problem for the locals - they will happily dance on the street to the music from the clubs.

ENJOYING PASTÉIS DE BELEM

The world's famous "Portuguese Egg Tart", so why not try one (or two) now that you are in the country of origin? A topping made of eggs and cream baked in a crispy puff pastry, and sprinkled with a little cinnamon, Pastéis de Belem, is a must for all sweets lovers.

LISTENING TO FADO MUSIC

The Fado is THE sound of Lisbon. In every piece "saudade" (Fado guitar) resonates with desire. If you want to listen to this melancholic but unique music, you can book tickets for a Fado concert, or simply look for a pub that is visited by locals. With luck, you may find the musicians spontaneously singing to the tunes.

EXPLORING THE CITY ON THE TRAM LINE 28

It jumps and twitches when the old tram 28 goes in the curves. She squeezes through the narrow streets and passes several interesting sights on her way from Martim Moniz to Campo Orique. The old transportation relics have been on the Rails of Lisbon since the 1940s.

APPRECIATE THE MAGNIFICENT LISBON FROM HIGH UP

You do not necessarily have to climb multiple steps of a hill to enjoy Lisbon from the top. Those looking for great views can see the city from here: Elevador de Santa Justa; Cristo Rei statue; Castelo de Sao Jorge; Santa Luzia; or at Miradouro da Graça.

#21 LJUBLJANA

A PROTECTED HISTORICAL CENTRE, SPLENDID BAROQUE BUILDINGS, BRIDGES WITH A TWIST OF SOMETHING SPECIAL AND THE NEWER ARCHITECTURE, DESIGNED BY A SLOVENIAN STAR ARCHITECT, LJUBLJANA IS FULL OF SURPRISES. THE CAPITAL OF SLOVENIA IS SITUATED ON THE BANK OF THE LJUBLJANICA, A SMALL RIVER THAT CLEARLY DIVIDES THE CITY INTO TWO HALVES. ON ONE SIDE IS THE OLD TOWN WITH ITS NARROW STREETS, CATHEDRAL AND EPISCOPAL PALACE. THESE ARE ARRANGED CLOSE TO EACH OTHER AROUND THREE CENTRAL SQUARES (STADTPLATZ, ALTER PLATZ, AND OBERER PLATZ) AND FORM THE OLDEST PART OF THE CITY. ON THE OTHER SIDE OF THE RIVER, LJUBLJANA IS BUSIER, WITH PREŠEREN SQUARE AND NUMEROUS COFFEE SHOPS, RESTAURANTS, PEDESTRIAN STREETS, BOUTIQUES AND DEPARTMENT STORES.

○ FRANCISCAN CHURCH

The Franciscan Church of the Annunciation dominates the landscape on the Prešeren Square in the centre of Ljubljana. The Baroque basilica was built between 1646 and 1660. The façade, however, did not receive its present appearance until around 1700, and the altar dated to the mid-18th century. An earthquake in 1895 damaged the ceiling, destroying much of the original frescoes. Impressionist Matej Sternen created a new one in the mid-1930s.

○ TROMOSTOVJE

Also on Prešeren Square is one of the main landmarks of Ljubljana, the Tromostovje (the "Three Bridges"). And indeed, the three bridges cross the river directly next to each other. After the original medieval wooden bridge burnt down in 1657, it was replaced by a new one. This finally had to give way to a new stone bridge in 1842. Between 1929 and 1932, two side pedestrian bridges were added according to plans by Jože Plecnik. Since then, the Three Bridges cross the Ljubljanica together.

○ COBBLER'S BRIDGE

The Cobbler's Bridge (Cevljarski Most) is also a work of Jože Plecnik. Reconstructions of the Cobbler's Bridge were quite frequent, due to fires or floods, so in 1867, an iron bridge was built replacing the original wooden one. The iron bridge was moved in 1931 further down the river where it is still in use, and is known as the Cobbler's Bridge of today. On the site of these earlier bridges, Plecnik erected a wider space above the water with his new bridge. The stone and concrete construction has simply formed railings, and on each side, a row of six high columns with round spheres at the tips. The bridge was built in the years 1931 and 1932, and looks more like a piazza than a classic bridge, combining the districts on both sides of the river.

○ OLD TOWN

On the Old Town side, where the Cobbler's Bridge flows into the Town Square (Mestni trg), there are also the first original street cafés. Here you are already in the middle of the oldest, and today's mostly traffic-calmed, part of the city. The surrounding houses are almost entirely Baroque structures. However, some show on the gable forms that they were originally Gothic. Important sights are not far away, such as the Town Hall from 1718 and the Fountain of the Three Rivers at the town square, and at the Upper Square (Gornji trg) lies St. Florian's Church, which was completed in 1672.

○ COLONNADES

From the Three Bridges to the Dragon Bridge, a long row of Colonnades runs directly along the banks of

Left: Since 1932, the Tromostovje ensemble - three closely spaced and almost parallel bridges - has crossed the Ljubljanica River in the shadow of the Franciscan church.

Right: With its balustrades and columns, the Cobbler's Bridge has the appearance of a piazza floating above the water.

WHERE TO STAY

City Hotel // The biggest plus of this hotel is its central location. With large-format photos of the city you are already taken on a sightseeing tour in your room. On the terrace, you can enjoy breakfast, lunch or dinner overlooking the castle.

// www.cityhotel.si

Celica Hostel // The former prison has been converted into a budget hostel by designers. There are two to three beds in each individual room, and no one has to go without a good breakfast here.

// www. hostelcelica.com

the Ljubljanica. Built in 1939 and 1940 by Jože Plecnik, it gives the city centre a charming Mediterranean feel. Easily missed, hiding behind the Colonnades are the Market Halls. These are also unmistakably the signature of a great architect. The elegant forms of the white arcades are reminiscent of Greek temples. The market sells fresh local produces from the surrounding countryside.

○ **SUMMER THEATRE KRIŽANKE**

The redesign of the former Monastery of the Teutonic Order on the site of the French Revolution (Trg francoske revolucije) is also to Plecnik's merit. From 1952 to 1956, the architect gave the complex a facelift, that was already once rebuilt in Baroque style. Today, there is the School for Design and Photography, and the popular Summer Theatre Križanke.

○ **NATIONAL GALLERY**

The building of the National Gallery was built in 1896 by a Czech architect, František Skabrout, as a venue for Slovenian associations and was called the "National House". The National Gallery has also been housed here since 1918.

GOING OUT

Julija // The Julija is located in the old town and is very down to earth. Here, the ambience is as great as the quality. On the menu you will find both traditional Slovenian dishes and Mediterranean dishes.

// www.julijarestaurant.com

SHOPPING

○ **BTC CITY**

This large shopping centre offers international brands, many restaurants, and leisure activities such as a cinema, a water park, plus many live events. The centre can be reached by bus lines 2, 7, 12 and 27.

// www.btc-city.com

NOT TO BE MISSED

BOAT TOUR THROUGH THE OLD TOWN

Especially to get a good overall feel of the city, it is worth taking a boat ride on the river Ljubljanica. A tour leads past promenades, eateries, and the key sights of the city. For a more romantic feel, you should book the special Sunset Tour, when the street lights reflect in the river and tranquillity reigns in the city. Some tours also offer few glasses of wine to enjoy while cruising down the river for an even more enjoyable experience.

SHOPPING AT THE WEEKLY MARKET

The lively weekly market at St. Nikolai Church is certainly worth a visit. Most of the market sellers source their products from the nearby area. With a selection from honey to schnapps, the market is greatly appreciated by the locals. In the summer, every Friday as part of the "Open Kitchen" event, the market turns into a culinary feast when top chefs from all over the country prepare delicious dishes right in front of the visitors.

EXPERIENCING DANCE, MUSIC AND CULTURE

The Ljubljana Festival is not a small event, but an event that lasts for several weeks and offers a great variety of cultural experiences, from orchestral or solo concerts to ballet and musical plays. If you visit the city in summer, you should not miss it!

THE CITY BEACH

The lively waterfront Trnovski Pristan is often referred to by locals as Ljubljana's "beach". During the day, families come here for picnics, sports and jogging, and those who just want to enjoy the summer outdoors. In the evening, it's the teenagers and the students who like to escape from their everyday learning - they gather here with guitars and friends, singing and chit-chats through balmy summer nights.

SAY HELLO TO THE DRAGONS

It is the main landmark of the city and probably captured on most holiday photos: the Dragon Bridge. Architecturally, it was a novelty at its time, but today most visitors are intrigued with these eponymous mythical creatures, which look quite frightening due to their detailed design and size.

#22   PARIS

HARDLY ANY OTHER CITY HAS BEEN SUNG MORE OFTEN IN SONGS, SERVED MORE OFTEN AS A BACKDROP FOR FILMS, NOVELS OR PLAYS THAN PARIS - THE CITY OF LIGHTS AND THE CITY OF LOVE. THE FRENCH CAPITAL ENCHANTS ITS VISITORS; IT IS OFTEN LOVE AT FIRST SIGHT. WHETHER ENJOYING PASTIS IN A SIDEWALK CAFÉ IN THE BUSTLING LATIN QUARTER, A BOAT TRIP ON THE SEINE, A STROLL IN THE JARDIN DU LUXEMBOURG OR IN FRONT OF ONE OF THE WORKS OF ART IN THE MUSEUMS - YOU CAN HARDLY ESCAPE THE MAGNETIC CHARM OF THIS CITY. FROM THE NUCLEUS OF FIRST SETTLEMENT ON THE ÎLE DE LA CITÉ HAS DEVELOPED A HUGE CITYSCAPE, WHOSE QUARTERS CAN STILL BE EXPLORED ON FOOT. THEN THERE IS THE MÉTRO, WHICH STATES THAT NO POINT IN PARIS IS MORE THAN 500 METRES FROM ONE STATION TO THE NEXT.

Above: No fewer than nine bridges connect the Seine Island Île de la Cité with the river banks and the neighboring Île Saint-Louis. In addition to the Notre Dame, there are a few other medieval buildings on the quieter river island: the Sainte-Chapelle Palace Chapel, the Conciergerie, and the Palais de la Cité.

Left: The glass pyramid of I. M. Pei in front of the building wings has marked the main entrance to The Louvre since 1989.

○ NOTRE-DAME

Construction of the cathedral, which began in 1163, lasted more than 150 years. The dimensions of the interior are considerable: 130 metres long, 48 metres wide and 35 metres high. Despite the size of the room, the coloured glass windows create a festive atmosphere.

○ SAINTE-CHAPELLE

It was originally the Castle Chapel of a defunct Royal Palace, and now sits on the grounds of the Palais de Justice. The upper Chapel, which at the request of Louis IX was to house valuable relics like the Crown of Thorns, is rather fascinating with its stained-glass paintings, from the 12th to the 14th century, depicting Biblical Scenes.

○ PLACE VENDÔME

This famous square, designed by Jules Hardouin-Mansart in the 18th century, is magnificent because of its harmonious design. It is the meeting place of the rich and beautiful from all over the world, as they shop at jewellery houses such as Cartier, or Van Cleef & Arpels.

○ PONT NEUF

The name - New Bridge - is misleading. The Pont Neuf is the Oldest Bridge in Paris, completed in 1607. At the same time, at 330 metres, it is the longest bridge in the city. It has also served as a work of art several times: Christo packed it in 1984, and the Japanese couturier Kenzo had it colourfully decorated with flowers.

○ THE LOUVRE

Once a huge city palace of the French kings, which has been constantly rebuilt for centuries, is today one of the most important art museums in the world. During the tour of the Louvre, you should pay attention not only to the numerous magnificent works of art, but also to the impressive rooms that the art pieces are housed in.

WHY VISIT IN SUMMER?

TO WATCH MOVIES UNDER THE STARS - AT THE CINÉMA EN PLEIN AIR: THE PARC DE LA VILLETTE IN THE NORTH-EASTERN CORNER OF THE 19TH ARRONDISSEMENT MAY NOT SOUND VERY ATTRACTIVE, BUT THIS 55-HECTARE AREA USED TO BE THE SLAUGHTERHOUSE OF THE CITY. BUT SINCE ITS REMODELLING IN 1979, IT HAS BECOME ONE OF THE MOST IMPORTANT LEISURE AND CULTURAL CENTRES IN PARIS WITH TEN THEMED GARDENS, THREE LARGE CONCERT STAGES, AND THE LARGEST SCIENCE MUSEUM IN EUROPE. A VISIT IS WORTH EVEN MORE WHEN THE CINÉMA EN PLEIN AIR TAKES PLACE. THEN A HUGE SCREEN IS SET UP AND A SELECTION OF GOOD FILMS ARE SHOWN - ADMISSION IS FREE AND TO RENT BEACH CHAIRS COSTS ONLY A FEW EUROS. THE FILMS ARE SHOWN IN THE ORIGINAL VERSION WITH FRENCH SUBTITLES, BUT EVEN THOSE WHO DO NOT UNDERSTAND EVERYTHING WILL ENJOY THE ATMOSPHERE. MILD PARISIAN EVENINGS WITH PICNIC BLANKETS, BAGUETTES AND A BOTTLE OF BORDEAUX - A SOCIABLE EVENING UNDER THE STARS.

○ OPÉRA GARNIER

This magnificent building by the architect Charles Garnier was built between 1860 and 1875 under Napoleon III, whose era here found its own "Neo-Baroque-Architectural" style. However, since the construction of the Opéra Bastille, the building has largely served its purpose as a venue for operas. Ballet performances by the in-house ensemble are also performed here.

○ LA MADELEINE

Under Louis XV, a Baroque church with a dome was to be built here. However, Louis XVI wanted a classical building like the Panthéon, but it was only under Napoleon that the plan for the ancient Greek temple designed to serve as a Temple à la Gloire, as a hall of fame, emerged. Under King Louis Philippe in 1842, the Church Sainte-Marie Madeleine was consecrated.

○ PLACE DE LA CONCORDE

The largest square in Paris, and the second largest in France, has a varied history. It was built as a Royal Square, but was renamed in 1792 as "Place de la Révolution". Here stood the guillotine, that famously took the life of Marie Antoinette and Louis XVI. The obelisk in the centre was a gift from the Egyptian Viceroy to France.

○ CHAMPS-ÉLYSÉES

The origins of the splendid boulevard, almost 2 kilometres long from Place de la Concorde to the Arc de Triomphe, dated back to the second half of the 17th century. Most of the buildings that characterise the streetscape dates back to the 19th century. The wide sidewalks are very inviting for a leisurely stroll.

○ ARC DE TRIOMPHE

Under Napoleons rule, the foundation stone was laid in 1806, but the inauguration did not take place until 1836. Since 1923, the famous "Eternal Flame" burns here at the tomb of the unknown soldiers.

○ JARDIN DU LUXEMBOURG

This park, which surrounds the Palais du Luxembourg, where the Senate meets today, is the green lung of Paris's 5th and 6th administrative districts. It offers plenty of recreational activities: for children,

Left: Open-air cinema with a unique atmosphere and a fantastic backdrop - this is what the Cinéma en Plein Air Film Festival offers in summer.

a puppet theatre, a carousel and an adventure playground; and for adults, there are tennis courts, a petanque court, a chess board and a café.

○ MUSÉE D'ORSAY

Located in a former train station, built for the 1900 World's Fair, works of art from the 19th century are collected here from several museums. Where once trains departed, today you will find one of the world's most important collections of art, focussing on the Impressionist and post-Impressionist paintings and sculptures.

○ HÔTEL AND DÔME DES INVALIDES

From 1671 to 1676, the Hôtel des Invalides was built on behalf of Louis XIV as a Home for War Veterans.

There was also a church here, but the Sun King considered it too simple and therefore ordered the Dome des invalided rebuilt into a more magnificent dome structure in 1675. Inside the cathedral, directly below the dome, is the Sarcophagus of Napoleon. The Hôtel des Invalides is also home to several museums.

○ EIFFEL TOWER

Today, it is difficult to imagine the outrage caused by the construction of the wonderfully filigree tower of about 10,000 tons of steel when it was built in 1889 during the World Fair. There probably isn't a structure of the French metropolis that is more well known worldwide than this 324-metre-high tower, designed by engineer Gustave Eiffel. Lifts lead to its platforms, which allow visitors a fantastic view over the city of Paris, and in clear weather, far into the Île-de-France.

○ SACRÉ-CŒUR

Two buildings dominate the skyline of Paris: the Eiffel Tower and the magnificent Sacré-Cœur Basilica. The white domes and the campanile glow far and wide above the city. Around Sacré-Cœur lies the heart of Montmartre with its small picturesque streets and restaurants.

GOING OUT

Au Pied de Cochon // A last relic from the big time of the Market Halls! When "Les Halles" still existed, suppliers came here to have a hearty meal early in the morning before returning home. Even today, a hearty cuisine is promoted: meat, as the name "To the Pigs Trotter" indicates, determines the main menu.

// www.pieddecochon.com

Café Marly // The big plus point of this café is its excellent location. Under the arcades of the Louvre, guests feel like they're travelling back to the time of Emperor Napoleon III.

// cafe-marly.com/fr

Benoit // Classic elegance characterises this bistro, which has existed for 100 years. It is also run by the world-famous chef Alain Ducasse. In the heart of the city, you can enjoy traditional French bistro cuisine in a splendid atmosphere. **// www.benoit-paris.com**

Right: The Mur de la Paix on Champ de Mars is a tribute to World Peace, and can be seen from the Eiffel Tower.

SHOPPING

○ **BAZAR DE L'HÔTEL DE VILLE**

The BHV is one of the oldest department stores in Paris. The range includes clothing as well as furniture and decorations.

// www.bhv.fr

○ **CENTRE COMMERCIAL DU CARROUSEL DU LOUVRE**

There are around 35 shops in various areas in the underground department store: fashion, jewellery and cosmetics, as well as glass and porcelain, and - in the Virgin Megastore - books and CDs. There is also food, a patisserie and a food court.

// carrouseldulouvre.com

○ **JEAN-PAUL HÉVIN CHOCOLATERIE**

In this chocolaterie, you can enjoy delicious chocolates and countless sweets as well as wonderful French pastries: from eclaires to Longchamp chocolat to macarons, leaves nothing to be desired.

// www.jeanpaulhevin.com

○ **LE BON MARCHÉ**

The most elegant Grand Magasin in the city. Here you do not just go shopping; you experience a piece of history. The founding of Bon Marché in 1838 marked the emergence of a new type of shop - the Department Store.

// www.24sevres.com/fr-fr/le-bon-marche

DAYTRIPS

○ **VERSAILLES**

At the gates of Paris, Versailles Palace is the prototype of the absolute ruler's residence and became the model for many European royal residences. Surrounded by the Baroque buildings, the Sun King Louis XIV built a large-scale park with perfectly manicured tress, hedges, and maze gardens.

WHERE TO STAY

Hôtel Caron de Beaumarchais // The poet Pierre August Caron de Beaumarchais once wrote his "Marriage of Figaro" in this house. With a fireplace in the style of Louis XVI. and historic candlesticks decorating guestrooms, you will feel as if you've been transported back to that grand era.

// **www.carondebeaumarchais.com**

Hotel de Bellechasse // Contemporary furniture, the atmosphere of an art gallery and the building in Neo-classical style. In addition, there is a small terrace in the pretty courtyard for guests to relax. With its central location, this hotel is surprisingly peaceful.

// **www.lebellechasse.com**

Amélie // Each of the rooms at this small, charming hotel, halfway between the Eiffel Tower and the Hôtel des Invalides, is decorated in different coloured shades. Many of the cities' sights are within walking distance.

// **www.hotelamelie-paris.com**

NOT TO BE MISSED

EXPERIENCING A SHOW AT THE CRAZY HORSE SALOON

The shows of this Revue Theatre, founded in 1951, are considered the most permissive in Paris. The dancers are chosen to be the same in size and stature, they are dressed primarily by the light from the amazing show. No food is served at the Crazy Horse itself, but some top restaurants in the area each offer a dinner, which can be booked in combination with the show.

.

ENJOY A SEINE RIVER TOUR OR TAKE A RIDE ON THE BATOBUS FERRY

The city grew outwards from the islands, so there are many of the most important sights along the Seine. From the cruise, you can admire these magnificent sights comfortably and perhaps get another very special perspective. Batobus offers the possibility to get on and off at about ten stops along the river.

LEARNING HOW TO COOK LIKE A FRENCH CHEF

Paris is the City of Love, and love also extends to the stomach. "Le Cordon Bleu" is THE place where professionals learn from professionals, but there are several cooking classes on offer. Also, very good for learning is the studio of the Sens.

VISIT SHAKESPEARE & COMPANY

The name Shakespeare & Company has been a tradition in Paris since 1919. At that time, the American Sylvia Beach opened her bookstore for English-language literature, which soon became the meeting place of literary greats such as F. Scott Fitzgerald, Ernest Hemingway, and James Joyce. In addition to a rich selection of English-language literature, today there are a variety of events such as author readings and workshops.

PLAY PÉTANQUE IN THE ARÈNES

In the Arènes de Lutèce, the Pétanque players meet every afternoon until early evening when the weather is good. Pétanque is a variant of the boules game. Many players join a club and annually compete in the Parisian championships.

#23 PROVENCE

THERE IS HARDLY ANOTHER REGION OF FRANCE THAT IS BURSTING WITH LIFE LIKE THE PROVENCE. THERE ARE A LOT OF FESTIVALS IN THE SUMMER, SUCH AS THE BIG OPERA FESTIVAL IN ORANGE, AND THE THEATRE FESTIVAL IN AVIGNON. IN PROVENCE, THE FOOD UNIQUELY COMES IN MANY SMALL PORTIONS, WHICH IS OFTEN REMINISCENT OF SPANISH TAPAS. THIS SHOULDN'T BE SURPRISING, THOUGH, AS THE BORDER IS VERY CLOSE BY. MOST OF ALL, IT IS THE PLAY OF ENCHANTING COLOURS THAT ENHANCES THE LANDSCAPE. WHETHER THE RED EARTH AT ROUSSILLON, THE DEEP PURPLE LAVENDER FIELDS NEAR VALENSOLE, OR THE BRIGHT YELLOW VAN GOGH CAFÉ IN ARLES - THE COLOURS SEEM TO BE CELEBRATING A FESTIVITY, AS ARE THE SCENTS. SOAPS AND HERB BOUQUETS, FRESH FLOWERS ARE SELLING AT THE COLOURFUL WEEKLY MARKETS AND UNVEIL THE FRAGRANCES OF THE WORLD.

Above: The Notre-Dame de Sénanque Monastery proves that one does not always need many decorations and ornaments to make a building look imposing. It dates back to the 12th century and was built by Cistercian monks.

Left: With its bright houses and narrow streets, Châteauneuf-du-Pape is typical of the Provence region.

○ MARSEILLE

The second largest city in France, and the most important port, Marseille has 2,500 years of history. The heart of the city lies, even today, at the port, in whose expansion the Canebière opens as the main axis of the city. The entrance to the Old Port is flanked on the north side by Fort St. Jean, and on the south side by Fort St. Nicolas. From the Plateau de la Croix, standing at the forecourt of the Basilique Notre-Dame-de-la-Garde, you have the best view over the harbour and the city.

○ CATHEDRALE

The Cathedral of Marseille was built in 1852. Napoleon himself laid the foundation for it, and the builders did not save on space. It is almost as big as St. Peter's Basilica in Rome, and it can accommodate 3,000 people. The dome alone is 70 metres high - and beautifully decorated with layers of stone and ornaments.

○ VIEUX PORT

The Old Port with its yachts and fishing boats is the central attraction for visitors to Marseilles. Around the harbour you will find cafés and restaurants where you can try fish specialties such as the legendary bouillabaisse.

○ AIX-EN-PROVENCE

The Spa and University Town was for centuries the capital of Provence. The Old Town lies between the Cours Mirabeau, a tree-lined avenue with beautiful 18th century city palaces, and the impressive St. Sauveur Cathedral (12th-17th centuries) with a Merovingian baptistery. Interesting sights include the Town Hall (17th century), the Musée des Tapisseries, and the Atelier de Paul Cézanne. A favourite motif of the town's most famous son is the Mont St. Victoire. On a specially designated city tour, one follows in the footsteps of the world-famous painter.

WHY VISIT IN SUMMER?

LAVENDER! NO OTHER REGION IN FRANCE SMELLS AS INTENSE AS PROVENCE WITH ITS LAVENDER FIELDS. EVEN IF THE FLOWERING HAS NOT STARTED OR IS OVER, THE AROMA OF ESSENTIAL OILS IS ALL OVER THE LANDSCAPE. THE FIELDS ARE STILL IN BLOOM FROM THE BEGINNING OF JUNE TO MID-AUGUST, AND THE LANDSCAPE IS CRISS-CROSSED BY PURPLE LINES, GIVING THE TYPICAL BUT STUNNING IMAGE OF PROVENCE.

○ ARLES

In Arles, one is inescapably reminded of Vincent van Gogh: The Yellow House with cobblestone streets and gardens. The painter has portrayed the city and its surroundings in more than 300 paintings betwwn 1888/89. Wherever he set up his easel is today marked as the Van Gogh way through the Rhone town. His motifs also included the Roman Arena. In the 1st century BC, the Romans had founded the colony of Arelate there, near a former Greek settlement - remnants of the ancient theatre, the forum including the Cryptoporticus and the Constantine Palace are still preserved.

○ ROUSSILLON

If you deduct the word "red" from the name, you wouldn't be wrong, because even then the Romans called the settlement Vicus Russulus ("Red Village"). The reason for this lies in the soil, which has a very special colour, a mixture of rusty brown, wine red and ochre. The latter was already mined by the Romans as a raw material for their pigments around Roussillon, and even today a factory refines the earthy compounds to colours. No wonder that the houses of this city are almost all plastered in the typical shade of red, as if someone has left a picturesque portrait behind.

Above: The wooden Bascule Bridge Pont de Langlois near Arles immortalizes Vincent van Gogh from several angles.

Top left: What an intense violet! Such magnificent lavender fields can only be found in the south of France.

Bottom left: One of the highlights in Lubéron is a visit to the town of Roussillon with its famous ochre quarry.

○ AVIGNON

During the "Babylonian Captivity", the Roman Curia found refuge from the political turmoil in Rome from 1309 to 1376 in the southern French city. Due to this, Avignon, which Pope Clement VI bought from Johanna of Naples in 1348, during the Pontificate of Seven Popes, became the centre of Christianity. By the 14th century, the city had been surrounded by a wall almost 5 kilometres long, reinforced by fortifications and towers, such as the Tour du Chiens, and the Tour du Châtelet. The latter controlled access to the world-famous bridge Saint-Bénézet, at the Pont d'Avignon, which, however, is the only piece left reaching into the Rhone.

○ PALAIS DES PAPES

The Residency of the Pope, built under Pope Benedict XII and Pope Clement VI in 1334, is one of the most important Gothic palaces in the world. The private rooms and premises have a total size similar to that of four cathedrals. The complex also includes liturgical spaces such as the Sacristie Nord with plaster figures of dignitaries, and splendid chapels painted by Matteo Giovanetti. The courtyard of the palace is today the backdrop of the famous Festival of Avignon.

○ ORANGE

In the territory of a conquered Celtic settlement in the Rhone Valley, the Romans founded the City of Arausio. From this period, there are still numerous remains of buildings, including the Theatre Romain - with its 103-metre-long and 37-metre-high façade front - it is one of the largest amphitheatres of ancient Roman times. Because of its spectacular location on a hill, some passages had to be dug into the rock. Up to 10,000 spectators can be accommodated with a beautifully decorated scene wall to watch stage plays, comedies, juggling or pantomime artists. Following centuries of decline and its past usage as a quarry and prison, it was restored in the 19th century. Today, the amphitheatre is being utilised again for festival performances.

GOING OUT

Arles: L'Atelier // This elegant restaurant in the heart of Arles is run by Jean-Luc Rabanel. His favorite ingredient is vegetables, which he literally use in every variation possible.

**//www.rabanel.com/
le-restaurant-l-atelier**

Marseille: Le Miramar // If you do not want a poor copy of the traditional fish soup bouillabaisse, but enjoy true tradition, then the Miramar is a must. The restaurant on the Vieux Port definitely complies with the 1980 Bouillabaisse Charter.

// www.lemiramar.fr

Aix-en-Provence: Au Verre Levé // France and wine are known to be inseparable. For all lovers of this fine liquid, it is worthwhile to visit the Au Verre Levé. The organic wine bar also has some outdoor tables - a lovely place to enjoy warm summer evenings.

// www.auverreleve.com

Right: The song "Sur le pont d'Avignon, IL'on y danse, l'on y danse...." - today, the famous Pont d'Avignon from this well-known children's song can only be found in parts.

SHOPPING

○ **MARSEILLE: LES TERRASSES DU PONT**

This modern shopping centre is located on the seafront, and the terraces invite you to take in at least a glimpse of the blue waters before heading to the nearest boutique, of which there are around 200 in addition to the restaurants and cafés.

// www.lesterrassesduport.com

○ **WEEKEND MARKET IN ARLES**

Almost everywhere in Provence, markets are open at weekends selling regionally grown produce, fabrics and ceramics. One of the largest, with around 450 sellers, takes place on Saturdays in Arles, on the Boulevard des Lices.

DAYTRIPS

○ **CAMARGUE**

The river delta between the two main estuaries arms of the Rhone, with 140,000 hectares of swamp, meadow and pasture land, as well as dune and salt fields. This is one of the largest wetlands in Europe, and offers a unique natural paradise. The lush grasslands of the delta are not only home to the well-known Camargue horses and wild life, but also the numerous water and marsh birds, including around 10,000 flamingo pairs.

○ **CALANQUES**

Is it the white limestone that makes the water so incredibly turquoise? Whatever the reason - the colours of the sea at the fjord-like indentations near Marseille are breathtakingly amazing. The national park is the youngest in France, and extends between Marseille and Cassis. It does not only cover the land side, but also far into the sea. Moreover, it is only a few kilometres outside the city of Marseille, and that alone makes it something very special.

Left: Dried rosemary, chives, fennel, star anise or thyme are sold at many markets - the famous "Herbs of Provence".

WHERE TO STAY

Avignon: La Banasterie // This almost luxurious bed and breakfast is located right in the Old Town and combines the flair of the old building with modern touches. The day starts with a delicious, hearty breakfast.

// **www.labanasterie.com**

Marseille: Hôtel la Résidence du Vieux Port // There are few accommodations in Marseille that offer a comparable view of the Vieux Port. And this designer hotel, perfectly highlights the view with its large windows.

//**www.hotel-residence-marseille.com**

Arles: Hôtel Particulier // The hotel is a small oasis in the middle of the city that draws its own charm with an added touch of luxury. A spa and restaurant complete the luxury that this hotel has to offered.

// **www.hotel-particulier.com**

NOT TO BE MISSED

ENJOY A COFFEE IN THE CAFÉ VAN GOGH IN ARLES

This café resembles an oil painting. If you're in front of the house for the first time, you'll probably have to blink for a moment. Why? Because it's almost everything that Vincent van Gogh once portrayed in his famous paintings, especially during the early dusk hours when the first stars are sparkling in the sky. It is this panorama as the artist saw it in September 1888 and immortalised on canvas.

VISITING MARIUS FABRE & RAMPAL-LATOUR

"Extra pure" it is written on the soaps, stamped in the olive-green colour of the fragrant pieces. While for years, soap was just a household product, the hand-crafted pieces with 72 percent olive oil, are currently experiencing a boom. They are made according to an ancient recipe in which the oil, mixed with vegetable ash, combine to a very special consistency. Even today, the distillers Rampal Latour and Fabre still make these fragant soaps by hand. Knowledge has passed from generation to generation, and so their workshops are like living museums.

TASTING A BOUILLABAISSE

Now a highly acclaimed specialty, the fish soup was once a poor fisherman's food, as the locals simply boiled up leftovers from their catch into a soup. Today, the preparation has deviated strongly from the origin: who wants to do it right, does not simply pour ingredients together, but prepares them separately depending on cooking times. The clear broth comes later in a dish with slices of white bread on the table. Fish and vegetables are served separately. A real ritual.

ENJOY THE SCENT OF THE FLOWER MARKET IN AIX-EN-PROVENCE

It is an extraordinary picture when the roses are jostling for the best fragrance and the wonderfully gaudy flowers are arranged in austere bundles on tables. Aix has two flower markets, one on Place des Prêcheurs on Mondays, Wednesdays, Fridays and Sundays, the other at Place de l'Hôtel de Ville on Tuesdays, Thursdays and Saturdays, both in the mornings. The Place des Prêcheurs also hosts a conventional weekly market on Tuesdays, Thursdays and Saturdays.

EXPERIENCE MEDITERRANEAN CULTURE IN THE MUCEM IN MARSEILLE

Between the Cathedral and the Old Fort stands a modern Cubist building, fully glazed and decorated with a concrete pattern that looks like lace. The MuCEM, created in 2013, is something out of the ordinary. It is the first museum dedicated to Mediterranean cultures - a hitherto unique facility. Not only from the outside the building is worth seeing, also inside exhibits are shown, which can not be seen anywhere else in the world.

#24   RIGA

800 YEARS AGO, RIGA WAS FOUNDED AS A CONVENIENTLY LOCATED MERCHANT'S BRANCH. TODAY, THE CAPITAL OF LATVIA BOASTS NUMEROUS HISTORIC BUILDINGS AND BEAUTIFUL PARK LANDSCAPES. RIGA IS LOCATED AT THE MOUTH OF THE DUNA, IN THE BALTIC SEA. AFTER SEVERAL CENTURIES OF FOREIGN RULE SINCE 1918, TODAY, WITH OVER 700,000 INHABITANTS AND A DIVERSIFIED INDUSTRY, SEVERAL UNIVERSITIES AND COLLEGES, RIGA IS ALSO THE LARGEST AND MOST IMPORTANT CITY IN THE COUNTRY. ON THE RIGHT BANK OF THE DUNA RISES THE OLD TOWN, AND ON THE LEFT, THE NEW TOWN THAT WAS BUILT IN THE 19TH CENTURY. BOTH DISTRICTS ARE RICH IN IMPORTANT ARCHITECTURAL MONUMENTS FROM DIFFERENT STYLISTIC PERIODS. WHILE RENAISSANCE AND BAROQUE PREDOMINATE IN THE OLD TOWN, IN THE NEW TOWN YOU CAN DISCOVER AN EXTRAORDINARY DENSITY OF UNIQUE ART NOUVEAU TESTIMONIES.

Above: Over the Düna you can see the characteristic multi-towered silhouette of the Old Town of Riga. In the historic centre of the Latvian capital, you will find Medieval Churches and Merchant Houses, as well as one of the most beautiful collections of Art Nouveau buildings in Europe.

Left: During the day, the streets of the Old Town are lively. Here you can shop at souvenir markets, enjoy art in galleries and history in museums or dine in one of the many restaurants and cafés.

○ OLD TOWN

Riga's Old Town is only about one square kilometre in size, a small and compact area on which the sights are tightly packed together: City Hall, Cat House, Big and Small Guild, Powder Tower, Petrikirche, and many more historic buildings. But those who hurry through the historic buildings will not experience the colourful flair of the city. In the sunshine, street cafés attract guests with kringels, the traditional sweet almond biscuits. The inhabitants of Riga rush by, always busy and smartly dressed. The Old Riga in Rozena Street is rather quiet and cosy, with houses just one arm's breadth apart.

○ ST. MARY'S CHURCH

The late Romanesque, from 1211 built from brick and repeatedly expanded, St. Mary's Cathedral is not only a church, but a witness of spiritual power, which competed with the rich Hanseatic merchants and the representatives of the Teutonic Order. The winner of the prestigious competition was the Cathedral of the Archbishop with its 140 metres high tower (1595), which has become dilapidated and in the 18th century had to give way to a Baroque tower, 90 metres high. The Gothic interior of the largest Church in the Baltics fell victim to the iconoclasm of the Reformation, but was renewed in the 17th century.

○ PETRI CHURCH

The Golden Rooster on the over 123-metre-high spire of St. Petri has the best view over the Old Town, the Duna and the Baltic Sea. The panoramic view, which visitors enjoy from the viewing platform at 72 metres height, is great. But the church towers did not seem to have much luck. The first collapsed, its successor, a splendid Baroque copy, and at 136 metres the world's highest timber construction at that time, was struck by lightning, and the following one destroyed by German bombs. The origins of St. Peter's

Church from 1209 still preserved are the outer walls of the aisle and a few pillars inside. Various alterations and new buildings gave the present appearance of the three-aisled basilica in the style of the 15th century Gothic brick. Today, the church serves as a space for exhibitions and concerts, which give the painted, Gothic glass windows a unique atmosphere.

○ BLACKHEADS HOUSE

The impressive building at the historic Town Hall Square was built in 1334 as a guild and meeting house. Originally built in Gothic style and later changed several times, it received its magnificent Renaissance façade in the 17th century with numerous figures and reliefs. The building is known as the "Blackheads House" since the second half of the 17th century. The namesake is the merchant association, which had used the house for more than two centuries. The members of a federation of merchants of predominantly German origin in Riga, and some other cities of the Baltic, called themselves "Blackheads". During the Second World War, the building was almost completely destroyed. About half a century later, from 1995 to 1999, the house was rebuilt true to the original.

Above: Next to the House of the Blackheads is the 13th-century Petri Church, which was extensively altered in the Middle Ages. The two historic buildings are among the most beautiful in the Baltic culture.

Left: Children in traditional costumes at the Latvian Youth Song and Dance Festival.

Right: The façade is splendid and stylish in Elizabetes iela 10b, designed by Mikhail Eisenstein. Female figures, floral and plant drawings, winding lines and masks are the typical elements of Riga's Art Nouveau.

○ NEW TOWN

Northeast of the 42 metres high Freedom Monument, which marks the border to the Old Town with the parks, begins the "Boulevardbogen". This is the name given to the central area of Riga New Town, which is defined by three large boulevards. Here you will find an impressive collection of magnificent buildings ranging from Classicism to Art Nouveau.

○ NATIONAL OPERA

South-east of the monumental statue is the Latvian National Opera. The Classicist building with its columns and allegorical statues was built between 1860 and 1863, the Nymph fountain on the forecourt was added in 1887.

○ PALACE OF CULTURE AND SCIENCES

The Palace of Culture and Science, which was completed in 1955, and once bore the name of Josef Stalin and today, among other institutions, houses the Academy of Sciences, rises high into the sky. Also visible from afar stands on the south-western tip of Dünundsel Za usala is the 368 metres tall television tower.

○ CENTRAL MARKET

Opposite is the Central Market, which was built between 1924 and 1930 using the building fabric from two large Zeppelin halls. Today, the market covers a huge area with an ensemble of five large market halls and many smaller ones with a commercial space of more than 70,000 square metres.

○ ART NOUVEAU ARCHITECTURE

Those exploring the New City of Riga discover a wealth of Art Nouveau buildings, which need not shy away in comparison of the more famous ensembles in Vienna or Prague. Overall, the city is decorated with 800 Art Nouveau buildings. After the demolition of the ramparts in 1863, the new open spaces were built on in the other side of the Old Town. Riga's Art Nouveau is associated with the name of Mikhail Eisenstein (1867-1921), the father of the famous film director Sergei Eisenstein. As director of the municipal construction office, the architect and engineer created a large

GOING OUT

Restaurant 3 // The restaurant places high demands on itself, which are reflected in the quality and creativity of the dishes. Sustainability and responsibility in the use of resources are a matter of course here. Main ingredients are fish, seafood and meat.

// www.restaurant3.lv

Café V. Kuze // Above all, the café is authentic! Decorated in the style of the 1930s, sweet delicacies are served, from cakes to pralines, truffles and hot chocolate. A place to relax and pamper your palate.

// www.kuze.lv

Coyote Fly // It is not just a popular place to party for the local night owls. Well-crafted cocktails, international DJs and a boisterous crowd make the Coyote Fly a club to return to.

// www.coyotefly.lv

number of the most outstanding buildings from 1893 onwards, with an immense wealth of forms and sculptures. One of the most famous is the exceptional house on Elizabetes iela 10b with its nine windows and oversized heads on the gable.

SHOPPING

○ CENTRAL MARKET

Visiting one of Europe's largest food markets is an experience for all the senses. It is housed in a former airship hangar and impresses not only by the size, but also by its liveliness. Numerous restaurants are just inviting you to linger a while.

○ GALLERIA RIGA

Located in the heart of the city, this mall offers everything the fashionista's heart desires. There is also a good rooftop café and a number of toys, homewares and accessories shops.

// galleriariga.lv/en

DAYTRIPS

○ PALACE RUNDALE

Rundale Palace is the largest Baroque ensemble in Latvia. Ernst Johann von Biron, Duke of Courland, and the favourite of Tsarina Anna, laid the foundation stone for his summer residence in 1736. The two-storey Baroque Palace was designed by the Italian architect, Bartolomeo Francesco Rastrelli, the builder of the Winter Palace in Saint Petersburg. Today, many of the 138 rooms can be visited.

WHERE TO STAY

Hotel Garden Palace // Wooden beams decorate the ceilings, and stylish furniture adds a classic feel to the hotel's 60 rooms and suites. The location in the middle of the Old Town contributes well to the success of the vacation as does the excellent breakfast.

// www.latvia.travel/de/unterkunft/
garden-palace

Rixwell Konventa Seta // A former Monastery from the 15th century has been converted into this neat three-star hotel in the heart of the Old Town.

// www.rixwell.com/en/
rixwell-hotel-konventa-seta

Neiburgs Hotel // Playful Art Nouveau welcomes guests to this boutique hotel. The rooms are elegant and spacious, the location is excellent between the Old and New Town, and a small restaurant spoils the taste buds.

// www.neiburgs.com

NOT TO BE MISSED

VISIT THE COLOURFUL AREA OF KALNCIEMA

Six 120-year-old wooden houses line the intersection of Kalnciema and Melnsila streets. For decades, they were abandoned and left to decay. In 2001, they began with a careful renovation using old techniques. Now the wooden houses are the heart of the living quarter. Flea and backyard markets enliven the scenery as well as numerous festivals and concerts. Workshops for children and guided tours are offered throughout the year, while small cafés and the restaurant "Maja" offer culinary delights.

TASTING "BLACK BALSAM"

Who has not tasted it, never really visited Riga - at least that's what many local bar owners say. Black Balsam is a herbal liqueur consisting of vodka and 24 different herbal ingredients. It is even said to have medicinal qualities.

TRAVEL BACK TO THE MIDDLE AGES IN THE "ROZENGRALS"

The Restaurant in the heart of the Old Town is housed in a building from the early 13th century and maintains this history as well - medieval traditions can be observed in the kitchen and service. Noble costumes and dishes based on original recipes from the Middle Ages make history come alive here.

A BOAT TRIP ON THE CANAL

Small wooden excursion boats offer one-hour tours on the city canal. This is the way to get to know the Old Town and the silhouette of modern Riga from the Daugava River on a leisurely tour.

EXPERIENCING HISTORY IN THE LATVIAN MUSEUM OF OCCUPATION

Between 1940 and 1941, Latvia had to suffer the occupation by the Soviet Union and by the National Socialists. This dark chapter of the history is conveyed very interestingly at the museum in a number of ways.

#25 SALZBURG

HUGO VON HOFMANNSTHAL CALLED THE CAPITAL OF THE PROVINCE OF SALZBURG THE "HEART OF THE HEART OF EUROPE". THIS CITY NOT ONLY PRODUCED WOLFGANG AMADEUS MOZART, BUT STILL TODAY CONTINUES TO INSPIRE ARTISTS FROM ALL OVER THE WORLD TO CREATIVE HEIGHTS. FORTRESS HOHENSALZBURG, CATHEDRAL, KOLLEGIENKIRCHE, RESIDENCE, ST. PETER AND MIRABELL PALACE. THE URBAN ARTISTRY ON THE SALZACH BETWEEN KAPUZINER - ALL INVIGORATE AND CAPTIVATE THE SENSES OF ITS VISITORS WITH ITS OVERFLOWING BAROQUE AMBIENCE AND ITS FASCINATING CULTURAL OFFERINGS. THIS GEM OF A CITY ESSENTIALLY OWES THEIR THANKS TO THE ARCHBISHOP WOLF DIETRICH VON RAITENAU. HE HAD DEMOLISHED HALF OF ITS MEDIEVAL CORE AROUND 1600 AND CREATED THE CENTRAL OPEN SPACES. AS A RESULT, HIS EQUALLY ARTISTIC FOLLOWERS COMPLETED THE UNIQUE ARCHITECTURAL ENSEMBLE OF SALZBURG AS IT LOOKS TODAY.

Above: The Old Town of Salzburg presents itself as a Baroque jewel, where Prince-Bishops who had become rich through salt mining in the 17th and 18th centuries built a hundred magnificent Churches and Palaces.

Left: Mirabell Gardens surrounding Mirabell Palace goes back to Fischer von Erlach. In 1730, it was then transformed into a Baroque garden, with emphasis on the main axis that aligns the gardens to the cathedral and the stronghold Hohensalzburg (in the background). Its essential elements are a central fountain and groups of figures, including historical dwarves.

○ FORTRESS HOHENSALZBURG

High above Salzburg, the landmark looks down onto its admirers with a watchful eye: Hohensalzburg Fortress is Central Europe's largest preserved Castle and the pride of Salzburg. This momumental landmark was built in the 11th century. The Fortress Mountain with its park at 120 metres high is ideal for a great walk with a breath-taking view. The castle is secured with a triple fortress ring wall and accessible only through three gates. Inside the inner wall, the defiant fortress is developed like a small town. There is also a fortress railway that brings visitors to the mountain.

○ CATHEDRAL ST. RUPERT UND ST. VIRGIL

Salzburg Cathedral, whose grand façade has been the backdrop for the Hugo von Hofmannsthal's "Everyman" performance since 1920 at the Salzburg Festival, is the oldest Bishop Church in present-day Austria. The roots of its architectural history go back to the early Middle Ages and can be found in the Cathedral Excavation Museum. There, under the Choir Crypt, archaeologists found remains of the first three-aisled basilica which after the 1181 fire disaster by Conrad III led to five-aisled construction. The current cathedral was built from 1614 to 1628 according to plans by the former court architect, Santino Solari. He was inspired by Italian churches and designed the front as a Baroque façade.

○ MOZART'S HOME AND BIRTHPLACE

If you want to walk in the footsteps of Salzburg's most famous son, visit Mozart's birthplace and the lavishly renovated residential building on Makartplatz. In Getreidegasse 9 stands the yellow-painted Hagenauerhaus, where the musical prodigy Wolfgang 1756 first saw the light of day. His parents

had moved in after their wedding in 1747, the family lived there until 1773. Today the house is a museum.

○ ST. PETER'S ABBEY
Above all, it is the architectural buildings of the Abbey Church of St. Peter from the 7th Century that are so impressive. But the real highlight is the cemetery - with the catacombs carved into the Mönchsberg.

○ HOUSE OF NATURE
Everyone who visits the House of Nature in Salzburg can experience extinct dinosaurs or a fascinating Underwater World.

○ PALACE AND RESIDENCE
If you want to feel like a king, visit Salzburg's former Palace Complex. The Residence, furnished with lavish splendour, and the Romantic Residence Square are true representations of Baroque architecture.

○ MIRABELL PALACE AND GARDENS
With the same mixture of lush Baroque and harsh Middle Ages as the City Centre on the left bank of the Salzach, is also on the other side of the river the district Neustadt. Take a walk through the State Rooms of the Prince-Archbishop's pleasure Palace Mirabell, the Baroque Museum, and the associated park with its Heckentheater (a kind of open-air stage, whose walls and alleys are made of hedges). Mirabell Palace was built in 1606 by

Above: Light marble from Untersberg defines the interior of the Salzburg Cathedral.

Left: The productions at the Salzburg Festival are elaborate (above: Mozart's "The Mildness of Titus"). The highlight, of course, is the play "Jedermann" (Everyman) by Hugo von Hofmannsthal (below).

Prince-Archbishop Wolf Dietrich von Raitenau for his mistress Salome Alt (with whom he fathered 15 children).

○ MOZARTS PLACE

It was created after the demolition of several town houses and is mainly dominated by the Mozart Monument. The Monument designed by Ludwig Schwanthaler was unveiled on September 5, 1842, in the presence of Mozart's sons.

○ MUSEUM OF MODERN ART

Anyone interested in Contemporary Art will find what they are looking for above the roofs of the city on the Mönchsberg. On altogether four levels, you can discover art from the 20th and 21st century right here.

○ PUPPET THEATRE

Surprisingly this is a place to marvel for both young and old. With a hand-carved dolls theatre and music performances, the highlight is, or course, Mozart's "Magic Flute".

○ MUSEUM OF TOYS

Trying out toys is expressly allowed in the Historical Toy Museum. The artistic toys are there for fun after all, and here even adult eyes will start to sparkle.

○ CASTLE HELLBRUNN

This magnificent "Palace of Pleasure" is an architectural masterpiece from the late Renaissance. In the sprawling Castle Park, the famous water features are delightful, especially when sparkling in the dreamy light of romantic summer evenings.

○ MONASTERY NONNBERG

Singing nuns, historical murals and Gothic architectural styles can be discovered in the Benedictine Monastery Nonnberg. Visit in the early morning hours because then the choir rehearsals take place.

○ HANGAR-7

Anyone interested in technology is in the right place at the airport at Hangar-7, and will be fascinated by the impressive collection of historic aircraft.

○ CASTLELEOPOLDSKRON

This place is a must for everyone who loves the "and they lived happily ever after". The park has a stun-

GOING OUT

Café Tomaselli // Over 300 years old and the longest permanently operated coffee house of the Danube Monarchy. Already visited by Wolfgang Amadeus Mozart and Herbert von Karajan. A well known „City Landmark". .
// **www.tomaselli.at**

Ikarus //Stylish venue at the airport in the futuristic hangar-7. The Patron is Eckart Witzigmann and every few weeks he amazes with conjuring up another world-famous Top Chef. Reservations must be made in advance.
// **www.hangar-7.com**

Right: In the former Home of the Mozart Family there is now a Museum that informs visitors about the life of Salzburgs most Famous Son.

ning romantic pond, and with beautiful mountains in the background, you will be enchanted.

○ CAPUCHIN CONVENT

If you want to visit the Capuchin Monastery on the Kapuzinerberg, this is best done on foot. The rewards are the view along the path where, at the top, the Historic Monastic Tombs awaits.

○ DOMQUARTIER SALZBURG

The DomQuartier Salzburg unites the exhibitions of five museums, which are located in the rooms of the residence, the Cathedral and the Monastery of St. Peter. During the tour, you will get stunning views of the city, and inside, get to admire the beautiful State Rooms and a multitude of invaluable art treasures.

SHOPPING

○ GETREIDEGASSE

International fashion in addition to traditional inns, and time-honoured crafts, can be found in the heart of the Old Town in the Getreidegasse. Exceptional are the wrought-iron guild signs, which can be seen in front of almost every shop.

○ CAFÉ-KONDITOREI FÜRST

Pralines and truffles at its best. The original Salzburg Mozartkugel, which was invented by pastry chef Paul Fürst in 1890, is still Salzburg's and Austria's number one souvenir and is in demand all over the world.

○ SCHRANNENMARKT

101 years old with 12,000 square metres of space and almost 200 stall holders, makes this place one of the largest weekly markets in the country.

○ DESIGNER OUTLET SALZBURG

If you like something more modern, visit the Designer Outlet at the airport. Even if you do not want to buy anything, it's worth a visit - the historical shopping scene is really worth seeing.

WHERE TO STAY

Goldener Hirsch // The Salzburg Festival Hall in the immediate vicinity, the world-famous Getreidegasse at the doorstep, and tradition on every square meter, this luxury hostel is in the centre of Mozart's city. Despite all the modern comforts, the 69 rooms have the charm of a 15th century hostel. Excellent food is available at the in-house restaurant "Goldener Hirsch".

// www.goldenerhirsch.com

Arte Vida // This smart boutique hotel takes you into the world of One Thousand and One Nights. An oriental-inspired oasis right in the Old Town, which offers rooms and apartments with kitchen.

// www.artevida.at

Wolf-Dietrich // The Hotel is in a beautiful Gründerzeit Villa in the middle of the Old Town, which has a well-designed spa area with indoor pool and an excellent breakfast.

// www.salzburg-hotel.at

NOT TO BE MISSED

VISIT A TRADITIONAL COFFEE HOUSE

If you really want to feel like you are from Salzburg on your journey, then you should start your day in one of the many traditional "coffee houses". Here, the locals meet to enjoy their coffee, chat, and of course for the latest town gossip.

ENJOYING A CLASSICAL CONCERT

When you are in what is known as Mozart's City, then of course you should attend a classical concert. The concerts are usually best enjoyed during the festival if you want the entire "Salzburg" feel. Even without any festivals happening, the city still offers numerous opportunities for all music lovers - goosebumps guaranteed!

A RIDE ON THE FIAKER

If you do not feel like walking then use a Fiaker. The famous horse-drawn carriages run through the Historic City, and will let you see the magnificent sights that Salzburg has to offer.

TASTE A SALZBURGER NOCKERL

When you order this famous "sweet ice-cream", you need to be patient, as this dessert is usually freshly made and takes its time. It is best to share the delicious but very powerful dessert with a friend and make sure you have a coffee to enjoy with it.

ENJOY THE VIEW FROM ONE OF THE MOUNTAINS

On a hike to one of Salzburg city mountains such as Mönchsberg, Fortress Mountain or Kapuzinerberg, you can trim off some of the calories from the Mozartkugeln and Nockerln and be rewarded with the breathtaking views of the city too.

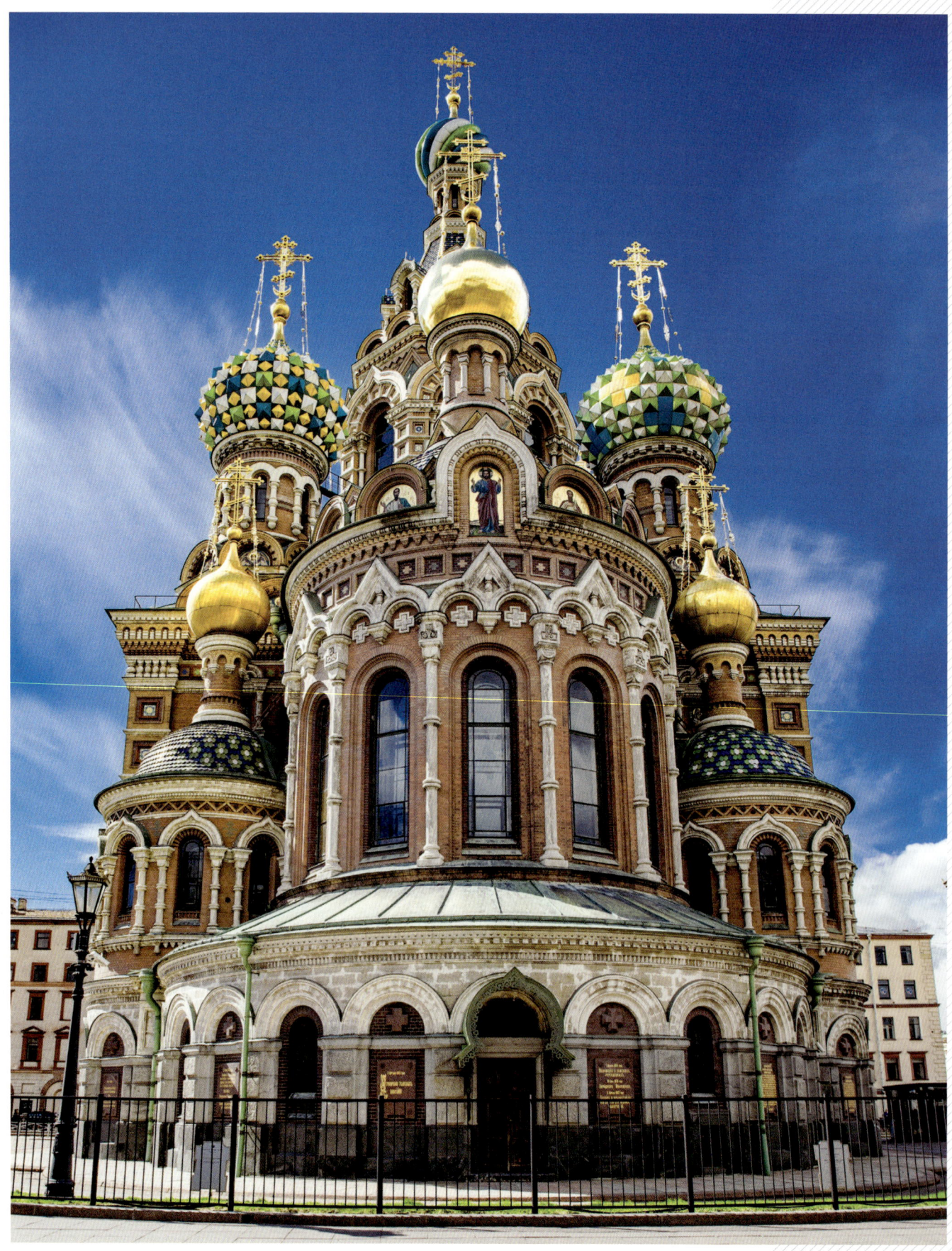

#26 ST. PETERSBURG

AFTER A WELL THOUGHT OUT PLAN, TSAR PETER THE GREAT BUILT HIS NEW CAPITAL, CHARACTERIZED BY HUNDREDS OF BAROQUE AND CLASSICAL BUILDINGS. AFTER PETER THE GREAT WRESTED THE COASTAL STRIP ON THE GULF OF FINLAND FROM THE SWEDISH KING KARL XII, HE HAD THE LONG-AWAITED ACCESS TO THE BALTIC SEA, AND THUS TO THE WEST. HE HAD A NEW CAPITAL BUILT, WHICH WAS TO SHINE ABOVE ALL EUROPEAN CITIES. NUMEROUS WESTERN AND CENTRAL EUROPEAN ARCHITECTS SUCH AS BARTOLOMEO RASTRELLI, DOMENICO TREZZINI AND ANDREAS SCHLÜTER PARTICIPATED IN THE CONSTRUCTION OF ST. PETERSBURG. THE CITY IMPRESSES WITH THE HARMONY OF ITS BAROQUE AND CLASSICIST BUILDINGS, THE PRESTIGIOUS SQUARES AND THE CANALS WITH MORE THAN 400 BRIDGES.

○ NEWSKI-PROSPEKT

In the evening light, it glows a yellow gold. This 4.5-kilometer-long road is one of the main arteries of St. Petersburg. It flourished in the middle of the 18th Century, when more and more nobles and dignitaries of the empire moved to the city centre of St. Petersburg, and built their own "city palaces" here. This, in turn, led to the construction of delis, jewellers, cafés and luxury hotels, which still give the street a stunning unique flair.

○ ST. ISAAC'S CATHEDRAL

St. Isaac's Cathedral is the largest and most magnificent church in St. Petersburg. In 1707, the first Church dedicated to St. Isaac of Dalmatia was built here. After defeating Napoleon, Tsar Alexander I decided to rebuild the church and transform it into a National Monument. For around 40 years, from 1818 to 1858, work was carried out on the building designed by the Neoclassical architect, Auguste Ricard de Montferrand. Magnificently finished in red granite and grey marble, the cathedral has a monumental gilded main dome and four mighty columned porticoes, whose pediments depict scenes from the "Life of Isaac" and the "History of Salvation".

○ PETER AND PAUL CATHEDRAL

On the grounds of the Peter and Paul Fortress is the Cathedral of the same name, built between 1712 and 1733 by Domenico Trezzini in the "Petrine Baroque". Externally, she stands out with the long golden tip of her 122-metre high bell tower with a weathervane in angelic form. Significantly, the cathedral is mainly a burial place of the Russian Tsars from Peter I to Alexander III, that are buried in a side chapel in marble coffins. It is also worth visiting: turrets, arches, columns - this cathedral is like a hidden object of design elements. Various brick colours are used, as well as golden onion turrets, copper-green roofs. Forms dissolve, then merge into something new, sometimes Classical, sometimes Art Nouveau.

○ ART CHAMBER

The reputation of being a House of Horrors precedes it - but the Art Chamber in St. Petersburg has much more to offer than just the preserved human miscarriages. Siamese twins, a double-headed calf and other abnormalities can be viewed here, as well as ritual objects from Africa and Asia. Extraordinary instruments, stuffed animals and a variety of minerals - this Museum was first opened to the public in 1719. The Art Chamber is considered to house

Left: The Resurrection Cathedral is the only Church in the centre of St. Petersburg built in the Old Russian style with the characteristic Onion Domes.

Right: With a diameter of 25 metres, the St. Isaac's Cathedral is the largest cantilevered church dome in the world after St. Peter's Cathedral. It offers rich figurative decoration and a magnificent ceiling painting.

WHY VISIT IN SUMMER?

TO EXPERIENCE THE WONDER OF THE WHITE NIGHTS. ST. PETERSBURG IS AT THE SAME LATITUDE AS GREENLAND, SO FAR TO THE NORTH THAT WONDERFUL LONG DAYS CAN BE EXPERIENCED FROM THE END OF MAY TO THE BEGINNING OF JULY, WITH THE BRIGHTEST TIME FALLING IN THE SECOND HALF OF JUNE. IT WILL NOT BE DARK AT NIGHT. INSTEAD, IN THE GHOST HOURS THERE IS A MAGICAL DIM LIGHT OVER THE CITY; THE STREET LIGHTS STAY OFF AND LOCALS DON'T NECESSARILY GO TO BED. THE CITY CAPITALISES ON THIS NATURAL MAGIC AND HOLDS A CULTURAL FESTIVAL IN THE CITY EVERY YEAR - WEALTH OF WORLD-CLASS OPERAS, BALLETS AND ORCHESTRAL PERFORMANCES, MANY IN THE GRAND MARIINSKY THEATRE. BUT YOU CAN ENJOY THE WHITE NIGHTS DIFFERENTLY - SPEND A DAY IN LETNIJ SAD (SUMMER GARDEN) AND ON THE NEVA, THEN CROSS FROM THERE INTO THE NIGHT AND WATCH AS THE LIFE OF THE CITY'S WATERFRONT GOES BY AND THE HUGE BRIDGES AS THEY OPEN. OR, GO TO ONE OF THE HIP NIGHT CLUBS - THERE ARE CELEBRATIONS WITHOUT THE SUN REALLY GOING DOWN.

the most comprehensive anthropological collections of its kind. One of the highlights of the collection is the Gottorf Giant Globe.

○ ADMIRALITY

Actually, it was supposed to be the shipyard for Peter the Great. The plans for the construction, which started in 1704, came from the Tzar himself. He chose the area, because the Neva was particularly deep here and therefore had enough room to let in even large ships from the fleet in. Such a strategically important position needed appropriate protection, and so the Admiralty soon built a fortress with ramparts and bastions. The main building was later rebuilt in Classicist style, and since 1823, it is the main line of sight between the Gorochowa Street, the Nevsky Prospect and the Wosnjesjenski Prospect.

○ WINTER PALACE

This is one of those incomparable building where Peter I died in 1725. The Winter Palace has 1,000 rooms and halls; the ballroom measures a proud 1,103 square metres. Gold plating gleams, large statues and pillars catch the eye, and visitors walk on thick, red carpets. The Winter Palace is considered the most important building of the Russian Baroque and is where the "Hermitage" proudly stands, one of the most important collections of paintings in the world.

○ HERMITAGE

Three million pieces need to be stored at the Hermitage, because in spite of the house's 350 rooms, there is only room for about 60,000 exhibits. Works by Rembrandt, Rubens, Leonardo da Vinci and Picasso can be found here. Katharina the Great laid the foundation for the collection when, in 1764, she acquired 225 paintings from a Berlin art dealer.

○ KASANER CATHEDRAL

The Roman St. Peter's Basilica was considered a model for this Russian Orthodox Cathedral. The semicircle colonnades that lead to the main building with the dome are an imposing sight. The church marks an important design aspect of the Nevsky prospect, so the portals were also aligned to the north.

Left: During the White Nights, the city celebrates with street parties, concerts and fireworks.

○ CHURCH OF THE RESURRECTION

On the Griboyedov Canal rises the colourful Church of the Resurrection, built on the spot where Tzar Alexander II fell victim to an assassination by the revolutionary organization Volkswille in 1881. Therefore, the church is also called the Redeemer Church of Blood. It was built from 1883 to 1907 according to plans by Alfred Parland in the old Russian style - in contrast to its classical environment. The main building is crowned by five domes. Next to it stands a bell tower with a gold dome. Both exterior and interior walls are extensively decorated with mosaics, some of them in the style of icons, while the pediments adorn works by the painter Viktor Wasnezow. In 1997, the building, which was never used as a church, was reopened as the "Museum of Russian Mosaics".

GOING OUT

Fasol // Although the name means "bean", this stylish café near St. Isaac's Cathedral offers much more: in addition to Russian dishes, such as pilaf, Italian cuisine is also on the menu here.

// 17 Ul. Gorokhovaya

Café Botanika // A vegetarian restaurant in meat-loving Russia? Yes, that's possible, and very good indeed. The Botanika, opposite the Stieglitz Museum, offers not only excellent food but also a rich selection of teas and freshly squeezed juices.

// www.cafe-botanika.ru

Katyusha // Quaint ambience with plush sofas and silk wallpaper. The restaurant, located directly on the Nevsky Prospect, not only impresses visually, but also serves delicious dishes with good Russian cuisine, modernly prepared and presented.

// en.ginza.ru/spb/restaurant/katyusha

Right: With its artfully designed gardens, the Peterhof residence is the most elegant of the Tsar palaces around St. Petersburg. Particular attention was paid to the sophisticated water features.

○ PETERHOF

Anyone who loves the Versailles Palace in France will also love the Peterhof Palace. Rightly, it is often compared to its French role model. About 30 kilometres from St. Petersburg, Tzar Peter the Great created a residence from 1714 to 1723, the dimensions of which he used to demonstrate his claim to power. In the following century, Peter's successors continued to expand the construction. In front of the huge building, there is a stunning park with the Baroque's typical circular lawns, hedges and variety of plants.

○ CATHERINE PALACE IN PUSHKIN

Like ballet dancers at a performance, they are perfectly tuned to each other - the pillared front of the richly decorated 300-metre-long façade of the Catherine Palace is a special architectural jewel of Russia. White columns, gilded atlases, arched windows and the sky-blue colour background of the building. A fairy tale castle, built in 1752 for Katharina, the wife of Peter the Great. Significantly, the style of the Baroque has been immortalized and married to Russian style. But much more popular is the palace's interior - with the world-famous Amber Room, which is considered as noe of the "8th Wonders of the World". The bright gallery, which measures around 800 square metres, is also worth noting.

SHOPPING

○ GOSTINY DWOR

The gigantic historic department store has only two floors, but each floor is a kilometre long. Strung together here are branded boutiques, smaller shops as well as small grocery stores. You can definitely spend hours on end here going from cheesy souvenirs stores, high-street fashion brands to haute couture!

○ DOM KNIGI

The" House of Books" has become an institution on Nevsky Prospect, with the most beautiful Art Nouveau ambience in the former Singers House, and you will find a huge bookstore and a great café with a fantastic view here.

○ KUSNETSCHNY RYNOK

This food market is the most stunning in the city. Here you will find all the herbs and ingredients for a real borscht, but also exotic ones from Uzbekistan and Kyrgyzstan.

WHERE TO STAY

Belmonde Grand Hotel Europe // This luxury hotel takes you back to the time of the Tsars or, alternatively, to the avant-garde artists. Depending on the desired style, guest can request a room or suites with avant-garde paintings or designer furniture, sumptuous marble or expressive colours.
//www.belmond.com/de/ grand-hotel-europe-st-petersburg

3mostA // This hotel is equipped with all the necessities. Key advantages are its central location, and the nice view from the restaurant on the fifth floor.
// www.3mosta.com

German B&B // For those who enjoy an intercultural atmosphere when traveling, this B & B is recommended. It is run by a German couple who have been living in St. Petersburg for a long time and can give so many insider tips - in German.
// www.rentroom.ru

DAY TRIPS

○ LOMONOSSOW (ORANGERY)

It was in 1710 that the idea was born and Prince Alexander Danilowitsch Menshikov decided to have a gigantic palace built by Italian and German architects. This construction would include an "orangery", and here you can find the explanation for the coat of arms and the original city name, Oranienbaum. Until 1917, numerous residences were added, but the idyll was reserved for nobility and the Tsar family, who used the suburb of St. Petersburg for their summer stays.

○ PAWLOWSK

Just 5 kilometres from Tsarskoye Selo (Pushkin), in the middle of one of Europe's largest landscape parks is another Tsar's castle, that of Pavlovsk. The name goes back to Tsar Paul I, who in 1780 commissioned the Scottish architect, Charles Cameron, with the planning and management of the construction of his Classicist summer residence. Special care has been taken in the completion of the English-style landscaped park with numerous pavilions, sculptures and bridges spread over an area of approximately 600 hectares.

NOT TO BE MISSED

SEE THE PERFORMANCE OF SWAN LAKE

The whole city seems to be inspired by art, but above all, it is the music that moves the soul. Tchaikovsky lived in St. Petersburg; his monumental tomb is in the Alexander Nevsky Monastery. His greatest legacy is "Swan Lake", so why not see this beautiful ballet performance right in its birth city. Every evening, there is a performance of this famous ballet in one of the city's many theatres. It's best to ask for tickets at one of the ticket booths.

TRADITIONAL SHOPPING ON NEVSKY PROSPECT

Bookshops, delicatessens, fashion boutiques, jewellers and literary cafés - Nevsky Prospect offers a wide range of shops. Many are designed in the finest Art Nouveau style, and it is certainly worthwhile to take a look inside.

VISIT MOIKA PALACE

The stately city palace of the princely family "Jussupow" is a popular destination for visitors. In the sumptuously and magnificently furnished rooms, you can trace the life - and the wealth - of this Russian aristocrat family of the late 19th century. Although, the palace is also known for its gruesome event: it is here that the "miracle healer", Rasputin, was murdered in 1916. Felix Jussupow and his co-conspirators probably acted at the behest of the Romanov clan. Allegedly, they first fed Rasputin with large amounts of cyanide, then beat him with an iron bar and finally shot him three times. When they, mistakenly, thought he was dead, they threw him into the Neva, where he eventually died of hypothermia.

CELEBRATE GRADUATION

Do not panic: no one has to go back to school to celebrate graduation in St. Petersburg. One simply participates in the great spectacle during the "White Nights" that the schools of the city put together. It is the Festival of Red Sails, and offers, among other things, a large fireworks display and a lot of live music.

#27   TUSCANY

CYPRESSES, SUNFLOWERS, GREEN HILLS AND THE SEA - ABOVE ALL, THE GRANDIOSE CULTURAL CITIES OF THIS REGION MERGE STUNNINGLY TOGETHER RIGHT IN FRONT OF OUR EYES. THE OLD CITY REPUBLICS SOUGHT TO OUTDO EACH OTHER WITH EVEN FINER BUILDINGS, AND THE LATER GRAND DUKE OFFERED HIMSELF TO ONLY THE BEST ARTISTS FOR SELF-PORTRAITS. THUS, CHURCHES, PALACES, AND WORLD RENOWN ENSEMBLES HAVE ARISEN, WITH EXQUISITE TREASURES, MOSTLY LOCATED IN THE OLD TOWN, ON STREETS AND SQUARES THAT SEEM TO BE FILLED WITH MAGIC. SHOPS AND MARKETS INVITE YOU TO TAKE A STROLL. THE TUSCAN CUISINE, ITS WINE, ITS RESTAURANTS AND CAFÈS ARE WORTH A TRIP IN THEMSELVES.

Above: Just with this view, you will automatically breathe deeply and feel at peace. So calming is the hilly landscape of Tuscany, through which a path winds up to La Foce.

Left: In the South of Tuscany, there is the Tuffsteindorf Pitigliano. Impressively built on the steep rocks, the origin of this picturesque town dates back to the time of the Etruscans.

○ LUCCA

If you want to know what a city might have looked like in the time of the Renaissance, you must visit Lucca. Here you can climb the city mandmark: the Torre dei Guinigi, a noble tower, on whose 44-metre-high platform, a large Holm Oak stands. Two areas of Lucca reveal the ancient history of the city: Piazza San Michele with the Church of San Michele in Foro which was built on the former City Centre, the Forum; and, the oval shape of Piazza dell'Anfiteatro which was created by building houses around the today no longer existing amphitheatre from the 2nd century.

○ PISA

The "Piazza dei Miracoli" or the "Square of Wonders", as it was called by the poet Gabriele d'Annunzio, was the world-famous ensemble of buildings around the Duomo Santa Maria Assunta, which had started in 1063. They had to first search for a dry area in the alluvial soil around Pisa for the ground of the "cathedral district". They chose a former graveyard beyond the old city walls - a not entirely happy choice, as the inclination of the campanile, the famous "Leaning Tower of Pisa", illustrates today. All in all, the work on the entire district took more than 200 years: in 1118, the cathedral was consecrated, in 1157, the baptistery was completed, in 1173, the campanile; and in 1278, the camposanto.

○ FLORENCE

Florence is not just the political capital of Tuscany. Its artful and historically unique Old Town was added in 1982 as the first place in the region to the list of UNESCO World Heritage Site. "The god who created the hills of Florence was an artist," said Anatole France.

○ SANTA MARIA DEL FIORE DOME

Brunelleschi's Renaissance Dome is the pride of the city. The Bell Tower goes back even to Giotto. Typical of Tuscany are the different coloured marble panels, which give both buildings their distinct

WHY VISIT IN SUMMER?
TO ATTEND A RACE OF MEDIEVAL BOATS IN PISA ON JUNE 17: PISA'S FURIOUS 1500-METRE BOAT RACE UP THE ARNO GOES BACK TO THE YEAR 1290. FOUR NARROW BOATS, ONE FOR EACH URBAN DISTRICT, RACE ON A WAGER. IN EACH BOAT SITS A HELMSMAN, A MONTATORE, AND EIGHT OARSMEN WHO FIGHT AGAINST THE WAVES. FINISH LINE IS A BOAT ANCHORED AT THE PALAZZO MEDICI, A PLACE ESTABLISHED IN 1737 AT THE WISH OF THE DUKE OF MONTÉLIMAR, WHO WAS THEN LODGING IN ONE OF THE PALACES. THE MONTATORE HAVE TO CLIMB A TEN-METRE-HIGH MAST AT THE FINISH LINE AND BRING DOWN A PALIOTTO (SILK BANNER). THE WINNERS WILL RECEIVE AN OX OR A ROOSTER, THE LOSERS IN DISGRACE ARE TEASED WITH A GOOSE.

characteristic. The dome fresco by Giorgio Vasari, the painted equestrian monuments by Paolo Uccello, and, Andrea del Castagno, as well as a depiction of Dante are particularly impressive in the interior of the dome.

○ BAPTISTRY

The Baptistery, one of the oldest buildings in the city, is famous for its doors. The Southern Door, designed by Andrea Pisano, has Gothic characteristic; the Northern Door, a work by Lorenzo Ghiberti of 1401, is referred to as "Paradise Door", as Michelangelo considered the scenes designed in the reliefs as extremely real-looking figures, worthy to decorate the gates of paradise.

○ PIAZZA DELLA SIGNORIA

Past the elegant shops of Via de Calzaiuoli, and the Master Sculptures of Donatello, and Ghiberti of Orsanmichele, you will reach the heart of the city. The Piazza, the old political centre, which is adorned with numerous statues. The depicted heroic exploits of David or Judith of Donatello symbolise the courage of the citizens.

○ UFFIZIEN

Built by Giorgio Vasari in 1559, the administrative buildings house one of the most important picture galleries in the world. Exhibits include masterpieces of the periods from Gothic to Baroque - from Giotto and Duccio through Botticelli, Leonardo, Titian; and, Dürer to Caravaggio and Rubens.

○ PONTE VECCHIO

As early as the 13th century, there were shops on the oldest bridge in Florence, but since 1593 only "worthier" craftsmen and goldsmiths were allowed to have business there. One should not only look into the inviting shop windows, but also over the city, and down the river, steer towards the elegant Ponte S. Trinità.

○ SIENA

Many consider Siena, with its red brick palaces and extraordinary flair, more pristine than its eternal competitor, Florence. The "Gothic City" stretches over three ridges in the heart of the Tuscan hills.

Left: The boats present themselves beautifully decorated with historical motifs at the summer race in Pisa.

○ DUOMO DI SIENNA SANTA MARIA

The medieval church was originally a Roman Catholic Marian church, but is now dedicated to Santa Maria Assunta (Assumption of Mary). Its richly decorated Gothic façade is amazing in red marble; and the exterior and interior with white and greenish-black marble in alternating stripes is equally stunning. Other treasures include the pulpit Nicola Pisanos; the sculptures of Donatello and Bernini; and the frescoes by Pinturicchio.

○ PIAZZA DEL CAMPO

The "shell-shaped" town square of Piazza Del Campo is considered as one of Europe's greatest medieval squares. Renowned worldwide for its beauty and architectural significance, it is also here where the stunning white marble "Fonte Gaia" (Fountain of the World) is. In addition, twice a year, the famous "Palio di Siena" horserace takes place around this square.

○ PALAZZO PUBBLICO

The old Town Hall, which is still used as such, made its mark: according to the city's plan, this Gothic construction with its small, Baldachin-like chapel had to be adapted to all the surrounding Palazzi - this was the only way to create the complete impression of the square that we admire today.

Top right: From the high Piazzale Michelangelo, you can enjoy a magnificent view of Florence with the Red Dome of the Santa Maria del Fiore, designed by Filippo Brunelleschi from 1420. It is indeed an overwhelming eye-catcher.

Bottom right: The Siena Cathedral is the main Church in the city, and is considered to be an important example of Gothic architecture. Its interior is impressive: the entire floor is covered with delicate panels depicting biblical themes as well as antique motifs. The church also contains true art treasures such as the octagonal pulpit by Niccolò Pisano.

GOING OUT

Florenz: La Dolce Vita // The bar with its integrated art gallery and cool terrace is a cult meeting place for the Florentine club scene.
// new.dolcevitafirenze.it

Siena: Alla Speranza // In the heart of Siena, on the Campo, you can enjoy dishes of Tuscan cuisine and fine wine.
// www.allasperanza.it

Lucca: La Vecchia Cucina di Soldano // This traditional trattoria serves traditional Tuscan dishes at very reasonable prices
// www.trattoriasoldano.it

Florenz: Da Nerbone // If you want to experience the real Florence up close, then right here, close to the lively Mercato Centrale, look for this simple trattoria. Everyone gets their meal at the bar, eats in a standing position, or if lucky, you might get one of the few places at a table.

○ SAN GIMIGNANO

The small town, with many medieval towers, is one of the most visited in Tuscany. The unique backdrop of the soaring towers, visible from afar, gave San Gimignano the nickname "Manhattan of the Middle Ages". These towers, which are up to 54 metres high, were built by the aristocratic families of the city, which became rich through commerce.

○ VOLTERRA

Volterra - situated on a hill with stunning views over the Val di Cecina - is known as the city of the Etruscans as well as the centre of Alabaster processing. The centre of the city is the medieval ensemble around the Piazza dei Priori that was built in the years 1208 to 1254, and the Cathedral of Santa Maria Assunta.

Left: In the middle of the beautiful Old Town of San Gimignano you will find the paved main square, Piazza della Cisterna. The triangular area is lined with medieval houses and the remains of columns from ancient palaces.

SHOPPING

○ FLORENZ: FARMACIA DI SANTA MARIA NOVELLA

The most famous Florentine Pharmacy is also one of the oldest in Europe (since 1612).

// www.smnovella.com

○ FLORENZ: MERCATO CENTRALE

The Food Market leaves nothing to be desired. On the ground floor fish, meat and poultry are offered; and, one level higher, you will find fruit, salad and vegetables.

// www.mercatocentrale.it

○ FLORENCE: VIA TORNABOUN

It is considered the city's most expensive street and is home to luxury fashion brands and top-notch jewellers. A stroll through this street is worthwhile, even if you're just window shopping.

○ SIENA: ANTICA PIZZICHERIA

This gourmet shop in the Palazzo della Chigiana sells local specialties from its own production at absolutely reasonable prices.

WHERE TO STAY

Florence: Beacci Tornabuoni // On the upper floors of a noble Town House you will find stylishly furnished rooms with old furniture. You can enjoy breakfast on the roof terrace overlooking Florence.

// www.tornabuonihotels.com

Siena: Palazzo Ravizza // An oasis of calm in the narrow streets of the Old Town. This charming hotel is housed within the walls of a Renaissance palace. The small salon with reading tables is inviting and comfortably furnished.

// www.palazzoravizza.it/de

San Gimignano: Bel Soggiorno // Located on the outskirts, many of the guest rooms offer beautiful sweeping views far beyond the picturesque Tuscan countryside.

// www.hotelbelsoggiorno.it

NOT TO BE MISSED

PARTICIPATE IN THE PALIO OF SIENA

The Piazza del Campo plays host to a traditional festival twice a year since the beginning of the 14th century: the Palio di Provenzano. This is held on the 2nd of July in honour of the Blessed Virgin, the Palio dell'Assunta as part of the Assumption Day on the 16th August. In the tournament, ten out of a total of 17 districts will compete against each other. Worth seeing at the Palio di Siena is also for the procession of the representatives of the Contraden who are dressed in historical robes.

RELAX IN THE THERMAL SPRINGS NEAR LUCCA

Bagni di Lucca is about 30 kilometres from Lucca. Its natural springs attracted travellers as early as the 19th century, such as Napoleon's sister Pauline, after whom the one grotto (Paolina) is named, or Heinrich Heine. Sick people often find relief here; while healthy people will truly get the full body & soul relaxation in the superb natural thermal spa. The location alone will already take your breaths away: exceptional caves with naturl thermal springs are the grottoes Grandale and Paolina.

VISITING VAL D'ORCIA BY STEAM TRAIN

Val d'Orcia, located about 25 kilometres southeast of Siena, is a man-made Renaissance landscape whose aesthetically pleasing design reflect the model of good care and respect to nature. Cypress trees, scattered farmhouses and small churches sitting on hills are still considered typical Tuscan. From Siena, you can take a leisurely ride on the Steam Train Ferrovia Val d'Orcia u. a. through the Orcia Valley, around the Amiata Mountain, and into the valley of the Ombrone.

TRACING THE LIFE OF NOBILITY IN PALAZZO DAVANZATI

If you want to know how they lived in an old Florentine city palace, Casa Forientina is the place to visit. It is a "house-style" museum, which displays furniture, sculptures and everyday objects from the Middle Ages, Renaissance to Baroque periods.

SIP A HOT CHOCOLATE IN CAFFÈ RIVOIRE

This Traditional Noble Café of the Florentines is located in Piazza della Signoria. The price should not put you off and you should absolutely try their speciality hot chocolate. This place has, since 1827, held an expert status for this noble drink - the hot chocolate "drink" is so dense that the spoon will stand on its own.

#28   VERONA

VERONA BECAME A PLACE OF PILGRIMAGE FOR LOVERS THANKS TO WILLIAM SHAKESPEARE – ALTHOUGH BEFORE HALF A DOZEN OTHER AUTHORS HAD ALREADY TOLD THE MELODRAMATIC STORY OF THE HAPPY-UNHAPPY-LOVE COUPLE. COUNTLESS GUESTS VISIT THE CASA GIULIETTA AND STROKE THE RIGHT BREAST OF THE BRONZE FIGURE OF JULIA IN THE HOPE OF LOVE AND HAPPINESS. BUT NOT ONLY BECAUSE OF ROMEO AND JULIET THAT DRAWS PEOPLE TO THIS PRETTY TOWN, IT IS ALSO BECAUSE OF THE OPERA FESTIVAL IN THE ANCIENT ARENA. IN THE YEAR 89 BC, THE ROMANS FOUNDED A COLONY HERE, WHICH SOON BECAME A MAJOR CITY. THE CHECKERBOARD FLOOR PLAN WITHIN THE RIVER LOOP OF THE ADIGE (ETSCH) STILL STRUCTURES THE OLD TOWN TODAY.

Above: The checkerboard layout within the river loop of the Adige (Etsch) still structures the Old Town with its famous Arena.

Left: The Ponte Pietra leads over the Adige and the Cathedral. On the façade of the church you can see the typical Veronese stripes - alternate stone and brick.

○ ARENA DI VERONA

Imposing monuments such as the huge Amphitheatre built in the 1st century, or the Porta dei Borsari, built in the same period, testify to the ancient origins of Verona. Opera fans celebrated their Centenary here: on August 10, 1913, the 100th birthday of Giuseppe Verdi, for the first time in the arena, the audience was passionately carried away. To Verdi's "Aida", thousands lit candles at dusk, introducing a ritual of light that is still today part of these festivals, which are as much a festival as a social event. The oval of the Arena - 152 metres long, 128 metres wide - holds 25,000 people. While there are comfortably upholstered armchairs with a backrest on the parquet floor, you can sit on higher levels, but you will need pillows, blankets, a picnic basket, and bring your own drinks.

○ PIAZZA DELL'ERBE

Piazza dell'Erbe, with the Fountain of the Madonna Verona, the Colosseum, and the Palazzo Maffei, is a bustling market square during the day. Even Goethe was fascinated by the vegetables and fruits here. Only in the evening does the market stalls come to rest.

○ DUOMO SANTA MARIA MATRICOLARE

After an earthquake had destroyed the previous Houses of Worship, they decided to construct a monumental building. The Duomo Santa Maria Matricolare was built as a Romanesque basilica in the 12th century. In 1187, priests consecrated the new church. But the style did not last long. From the Romanesque period, the cloister has remained on the left side of the cathedral, dating back to 1123. In the 15th century, the Duomo was Gothicized and fitted with up-and-coming windows. Baroque elements can also be found. The richly decorated chapels in the three-nave building are certainly striking. Red marble and frescoes are as much a sign of the craftsmanship of past centuries as the bas-reliefs on the façade. In the Capella Nichesola, there is a picture of Titian, and in the Mazzanti Chapel, the sarcophagus of St. Agathe.

○ BASILICA DI SAN ZENO

One of the most important Romanesque churches in northern Italy is the Basilica San Zeno which was built in the 12th and 13th centuries on top of a previous building. The relics of the eponymous Bishop Zeno of Verona are kept in a crypt from the 10th century, above which the stage choir of the high choir rises. There is the San Zeno Altar, a masterpiece by the Renaissance painter, Andrea Mantegna. The three-part painting shows the Mother of God. A late Gothic coloured wooden ceiling from the 14th century arches over the central aisle. Like the nave walls, the free-standing bell tower (Campanile), which was completed in the 12th century, alternates between light tuff stone and red brick in striped layers. One of the earliest Romanesque examples of the rose-rose motif is found on the façade.

○ PONTE PIETRA

The five-arched Ponte Pietra leads over the Adige. Due to recurring destruction and restoration, the bridge today consists of various buildings, each of which has characteristics of its respective era.

SHOPPING

○ VIA MAZZINI

A shopping mile, as it is portrayed in a book: brand shops line up along this pedestrian zone next to less expensive shops. It is amazingly very busy at all times of the day.

// www.kaashuistromp.nl

○ CORSO SANT'ANASTASIA

Around Corso Sant'Anastasia, antique shops and galleries will certainly make the hearts of collectors and art lovers skip a beat! A great place to even just stroll and look at some interesting art pieces.

DAYTRIPS

○ SOAVE

White wine grapes ripen on the hills around the small town, which gave the wine its name and made it world famous. Medieval elements are still preserved around the main square until today, the Town Hall (formerly Palazzo di Giustizia) is striking with a stately late Gothic marble staircase. The Scaliger family, keen castle builders, also constructed a castle in Soave, and a fortified wall surrounding the city with 24 towers.

WHERE TO STAY

Grand Relais The Gentleman // This luxury hotel lives up to its name: like a true gentleman of yesteryear, wishing to fulfill the wishes of every guest.
// www.thegentlemanofverona.com

Hotel Il Sogno di Giulietta // For the complete romantic package, a night in the Sogno di Giulietta is a must, because from the rooms you have a direct view of Verona's most famous balcony and the courtyard, which is closed to tourists at night.
// www.sognodigiulietta.it

Albergo Mazzanti // The hotel is very centrally location, and has a cosy ambience with its wooden floors and ceiling beams. Best of all, a very friendly service.
// www.albergomazzanti.it

NOT TO BE MISSED

ENJOY AN AMAZING OPERA

Built by the Romans in 30 AD, the Arena of Verona at that time had 30,000 spectators. Even today, once the Summer Opera season starts, many remarkable performances are on offer. Events are available from June to the beginning of September. It's an uplifting moment when a world-class diva slams a passage from "Aida" into these historic walls. Even those who do not understand a single word can enjoy the balmy evenings by the light of the candles that are always lit at sunset, with the "Bravo!" calling out from the audiences. Just do not forget to bring a pillow for more comfortable seating.

ADMIRE THE ARCHITECTURE

The courtyard of the Palazzo del Mercato Vecchio is well worth a visit due to its amazing architecture. You can also climb the 84-metre-high stairs up the tower "Torre dei Lamberti".

VISIT THE POET PRINCE

No, this does not mean Shakespeare, but it is actually Dante Alighieri. He raises his hand thoughtfully to his chin, day after day, in the Piazza dei Signori. The statue of the famous author of the "Divine Comedy", who lived in exile for a while in Verona, was created by Ugo Zannoni.

RISOTTO AND WINE

They are the most famous specialties of the region: Risotto and Wine. A visit to a traditional Osteria in Verona is easily organised. If you want to devote a bit more time to the fine wine, you can easily arrange a trip to the vineyards around the city.

AUTUMN

Enjoying the breeze while sitting in a beach chair - Sylt offers this experience to its visitors in autumn, when the island shows off its rougher side.

#29 THE AMALFI COAST

THE ROAD ALONG THE COAST AMALFITANA, ONE OF THE MOST BEAUTIFUL CLIFFS IN ITALY, SHOWCASES AMAZING VIEWS OF THE BLUE MEDITERRANEAN SEA, BEAUTIFUL BAYS AND PICTURESQUE SURROUNDINGS. THE COASTAL ROAD RUNS ABOUT 45 KILOMETRES IN ITS WINDING SERPENTINE. HERE, ITALY IS INDEED THE LAND WHERE THE LEMONS BLOOM! SINCE THE 19TH CENTURY, ARTISTS LIKE RICHARD WAGNER, WALTER BENJAMIN, GRETA GARBO OR WILHELM KEMPFF TREASURED THE CHARMS OF THIS COAST; THEY CHOSE PLACES LIKE RAVELLO, ATRANI OR POSITANO FOR THEIR HOLIDAY HOMES OR RETIREMENT RESIDENCES. THE MAIN TOWN OF AMALFI RECEIVES MUCH ATTENTION WITH ITS NORMAN-ARAB STYLE MARINA, CATHEDRAL IN ITS MAGNIFICENT MOSAIC FAÇADE, AND THE MAJOLICA-DECORATED BELL TOWER.

The region around Amalfi, with its breath-taking cliffs, is one of Italy's greatest natural beauties. It has been a UNESCO World Heritage Site since 1997. The site includes the stretch of coast between Positano (above and left) and Vietri sul Mare with the mountain villages of Scala, Tramonti and Ravello.
Right: The Cathedral is one of the main tourist attractions of the town of Amalfi, which lies on the south-side of the Sorrento Peninsula.

○ AMALFI

Amalfi, today a pretty seaside resort with 6,000 inhabitants, was a major maritime republic from the 9th to the 11th century, with 50,000 inhabitants. It was a key competitor to cities such as Genoa, Pisa

and Venice, and what remains today to remind us of the town's former splendour is the rowing regatta against its former rival cities, which takes place every four years. In the 14th century, Amalfi was largely destroyed by a tidal storm that wiped out a number of significant historical landmarks. Fortunately, the beautiful Amalfi Cathedral remains, located in the maze of narrow streets with its many stairs that take you up to the Cathedral itself. The structure dates back to the 9th century; it was rebuilt in 1203 in the Arab-Norman-Sizilia-African style. There are two beautiful former monasteries which now house luxury hotels, where Henrik Ibsen and Ingrid Bergman spent the night.

○ POSITANO

Famous for its picturesque location, Positano commands one of the most beautiful spots off the Amalfi Coast, starting at the beginning of the Amalfitana. Discovered during the Roman times, this seafaring village has a dreamlike beauty that comes from many colourful houses build stepwise along the two slopes of Monte Angelo a Tre Pizzi (1,443 metres). There are countless narrow streets where pretty little boutiques, cafés and restaurants can be found. In the evening, take a leisurely stroll at the harbour and soak in Positano's evening charm while you enjoy your dinner at one of the cafés or restaurants. Positano is also known as a fashionable seaside resort, over whose beach Spiaggia Grande rises the 10th century church of Santa Maria Assunta - a majestic landmark with its eye-catching central dome made of yellow, green and blue majolica tiles.

WHERE TO STAY

Belmond Hotel Caruso // In Ravello, at more than 1,000 metres high on a rocky overhang, this hotel offers every luxury imaginable. These include a wellness centre and enjoy a dream dinner, where your table is set in the infinity pool!
// **www.belmond.com/hotels/ europe/italy/amalfi-coast/belmond-ho-tel-caruso**

Santa Caterina Hotel // This 19th century villa is picturesquely located on the Amalfi Coast, overlooking the wide slopes in front of the town. Relax in the seawater pool, enjoy first-class Mediterranean food in the evening - what could you want more?
// **www.hotelsantacaterina.it**

Il Pettirosso Agriturismo // Holiday on the farm? Not quite, this so-called Agriturismo means that you travel "green". This rural property in Agerola offers delicious home-made natural organic products such as jams, honey and cheese.
// **www.ilpettirossoagriturismo.it**

SHOPPING

○ **VIALE PASITEA IN POSITANO**
Located in the city centre, this shopping street showcases many small local boutiques, as well as luxury brands. Shops selling local delicacies such as wine, jams and limoncello can also be found here.
// www.positano.com/en/shopping

○ **CERAMICS**
If you are looking for beautiful ceramics, then you are at the right place on the Amalfi coast. Make sure you have a stop in Vietri sul Mare, which is considered the capital of ceramics making.
// www.ceramicasolimene.it

○ **SANDALI TIPICI DI ALFONSO DATTILO**
Summer, sun, sandals! In Maiori, for over three generations the typical leather sandals have been made in this workshop.
// www.sandalitipici.it

GOING OUT

Africana Famous Club // Since 1962, this club is a must for those who enjoy good music until the wee hours of the morning. Its location alone is absolutely breathtaking as the club sits in a natural cave.// **www.africana-famousclub.com**

Positano: Music on the Rocks // The biggest club in Positano, offering the very best mix of hits and good (although pricey) drinks. The club also has is an amazing sea view.
// **www.musicontherocks.it**

NOT TO BE MISSED

TAKE A ROAD-TRIP DOWN THE PANORAMIC AMALFITANA

This is a magnificent driving experience with spectacular views of the coast and the Gulf of Salerno. To fully appreciate the exhilarating 50 kilometres drive, you should rent a car in Naples or Vietri sul Mare. Certain sections of Amalfitana road can be very narrow so that two cars can hardly pass each other, but there are several small lay-bys that make it possible to stop safely and provide an amazing photo opportunity. Although, if you have vertigo or are scared of heights, this drive may not be as enjoyable.

TAKE A HIKE IN THE "VALLEY OF THE MILLS"

If you like to do something a little off the beaten tourist tracks, then a hike from Amalfi to Valle dei Mulini ("Valley of the Mills") is definitely worth every step. In days gone by, numerous paper mills were built in this valley, thanks to the abundance of flowing water, some being the oldest in Europe. Not ideal for the faint-hearted as it is a five-hour walk, but the walk itself can be very relaxing as you breathe in the fresh coastal air while withnessing mother nature at her splendid best. The walk follows the path from Amalfi that leads into this famous valley.

GROTTA DELLO SMERALDO

The enchanting feature of this cave at Conca dei Marini is its radiant emerald green water. The gorgeous colour is created from the sea water which sparkles in the sunlight, as if the entire cave is filled with gemstones. Access to the cave is only by boat.

ATRANI

Certainly, worth a visit! This little town with its pretty winding streets is one of the most beautiful locations in Italy ("i borghi più belli d'Italia"). Situated in a natural bay, the central square of Atrani leads directly to the beach and the sea by crossing an antique passageway created to save boats from storms. Until now, this place is still considered an insider tip, as not many tourists have yet discovered the area.

VILLA RUFOLO

If you are in Ravello and still have some spare time, then you should visit this 13th century villa. Villa Rufolo was gloriously restored to its grandeur in the 19th century, with beautiful lanscaped gardens. In addition, you will find a number of interesting exhibitions in some of the rooms.

#30   BARCELONA

A CONSTANTLY EVOLVING CITY, BARCELONA IS A "CITY OF WONDERS", AS THE WRITER EDUARDO MENDOZA ONCE CALLED IT. THE CAPITAL OF CATALONIA, BARCELONA IS FILLED WITH TREASURED BUILDINGS AND PALACES THAT SHOWCASE A MAGNIFICENT HISTORY WHICH HAS BECOME ENSHRINED THROUGHOUT THE CITY. THE MAGICAL BARCELONA IS DEPICTED IN CARLOS RUIZ ZAFÓN'S "THE SHADOW OF THE WIND", WHO LOSES HIMSELF IN THE MAZE OF ALLEYS IN THE BARRI GÒTIC. NEVERTHELESS, BARCELONA HAS MANY FACETS - THE OBVIOUS TRADITIONAL OLD CITY IS JUXTAPOSED WITH A LIVELY COSMOPOLITAN FLAIR. IT IS A CITY WHERE POSTMODERN ARCHITECTURE CAN BE FOUND NEXT TO THE ART NOUVEAU BUILDINGS OF THE CATALAN MASTERS OF MODERNISM. THE DIVERSITY OF BARCELONA RANGES FROM THE ROMAN RUINS OVER THE STREETS, AND HISTORIC SITES OF THE CITY'S HEYDAY IN THE MIDDLE AGES, TO THE BUILDINGS IN THE EIXAMPLE DISTRICT OF ANTONI GAUDÍ. THE CITY IS A MAJOR CULTURAL AND ECONOMIC CENTRE WHICH HOSTED TWO WORLD EXHIBITIONS AND THE OLYMPIC GAMES IN 1992. ALL OF THESE FACTORS, TOGETHER WITH PEOPLE OF VARIOUS ORIGINS, HAVE TRULY ASCENDED THIS CHARMING, LIVELY AND MAGICAL PORT CITY THAT IS BARCELONA TODAY, AS ONE OF THE WORLD'S MAJOR GLOBAL CITIES.

Left: The foundation stone of the Sagrada Family, the Atonement Church of the Holy Family, was laid on 19 March 1882. The original Neo-Gothic design was designed by Antoni Gaudi in his typically imaginative, organic style of Modernism. In the year 2026, when Gaudi's death anniversary marks the 100th Centennial, the construction, which is still unfinished, should be completed.

Right: The Palau de la Música Catalana Music Palace holds Barcelona's most important concert hall, designed by Domènech i Montaner in 1908 for the choir "Orfeó Català". The steel construction of this Art Nouveau building is covered with colourful ceramics and coloured glass.

○ BARRI GÒTIC
This gothic quarter with its narrow streets and decorated facades is certainly worth a visit. With its old Roman ruins, narrow medieval streets and La Seu Cathedral, it is the oldest part of Barcelona.

○ LA SEU
Buried in the crypt of this church, in the Gothic quarter, lies the patron saint of Barcelona. A truly interesting sight here is a flock of geese in the cloister courtyard where the birds have made this place their homes since the Middle Ages.

○ PALAU DE LA MÚSICA CATALANA
Nobody should leave Barcelona without having seen this colourful and playful musical palace. Step inside and you will find a magnificent Art Nouveau decor of the concert hall that guarantees to take your breath away.

○ LAS RAMBLAS
This is the pulsating artery of Barcelona; you could not imagine the city without it. Stretching over more than one kilometre, this is a sensational pedestrian boulevard where you see people from all around the world mix in a wonderful multicultural coexistence, surrounded by unique shops, interesting stalls, and cafés.

○ PLAÇA DE CATALUNYA
As big in area as St. Peter's Square in Rome, this is considered to be the heart of the city, where all important streets and avenues converge. It is also well known for beautiful fountains, historical statues, and showcasing some of Barcelona's most popular attractions, such as the flocks of pigeons that always gather in the centre of the square.

○ PARC GÜELL
The park, which was created in 1900 as part of a garden city, is vividly colourful and inviting. Gaudí was commissioned by Eusebi Güell to build a housing estate for the wealthy alongside of the park, modelled after an English country town. However, only the park and the wall with guarded entrances were fully finished. Only three houses were built, one of which was Gaudí's house and has now been turned into his museum.

WHY VISIT IN AUTUMN?

"FESTA DE LA MERCÈ", HELD ON 24TH SEPTEMBER, SPANS OVER FIVE DAYS TO CELEBRATE THE PATRON SAINT OF BARCELONA, NOSTRA SENYORA DE LA MERCÈ (OUR LADY OF THE BLESSED VIRGIN MARY). WITH FESTIVITIES HAPPENING ACROSS THE ENTIRE CITY - GIANTS AND DWARFS DANCE TO THE TUNES "BALL OF GEGANTS" WITH MARCHING BANDS AND HORSEMEN. HUMAN TOWERS (CASTELLS); PYROTECHNICAL SHOWS OF FIRE-BREATHING DRAGONS, DEMONS AND WILDFIRES (CORREFOC) MESMERISE THE SPECTATORS WITH FLAMES AND HELLISH NOISE UNTIL ST. GEORGE, THE HERO, PUTS AN END TO THIS VIVID TERROR.

○ SAGRADA FAMÍLIA

This world-famous sacred building, whose full name is Temple Expiatori de la Sagrada Família, is considered to be Gaudí's masterpiece - idiosyncratic and individualistic, like the architect himself. The Neo-Gothic cathedral has become a symbol of Barcelona – although it is still a permanent construction site. The extraordinary structure will probably be completed sometime in the middle of the 21st century; then there will be a total of 18 towers rising into the sky. Gaudí, who devoted himself completely to this project during the last decades of his life, found his last rest in the crypt.

○ CASA MILÀ

Named the quarry house, this is the last work of Gaudí before he dedicated himself to the Sagrada Família. There is an art museum, an exhibition about the architect himself, and an apartment still fully furnished with the original furniture for when Gaudi used to visit.

○ CASA BATLLÓ

Gaudí completely redesigned this building for the industrialist Batlló. The beautifully crafted facade tells a legend of the patron saint of Catalonia, who fought against a dragon.

Above: Sculpture by artist Rebecca Horn on the Passeig Maritim. The beautifully landscaped beach promenade with shady palm trees in La Barceloneta serves as a daytime stroll for walkers, skaters and cyclists. Left: This five-day "Festa de la Mercè" has been held since 1902, to honour Barcelona's patron saint. With music, folklore events, and acrobatics such as the Castellers (human towers), autumn in Barcelona is spectacularly welcomed.

○ LA BARCELONETA

Barcelona's "fishing village" was established on a tri-angular peninsula and developed from a former slum, which was demolished in the mid-18th century. At that time, a new living quarter with two- to three-storey houses would provide housing for dock workers and fishermen. Its design is that of a chess board-like ground plan. The centre of this popular district is the Plaça de la Barceloneta, with quaint fish taverns, and the beautiful Church of Sant Miguel del Port nearby.

○ L'AQUÀRIUM

The largest maritime museum in Europe - with an 80-metre underwater tunnel where you can get very close to sharks and many other intriguing marine life.

GOING OUT

El Pintor // This rustic restaurant serves Catalan dishes, especially the seasonal specialties.

// Carrer de Sant Honorat, 7

Pinotxo Bar // Located on the Boqueria, serving seafood tapas such as bacalao or calamari. The braised lamb is also delicious.

// pinotxobar.com

El Vaso de Oro // Here you will find delicious tapas and a good ice cold Catalan beer. Many locals from the harbour district appreciate that.

// www.vasodeoro.com

Bar Marsella // This bar exists here since 1820. For locals, it is also known as Absinth Bar. She became even more famous with Woody Allen's "Vicky Cristina Barcelona". The old chandeliers and mirrors just ooze with nostalgia.

// Carrer de Sant Pau, 65

Right: Opened in 1931, the cable car departs from Montjuïc's Mountain station to Torre Sant Sebastià in Barceloneta. Halfway up is the 119 metres high Torre Jaume I, a steel-framed tower named after the 13th century Jaume I, the Count of Barcelona and King of Aragón.

○ PORT OLÍMPIC

The port was built in its present form for the 1992 Olympic Games, and is now popular for colourful nightlife.

○ SANTA MARIA DEL MAR

An imposing structure built in the late 13th century, at the height of Aragon Kingdom, this Catalan Gothic church is both magnificent from the outside and inside. The purity and unity of Gothic style that this church encapsulates is considered very unusal for such large medieval structures. Legend has it that the apostle James the Elder preached at this church.

○ MUSEU PICASSO

Pablo Picasso studied in Barcelona; this museum is housed in five old city palaces and focuses on Picasso's early works. A must for art lovers.

○ MUSEU NACIONAL D'ARTE DE CATALUNYA

The Neo-Baroque Temple was built to represent Spain for the 1929 World's Fair. Now it is home to an impressive collection of Romanesque, Gothic and Catalan art.

○ CASTELL DEL MONTJUÏC

An old military fortress, dating back to 1640. The castle became a museum of military history, but now serves for cultural activities and events.

○ TRANSBORDADOR AERI

The old harbour cable car ride starts from Torre San Sebastià and is an exhilarating experience from the moment you take a lift to the top of the cable car tower.

○ TIBIDABO

A charming amusement park at 500 metre high on a mountain, and the church Sagrat Cor to visit.

○ FUNDACIÓ JOAN MIRÓ

Artist Joan Miró studied here. A must see is the impressive mercury-flowing fountain and a terrace overlooking the city.

WHERE TO STAY

Casa Camper // A boutique hotel located in the Raval. The modern 25 rooms are functionally well designed and creatively furnished. Each room is divided into a bedroom and a sitting room to relax or work.
// **www.casacamper.com/Barcelona**

Hotel Oriente Atiram // This hotel, a former 17th-century convent, is considered an institution in the Barri Gòtic. Since its opening in 1942, many great opera singers and musicians that have performed in the Gran Teatre de Liceu have stayed here.
// **www.atiramhotels.com**

Le Méridien Barcelona // An internationally well known five-star brand, the hotel is modern and a magnet for celebrities. Luxurious foyer, well-appointed rooms, a restaurant, a piano bar, a gym, and everything else that a luxury hotel can offer.
// **www.lemeridienbarcelona.com**

SHOPPING

○ PASSEIG DE GRÀCIA

This 60-metre-wide boulevard is considered to be the most prestigious shopping street in the city.

○ LAIE LIBRERIA-CAFÉ

The bookshop specialises in international art books, with a nice café where you can sit and watch people.
// www.laie.es

○ B.D. EDICIONES DE DISEÑO

Lovers of fine art and elegant design will get their money's worth in this gallery: from furniture, art objects and accessories. The gallery has been here for over 70 years.

// bdbarcelona.com

○ CASA GISPERT

A splendid colonial shop from 1851, with a long narrow corridor, full of fragrant edible treasures. Here they still dry the fruits themselves.

// www.casagispert.com

GOING OUT

○ CATALAN MONESTARY TOUR

The surrounding towns not far from Barcelona offers some of the most important monasteries in Catalonia. There is the Cistercian Monastery of Santes Creus with its lavish cloister and well-preserved wine cellar. The Monestir Santa María de Poblet is still used by Cistercians, with guest houses. The Benedictine Monastery of Montserrat, founded in 880, is situated in scenic mountains. It houses the revere Black Madonna, who is the patron saint of Catalonia.

NOT TO BE MISSED

MAGIC OF THE FONT MÀGICA

Built by Carles Buïgas for the 1929 World's Fair, this "Magic Fountain" is located at the head of Avinguda Maria Cristina. The fountain transforms into a magnificent water show – changing its shape and height, while being illuminated in vivid colours. The colourful fountain water "dances" to a perfectly mixed of classical music, modern pop hits and famous film tunes, such as "The Lord of The Rings" and "The Godfather". The baroque Museu Nacional d'Arte de Catalunya lights up in the evening, and provides a perfect background to the Magic Fountain.

HARBOUR TOUR IN GLASS-BOTTOM CATAMARAN

Get a closer look and enjoy wonders of the underwater world of Bacelona harbour, and along its coast, with this ninety minutes cruise. The floor on the lower deck of the catamaran is made of glass, which provides a fascinating uninterrupted view of the underworld.

IMMERSE IN THE BUSTLE OF PLAÇA D'ESPANYA

If you really want to experience the "cosmopolitant Barcelona", this is the place to be. This location is one of the city's biggest squares where several major thoroughfares meet. There are two colossal red towers, reminiscent of a Venetian Campanile, standing at one end of the square, amongst other impressive art structures, such as the twenty-two meter tall statue "Donna i Ocell" (Woman and Bird). The best way to observe the bustle and vibrant life around this square is from the Las Arenas department store that was built in 1900 and was formerly used as bull-fighting ring.

TAKE A STROLL THROUGH THE MERCAT DE LA BOQUERIA

The Rambla Market is opened from Monday to Saturday, closed Sunday. Since 1914, this solid structure with tiled roof is the "go-to" market for locals and tourists for its amazing arrays of fresh produces, spices, assorted dried fruits and jams, as well as meat. The market is actually called Mercat de Sant Joseph, but for most it is called the Mercat de la Boqueria or simply La Boqueria. To get through this maze of amazing freshness, it is best to take your time and follow your nose!

SEE A FLAMENCO-SHOW

Flamenco is a Spanish art form of guitar, song and dance in which the Spaniard's temperament comes into its own. Places like the "Tablao Cordobes", in the beautiful old Palacio del Flamenco, will guarantee you a stunning and elaborate show as the artists and performers are at a superior level.

#31

BERN

TRUE TO THE CITY'S MOTTO "THE WORLD PASSES, BERN EXISTS", BERN HAS HELD THE FEDERAL AUTHORITY SINCE 1848. THE "GRACIOUS LORDS" OF BERN, AS MEMBERS OF THE GOVERNMENT CALLED THEMSELVES, RULED OVER THIS AREA NORTH OF THE APLS, WHICH IS THE LARGEST PART OF SWISS TERRITORY. THE GLITTERING EPOCH IS REMINISCENT OF THE OLD CITY BUILT OVER THE AARE RIVER. BERN IS KNOWN AS THE "CLEANEST AND MOST BEAUTIFUL CITY" IN SWITZERLAND. IN 1983, THE HISTORIC OLD TOWN, AT THE CENTRE OF BERN, RECEIVED "UNESCO WORLD HERITAGE SITE" STATUS. THE CITY'S ARCHITECTURE IS LARGELY MEDIEVAL, WITH MILES OF ARCADES IN THE CITY CENTRE. ENVELOPED BY THE AARE RIVER ON THREE SIDES, BERN IS STUNNINGLY BEAUTIFUL.

Above: The Bern Cathedral Tower stands over the Old Town at almost 100 metres high. Up until late 20th century, a tower guard would keep watch over the city and raise the alarm when there's a fire.
Left: Nydegg Bridge and Untertor Bridge connect the Old Town of Bern with the opposite bank near the Bärengraben.

○ OLD TOWN

Now a UNESCO World Heritage Site, the Old Town of Bern was once the largest city state north of the Alps. A major fire in 1405 resulted in a rebuild in many parts of the Old Town, and more construction took place in the 18th century. Despite development at different time period, the Old Town remains quintessentially medieval. A stand-out characteristic of the town centre is the stately gilded town houses with a total of 6 kilometres of arcades. One of the most elegant works of Burgundy late Gothic structure is the Town Hall, whose exterior staircase and coats of arms decoration were lovingly restored. It was built from 1406 to 1417 in late Gothic style and renovated in 1942. The Holy Spirit Church of 1729 is considered the most important Protestant Baroque building in the country. However, the city's landmark is the former city gate Zytgloggeturm (Clock Tower), which was built

from the remains of the city wall. On the hour, many people gather in front of the Clock Tower to watch the clock mechanism from the 16th century perform its unique spectacle. Among the many beautiful historic residential buildings, the Ensemble in the Gerechtigkeitsgasse is most special - the houses are still intact from the 16th Century.

○ MÜNSTER

The Bern Cathedral St. Vincent is the largest and most important late Gothic church in Switzerland. The foundation stone for the three-aisled pillar basilica church was laid in 1421, and then the tower was completed in 1893. Builders were the actual citizens of Bern, who also funded the twelve-sided chapel. The cathedral is well-known for housing a rare complete collection of Gothic sculptures, which represent the Last Judgment. The statues were created similar to those

WHY VISIT IN AUTMN ?

THE "ZIBELEMÄRIT" (ONION MARKET) IN NOVEMBER IS BOTH BEAUTIFUL AND INTRIGUING. A MARKET FOR THE EARLY BIRDS, AS AT FOUR O'CLOCK IN THE MORNING, THE STANDS ARE ALREADY SET UP. UNDER CANDLE-LIGHTS, MOUNTAINS OF YELLOW AND RED ONIONS SHIMMER; SOME ARE TIED TOGETHER INTO WREATHS, BRAIDS AND ALL SORTS OF OTHER FANTASTIC CREATIONS.

Left: In the autumn Zibele-märit you will find onions galore.

At the top: Grand city gates and arcades are the distinguishing features of the old town. Here is the view of the cage tower.

Above: In the Paul Klee Museum, you can learn everything about the life and extensive work of this Expressionist artist.

Right: Powerful figure of the Kindlifresser, which means child eater, crowns the top of the fountain of the same name.

in the main lobby, by Erhard Küng. Inside, the tall choir windows, the oldest of which dated back to around 1450, create an almost stage-like lighting with their stained glass. In 1523, the cathedral was richly decorated with apostles, prophets and everyday figures choir stalls, in which the baptismal font of the master Albrecht of Nuremberg followed in 1524. The tower also houses the heaviest bell in Switzerland; weighing at 10 tons, the bell echoes one of the lowest tones in the world.

○ LAUBENGÄNGE

Typical for patrician buildings of Alt-Bern are the 6 kilometres long arcades (Pavilions). They once served as covered workplaces for traders and craftsmen. The numerous vaulted cellars are now occupied with shops, restaurants and theatres.

○ FOUNTAINS

There are over 100 fountains in Bern, however 11 fountains are really well worth a visit. These fountains are crowned with dramatic Renaissance statues; three of them were created by the Freiburg master sculptor Hans Gieng, and the others are attributed to his workshop. The Kindlifresserbrunnen "Child Eater Fountain" is most interesting, and perhaps scariest, as it's a statue of a giant swallowing a child. This statue is meant to scare disobedient children.

○ FOUNTAIN OF JUSTICE

Built by Hans Gieng in 1543, Justitia raises her scales in one hand and a sword of truth in another, she stands above the heads of the most powerful rulers of the Middle Ages: Pope, Emperor, Sultan and Lord Mayor. The statue symbolises that the power of justice is higher than any rulers and any political systems.

○ MUSEUMS

In contrast to the Medieval characteristic of Bern, the city also displays fondness to modern art. Sophisticated exhibitions on artists such as Giacometti, Moore, Johns or Nauman are shown in the Kunsthalle Bern. One of the biggest is the Paul Klee Museum which has the world's most important collection of paintings, watercolours and drawings by the artist – 4,000 pieces in all.

GOING OUT

Restaurant Harmonie // This restaurant has been in existence for 170 years, and was frequented by Albert Einstein who lived nearby. There is a special dish to honour him, which has no meat, as Einstein was a "die-hard" vegetarian.

// www.harmonie.ch

Kornhauskeller // Wine was once stored under the classic vaulted arches. Today, the space is also a restaurant serving distinguished international cuisine.

// www.bindella.ch

Mahogany Hall // Rumour has it that the Bernese get up early and go to bed early. But Bern also offers life after dark. Anyone looking to enjoy a few drinks and listen to live music, the Mahogany Hall is Bern's "go to" venue. This traditional place is truly for lovers of live music as it offers a program that will be sure to satisfy even the highest of demands.

// www.mahogany.ch

SHOPPING

○ **KRAM- UND GERECHTIGKEITSGASSE**

This is a shopping paradise located in the middle of Bern's old town. The arcades extend over 6 kilometres and house numerous shops. There is shelter from the sun and rain so your shopping trip in this historic atmosphere will not be spoilt.

○ **WESTSIDE**

It was none other than Daniel Libeskind who created the plans for this gigantic shopping centre. There are over fifty shops, a hotel, a cinema, as well as a water park, which will sure make everyone's day perfect.

// www.westside.ch

○ **MARKETS ON THE ORPHANAGE SQUARE**

There are several markets selling all sorts of nik-nak at the Orphanage Square. One market is opened every Tuesdays and Saturdays from January to November; and, the Bärenmärit (Bear Market) is held daily from April to October. It will be difficult to find a more colourful market experience than these ones.

// www.marktbern.ch

WHERE TO STAY

Hotel Allegro // A "designer" hotel located in the city centre that also has wonderful mountain views. The hotel is unique in its different "style" of rooms available, including the Asian-style Atrium trend and Broadway-style Atrium event. The crowning glory is the Paul Klee Suite with copies of the painter's most famous works.

// www.kursaal-bern.ch/hotel

Hotel Bellevue Palace // Located next to the Bundeshaus, this five-star hotel offers rooms with amazing views of the Aare River and Alps. Foodies will appreciate the restaurants "Bellevue-Grill La Terrasse" and "Zur Münz".

// www.bellevue-palace.ch

Beauvilla Bern // This is a Cultural Heritage listed Art Nouveau villa from 1902, located in the centre of Kirchenfeld. The villa offers finest level of luxury and comfort to discerning guests, particularly with an in-house restaurant serving marvelous dishes.

// www.beauvilla-bern.com

GOING OUT

○ **MURTEN**

A beautiful town on the lake of the same name, whose name derives from a Latin word "murus" (wall), showcases a 13th to 15th century ring wall that is very well-preserved. There is a tour that will take you through this very picturesque old town. The significance of Murten is the well-documented history written in 1476 by the Confederates about their victory over the Burgundian. More interesting historical facts and figures can be viewed at a museum in the town council house.

○ **THUN AND LAKE THUN**

The old bridge town Thun is situated at the mouth of the Aare River, which flows from the Thun Lake. The town is known as the "Gateway to the Bernese Oberland". It is the third largest city in the Canton of Bern as it is an economic and cultural centre of this region. Situated above the late medieval Old Town, Thun Castle built in the 12th century is now a fascinating museum with medieval armour and weaponary. With Lake Thun and its breathtaking view of the Bernese Alps, a 14th century town church, and several medieval "Sässhäuser", all these in one town that makes Thun an interesting place to visit.

NOT TO BE MISSED

THE BEAR RESERVE

This Bear Enclosure belongs to Bern as the Eiffel Tower to Paris and the Big Ben to London. This is a place of such significance to Bern that a pathway from the Old Town to the end of the Aare Bridge directly leads to the residence of these symbolic animals - they are represented in Bern's coat of arms. The reserve was expanded and renovated to ensure utmost comfort and wellness of the bears. The expansion was also to provide Mr Brown, a celebrity of this reserve, more leisure space as well as a place to hide when the onslaught of other resident bears get on his nerves.

THE CELLAR THEATRE KATAKÖMBLI

For over 40 years, Katakömbli has been part of the cabaret scene in the Old Town. This theatre operates as a non-profit-making enterprise and therefore has greater freedom in designing the repertoire than comparable institutions.

TAKE A SWIM IN BERNER MARZILIBAD

As a traditional leisure institution, the Bernese Marzilibad on the Aare River first made headlines during the sexual revolution of the 1960s, when the first topless ladies were sighted there. However today, this is nothing unusual. Enjoy the fine autumn weather and take a dip in the warm water of the outdoor pool, or let yourself be carried away with the Aare River currents. The choice is yours!

DRINK THE FOUNTAIN WATER

What would Bern be without its many fountains? More than 100 fountains were built in mid-16th century as public water supply. Although some have expanded in size and adorned with interesting statues, they are all still used today as water dispensers. Bern's water is of the highest drinking quality and refreshingly tasty for any thirsty passers-by. With so many fountains around worth visiting for their medieval tableaus and statues (oldest is the 13th century Lenbrunnen, which today can only be admired on a guided tour), this is definitely a unique thirst-quenching experience that everyone should try.

VISIT THE ROSE GARDEN

Take a stroll and smell the roses! Once a cemetery (1765-1877) then turned into a public park in 1913, the Rose Garden near the Bärengraben (Bear Reserve) is a must for all nature lovers. You also get a spectacular view of Bern.

#32   BUDAPEST

MAGNIFICENT BUILDINGS AND WIDE BOULEVARDS, ELEGANT COFFEE HOUSES AND LAVISH ART NOUVEAU BATH HOUSES AS IF YOU ARE IN THE "1001 ARABIAN NIGHTS". BUDAPEST IS OFTEN CALLED "PARIS OF THE EAST" FOR ITS SPLENDID MUSIC, MAJESTIC THEATRES AND WONDROUS CULTURAL LIFE. THE DANUBE DIVIDES HUNGARY'S CAPITAL INTO THE MOUNTAINOUS "BUDA" WITH THE CASTLE DISTRICT ON ONE SIDE, AND THE FLAT AREA OF "PEST" WITH THE CUPOLA-CROWNED PARLIAMENT BUILDING ON THE OTHER SIDE.

○ BURGBERG AND FISCHERBASTEI

"Castle Hill" and the "Castle District" is famous for medieval, Baroque and 19th century houses, churches and government buildings. This location also houses the "Buda Castle". The Castle District extends over about two-thirds of the plateau, from the Vienna Gate in the north to St. George's Square. Sadly, most buildings were destroyed in the Turkish wars, and the entire district had to be rebuilt. The Fischerbastei - a castle-like fisherman's bastion, built in 1902, stands at the edge of the forecourt of the Matthias Church on the steep slope to the Danube. It was built mainly for decorative purposes by a Budapest architect, Frigyes Schulek, who combined Romanesque style with those of other eras. The Fischerbastei provides a wonderful panoramic view of Budapest. Directly below, from the Wasserstadt district, there is a grand staircase which leads up the surrounding hills.

○ BURGPALAST

Known in English as the "Buda Castle", it was originally built to be a fortress at the southern tip of the Castle Hill. However, soon after its completion in 1265, it was chosen as the Royal Castle, and comprises of

smaller castles and palaces - residences for Hungarian kings and the royal family. The magnificent complex spans almost the entire southern hill; 400 metres long and 200 metres wide, it is the largest castle in Hungary. The history of Buda Castle extends more than 800 years and battered through many was, so it's not surprising that the castle which started in medieval, Gothic style, then to Barogue Revival, and Modernist after the World War II.

○ HUNGARIAN NATIONAL GALLERY

Established in 1957 and rightfully located in the Buda Castle, the gallery showcases Hungarian art collections in all genres.

○ MATTHIASKIRCHE

The 1255-1269 Romanesque basilica church on Buda Castle was consecrated as Our Lady's Church. Her unofficial name goes back to Matthias I. Corvinus. The church, thanks to him, was converted into a three-aisled Gothic hall church in the 14th century, with an impressive 80 metres high south tower. The Matthias Church, with its roof of colourful ceramic tiles, seems to have survived the times unscathed. But this

is far from the truth, its present structure has gone
through a comprehensive restoration (1874-1896) in
the style of Neo-Gothic.

○ GELLÉRTBAD

References to thermal springs with "healing properties" surrounding the Gellért Hill can be dated back
to the 13th century. During the Ottoman Empire in
the 16th and 17th century, baths were also built at
this site. The Gellért Baths complex was built between
1912 and 1918, it is by far one of the most beautiful
thermal baths in Budapest. Built eclectically in the Art
Nouveau style, the bathhouse is beautifully decorated with stained glass and handmade mosaic tiles.
There are three indoor and ten outdoor swimming
pools, plus various spa treatments. The famous Hotel Gellért was also built next to the complex.

○ GELLÉRTBERG

Named after Bishop Gellért, this mountain is 235 metres high and offers a magnificent view of the city. At
the top, a memorial was erected to the martyr himself. The citadel brings back memories from the independence revolution of 1848/49. On the southern
slope of the mountain, a small chapel was built in
1926 inside of a cave.

○ THE GREAT SYNAGOGUE

Judaism has a long, sad history in Hungary. This synagogue is the second largest in the world, and can
be visited as part of a guided tour. Here, there is a
Jewish Museum and the Holocaust Memorial in the
courtyard. This is a sacred and undeniably very emotional place to visit as thousands of victims of fascism
are buried here.

○ KETTENBRÜCKE

Winter can be very cold in Hungary and it is not unusual for the Danube to turn into a glistening river of
ice. Even the strongest wooden pillars are not be able
to withstand the strong current and water pressure,
so in the summer, the citizens of Budapest put together a bridge of pontoons between their two districts, in preparation for winter with the frozen Danube. It was the reformer István Széchenyi who took
the challenge, for a unique project at that time in Europe, to build a bridge over a wide river with such a
strong current. The construction began in 1839;
Széchenyi organized tons of steel and put the project

*Left: High spirited dancing
in the streets is not unusual at many of the festivals
that take place in summer
and autumn in Budapest.*

under an English construction management. Ten years later, the bridge was finally inaugurated.

○ PARLIAMENT

An impressive building festooned with 365 towers and 88 statues and figures. The building consists of a central wing and two symmetrical side wings with a Neo-Gothic façade, which also display Baroque and Renaissance stylistic elements. The top of the dome hovers 96 metres above the ground, and the ceiling of the dome hall, resting on pillars, reaches a clear height of 27 metres. This makes it one of the largest parliament buildings in the world.

Right: The model for the construction of the Parliament building was the Palace of Westminster in London. The complex, which is located in a prominent position directly on the banks of the Danube, forms a counterweight to the Buda Castle on the opposite side of the river. The ornate frescoes and ceiling paintings inside are kept in Classicist style and represent the history of Hungary. There are numerous golden ornaments, weighing more than 40 kilograms of gold.

GOING OUT

New York Kávéház // Here the owners describe their restaurant as one of the most beautiful in Budapest. They are not exaggerating and is really worth a visit. High rooms, amazing decorative pieces, lots of marble, gold and a menu that leaves nothing to be desired.

// www.newyorkcafe.hu

Szimpla kert // Szimpla kert is one of the city's first "Ruins Pub" which opened almost 20 years ago. Here you can experience a lot of Hungarian culture with a cold beer or two.

// szimpla.eu

A38 // This place has three floors with an excellent restaurant. It also offers perhaps the hippest concerts and exhibitions in the city.
// www.a38.hu/en

Gozsdu udvar // An inspiring complex, reminiscent of the Hackesche Höfe Berlin, features bars, cafés, restaurants and galleries.
// gozsduudvar.hu

○ ST. STEPHEN'S BASILICA

The construction of St. Stephen's Basilica started in 1848, however the work had to stop due to the revolution that broke out that same year. Three years later, work continued by master builder, Jószef Hild, and after his death, it was handed over to master builder Miklós Ybl. It took 54 years for this Neo-Classical church to be completed. This is the most important church in Hungary, and standing almost equal to the Paliament building, its dome is 96 metres high. The most important relic of the Basilica is the embalmed right hand of St. Stephen, who actually was the first Christian King of Hungary.

○ HELDENPLATZ

Budapest's "Heroes' Square" houses the Millennium Monument, a 36-metre high pillar carrying an impressive statue of the Archangel Gabriel. According to a legend, he appeared to St. Stephen and gave him the crown. The Heroes' Square is adorned with statues of significant personalities in the long Hungarian history.

○ HUNGARIAN STATE OPERA

The Hungarian State Opera House is well known as one of the most magnificent opera houses in Europe. Located in the district of Pest, the opera house is built in a Neo-Renaissance style, entirely in accordance with the requirements ordered by the Austrian Emperor Franz Joseph. It was also at the Emperor's command that the stage be built to the same glorious level as the one in Vienna. He commissioned the famous architect, Miklós Ybl, to travel to Budapest, and for the best artists of his time to paint the frescoes and marble works. World famous for its first-class acoustics, it has seatings for 1,200 people in the hall.

○ **MARGARETE ISLAND**
In the middle of the Danube lies Budapest's car-free park. Here you have access to beaches, jogging zones, a swimming pool, a rose garden, as well as historical ruins of some old monasteries. The Zentenarium monument proudly commemorates the union of Buda and Pest, and there is a pretty spring water fountain with its musical accompaniment.

SHOPPING

○ **VÁCI UTCA**
To the south and north of Elisabeth Bridge, the promenade is divided into two halves. High rents in the fancy houses are mostly responsible for the fact that luxury shops have settled here, but if you look closely you can find some cheap shops, beautiful buildings and relaxing cafés too.

○ **CULINARIS**
There are two branches of this specialty shop in Budapest, and one has a restaurant offering breakfast and lunch. The menu includes local and international cuisine.

○ **VASS**
Budapest is the epitome of elegant men's shoes. The famous handmade, welted leather shoes can be found in the shop of László Vass.

○ **ZENTRALE MARKTHALLE**
The "Great Market Hall" is 150 meters long and somwhat resembles a train station with its two aisles. Here, you can just stroll and look around while locals are usually busy buying their food. Fish and aquariums are in the basement, souvenirs on the first floor. But whatever you want to buy here, remember to haggle!

Left: This is how an Opera House should be - with unique golden ornaments, a Baroque design and carpeted floor of red velvet. It is no surprise that the Hungarian State Opera soon after its opening became the backdrop for the film "Phantom of the Opera".

WHERE TO STAY

Four Seasons Gresham Palace // Thick lush carpets and warming log fires, crystal chandeliers and marble busts. The Art Nouveau palace in the district Pest with a view of the Danube, offers more than your heart desires. Plus, there is an excellent restaurant and inviting spa area.
// www.fourseasons.com/budapest

Boscolo Budapest // You will be astonished by the glass-roofed courtyard, and the interior of the Belle Époque hotel is also really impressive. Even the spa presents a futuristic look with its jungle decoration and glacier walls.
// budapest.boscolohotels.com

Gerlóczy Cafe & Rooms de Lux // Very centrally located but in a quiet street, you can find an excellent café and rooms fit for a Prince. The guests can choose between 19 individually designed rooms with luxurious amenities.
// www.gerloczy.hu

NOT TO BE MISSED

ADMIRE THE ART NOUVEAU

Every country has its own interpretation of Art Nouveau, but the Art Nouveau in Hungary remains remarkably different. It starts with the roofs, which are laid in colourful mosaics and protrude from the sea of red and grey bricks. Paintings, stone carvings of intricate tendrils or intricately designed entrances can be found in many houses. The Budapest Art Nouveau has a distinct style. This is mainly due to Ödön Lechner, probably the most important Art Nouveau artist in Hungary; the architect invented the pyrogranite ceramics process, an artificial stone that could be extravagantly colourfully painted. Among other things, he experimented with Budapest's rooftops and turned the tiles into stunningly bright and colourful mosaics.

ENJOY THE EVENING VIEW FROM THE KETTENBRÜCKE

Not only will you get a fantastic view but also a great photo opportunity of the impressive bridge whose pillars are modelled on triumphal arches. Especially after dusk as all the lights are reflected in the Danube.

EXPERIENCE A KLEZMER CONCERT

The music, which was once shaped by Jewish traveling musicians, is experiencing a renaissance in Budapest. A good place to experience this is at Spinoza, on every Friday evening (the place also has a delicious menu).

CLIMB ONTO THE ELIZABETH TOWER ON THE JÁNOSHEGY

The Buda Mountain is over 500 metres high, and at the highest point stands a monumental tower. A cable car will take you most of the way up, then it is by foot to the building, which resembles a decorative multi-storey wedding cake. This location guarantees you one of the best views over Budapest!

GO TO A THERMAL BATH

A visit to the spa should not be missed. The Gellért Bath is very large and has perfect-tempered warm water, which is particularly good for joint and vascular ailments. The Rudas Bath has the feel of an exotic Turkish temple.

#33   DUBROVNIK

THE RED ROOFS OF THE HOUSES SHINING FROM AFAR ARE MOSTLY BUILT WITH NEW BRICKS AS AROUND 1667 A DEVASTATING EARTHQUAKE HAD DESTROYED MOST OF THE CITY, SO EVERYTHING HAD TO BE REBUILT. IT WAS TO BE RESTORED AS IT WAS, WHEN RAGUSA - THAT WAS DUBROVNIK'S NAME UNTIL 1921 - WAS STILL IN ITS FULL GLORY. STROLLING ACROSS THE STRADUN, LOOKING AT THE BLUE SEA ALL AROUND, ADMIRING THE RENAISSANCE PALACES OR EXPLORING THE NARROW STREETS, YOU WILL QUICKLY SUCCUMB TO THE CHARM OF THIS WONDERFUL CITY. EVEN IN HIGH SEASON, "IF YOU ARE LOOKING FOR PARADISE ON EARTH, COME TO DUBROVNIK", GEORGE BERNARD SHAW ONCE WROTE.

Left: At the heart of the Old Town, in addition to the almost 2,000-metre-long city wall, is the Baroque Cathedral of Dubrovnik. In the Old Town itself, the historic houses feature Gothic, Renaissance and Baroque styles.
Right: The up to 25 metres high and 1,940 metres long middle-age city wall of Dubrovnik is still completely preserved. The fortifications include several bastions, towers and forts.

○ CITY FORTIFICATION

The best first impression of Dubrovnik is from the top while walking along the city wall. It once ran around the whole city as protection on both the land and the water sides. On the land side, the walls are 4 to 6 metres thick, and up to 3 metres thick on the water side. The city wall is around 25 metres high everywhere around. The complete wall with three round and twelve quadrangular defence towers extends over 1,954 metres. Today, some of the houses actually lean against the wall meaning that visitors can look into their windows as they walk high above the sea around the formidable Bokar Fortress.

○ OLD TOWN

An impressive walk should start at the Pile Gate (Pile Vrata) in the west or one of the two landside accesses next to the Ploce Gate (Vrata od Ploce) in the northeast. Watching over both is the patron saint of Dubrovnik, Sveti Vlaho, St. Blaise, who holds a model of the city in his hands. Behind it begins an unusual world of stone. Wooden houses had been banned by the city administration in the Middle Ages because of the fire hazard, and balconies were not allowed to take the light off the narrow streets. Road width, floor height, roof pitch and window size were all set by law.

○ DOMINIKANERKLOSTER

The Dominican Monastery is one of the most beautiful buildings in Dubrovnik. Construction began in the 13th century and was slowly completed piece by piece until the 16th century. It is especially worth visiting the cloister.

○ SPONZAPALAST

Here, too, the architectural style typical of Dalmatia is visible in the transition from late Gothic to Renaissance. Erected between 1516 and 1522, the Sponza Palace has an ornate, open arcade hall on the ground floor and filigree tracery windows on the upper floor. The courtyard itself is supported by columns and is worth a visit. The Palaca Sponza is one of the few buildings that survived the 1667 earthquake. It has been used as a warehouse, customs office and even a prison.

○ REKTORENPALAST

The Rector's Palace (Knežev dvor), built from 1435 to 1451, has four building wings, which are also grouped around a courtyard. Splendid Baroque and Rococo halls have been well preserved, as well as the elegantly furnished living rooms of the rectors, which the Grand Council each could chose for the duration of a month. Visitors can look inside on a tour of the city museum.

○ CATHEDRAL

If you believe the traditional story, it was Richard the Lionheart who made the construction of the

Cathedral possible. When the English King returned from a crusade in 1192, he passed Dubrovnik and was rescued with his ship in a heavy storm. In gratitude, he gave the Dubrovnikians money to fulfil his vow; the citizens were to build a cathedral with this donation. Between 1673 to 1713, the Cathedral of the Assumption, Velika Gospa, was rebuilt in the style of Roman Baroque after being destroyed by an earthquake in 1667. The treasury was one of the richest of its kind in Europe before the quake, including 138 relics containing in boxes and statues of gold, silver and precious stones, which are still preserved today.

○ ST. BLASIUS

Since 972 he is the patron saint of the city, St. Blaise, Sveti Vlaho. His gilded statue can be found in the church of St. Blaise on the high altar below the Baroque organ. A goldsmith from Dubrovnik made it in the 15th century. The precious piece was always carried on the 3rd February each year in a large procession through the city. The present church was built between 1706 and 1715 because a fire had destroyed the previous one.

○ STRADUN

The Stradun shines like new in the sun. No wonder, after all, as it has been polished by the thousands of shoes that walk through the historical centre on the smooth-cut stone floor. The Stradun, also called

Above: Supposedly, the Ascension Cathedral was commissioned by Richard the Lionheart. He was shipwrecked and stranded on the island of Lokrum off Dubrovnik. Out of gratitude he financed the construction of a cathedral. In 1667, it was destroyed by an earthquake. The new building was built in the style of Roman Baroque.

Left: Near Dubrovnik is the village of Ston, which has had a certain culinary effect on Dubrovnik: salt and mussels are sourced from here, which should not be missed at the Autumn Food Festival.

Placa, leads straight from the Pile Gate to Placa Luža, and past numerous shops, cafés and bars. Luža Square is the most important of the Old Town, most public life takes place here and the lake gate opens the way to the sea. The road runs exactly in the place of the filled canal, which originally separated the two settlements - Ragusa and Dubrava - in the beginning of the town's history. Over time, this inlet had been "buried", and Dubrovnik grew together as one city. Incidentally, the smooth-cut stone slabs were not laid by the Romans on the Stradun, but by the citizens themselves in 1468.

○ ONOFRIOBRUNNEN

The Neapolitan master builder, Onofrio della Cava, built the round fountain in the small square on the Pile Gate in the 15th century. Before the great earthquake in 1667, the Onofriobrunnen supplied the citizens of Dubrovnik with fresh drinking water, which was directed from a spring outside the city and into the well.

○ ERLÖSERKIRCHE (SVETI SPAS)

On the square in front of the Pile Gate is also the Erlöserkirche Sveti Spas. The citizens of Dubrovnik had them built in 1520 in gratitude because the city was spared the earthquake that year. Surprisingly, the church was also left intact during the great earthquake in 1667.

○ ST. IGNATIUS

At first, it is a small lane full of steps, then the path turns into a splendid Baroque staircase. At the end of it stands the Jesuit church Sveti Ignacijo, St. Ignatius. It rises proudly at the southern end of the old town and is one of the few buildings that were not authentically rebuilt after its destruction by the earthquake. Instead, one of the largest Baroque churches in Dalmatia was built between 1699 and 1735 according to the designs of the Roman architect, Andrea Pozzo. The single-nave interior spans a barrel vault - following the example of Jesuit religious architecture.

○ FRANZISKANERKLOSTER

A pharmacy and a nursing home - both facilities existed in Dubrovnik as early as the 14th century. Early on especially in the Franciscan Monastery, monks worked with mortars, pots and medicines. In 1317, construction began on this church, which is sepa-

GOING OUT

Konoba Dalmatino // This tavern is tucked away in a side street of the old town. Here you are at the right address when it comes to traditional meat and fish dishes from Southern Dalmatia: cooked the old fashioned way using grandmother's recipes.

// Prijeko ul. 15

Nishta // A Swiss-Croatian couple has dared to open a vegetarian restaurant in meat-loving Dalmatia. It became a success. Now Nishta has an excellent reputation for serving good food at fair prices in a relaxing atmosphere.

// www.nishtarestaurant.com

360° // Dinner with a panoramic view? This extraordinary restaurant makes it possible. You dine overlooking the harbor and enjoy first-class Mediterranean food. Especially the fish dishes are delicious! Add a fine drop from the wine cellar.

// www.360dubrovnik.com

Right: The monumental Onofrio Fountain on the small rectangular plaza lost much of its Renaissance decorations during the 1667 earthquake, only the 16 water-streaming masks have been preserved.

rated from the Erlöserkirche Sveti Spas only by a narrow corridor. The lush green cloister from 1360 astounds with double columns and the decoratively masked pillars.

SHOPPING

○ LJEKARNA MALE BRAĆE

The monastery pharmacy at the Franciscan Monastery is the longest-serving pharmacy in Europe and has been in operation since 1317. At the counter, there are also remedies and cosmetics, made according to ancient monastery recipes.

// ljekarna-dubrovnik.hr/mala-braca

○ MARKET

Every day from 7 am to 1 pm, Gunduli eva Poljana, near the cathedral, holds a market selling fresh fruits and vegetables as well as other regional produce.

○ KRAŠ

Chocolates, bonbons, sweets, biscuits, pastries ... If you have a sweet tooth, you will not be leaving this store fast.

// kras-trgovina.hr

GOING OUT

○ ELAFITI ISLANDS

Eight large, five smaller and numerous tiny islets and reefs are among the Elafiti Islands - these are practically at the doorstep of Dubrovnik. Šipan, Lopud and Kolo ep are inhabited and known for their beautiful beaches and lush, almost subtropical vegetation.

WHERE TO STAY

Villa Sigurata // In the heart of the old town, just two minutes from the Stradun, lies this hotel, whose construction dated back to the 17th century. The rooms are rather small, but the medieval stone walls make up for the atmosphere. Lovable service - thanks to the boss, Nikolina.

// **villasigurata.com**

The Pucic Palace // Those seeking luxury can find it in the old town. This hotel has retained the character of a former Palazzos despite modern facilities. Chandeliers, antiques and the plush interior design of the rooms fit perfectly into the cultural heritage building.

// **www.thepucicpalace.com**

Stari Grad // Small but nice, this boutique hotel is in the middle of the old town. Completely redesigned in 2013, the old noble palace from the 16th century flourishes in its new splendour.

// **hotelstarigrad.com**

NOT TO BE MISSED

TAKE A WALK ON THE OLD CITY WALL

The medieval city wall of Dubrovnik is 2 kilometres long, and a tour of this wall is really spectacular. You can start the walk at either end. Up the stairs, past watchtowers, sometimes narrow, sometimes wide paths, but always with the beautiful views of the sea and the island of Lokrum. This is truly a breathtaking excursion that is a "must do". Although caution is advised - because the wall is very high, you should not lean too far over it!

DINE IN THE POKLISAR

The terrace of the restaurant is just in front of the old city wall - the view of the sea, the white boats in the harbour and people watching is included. The kitchen offers typical local fish and meat dishes, pizza and pasta. Poklisar is also famous for the delicious homemade ice cream.

TASTE THE BEST WINES

Dubrovnik's first wine bar, the D'Vino, has only been in existence since 2008. Here you can choose from among 100 different local wines, all Dalmatian, Istrian and Slavonian varieties, including Grgi Plavac Mali and Zlatan Plavac. The city of Dubrovnik also offers very interesting wine tours.

A VISIT TO THE AQUARIUM

Set in the thick walls of the fortress of Sveti Ivan of Dubrovnik are 31 aquariums. You can see much of the local Adriatic fauna: lobsters, colourful starfish and corals, octopus, rays, moray eels, to name a few. The aquarium is a nice side trip on a city tour with children.

TAKE A RIDE IN THE CABLE CAR

The drive up to the mountain is worthwhile just for the view of the beautiful old town. Above are two panoramic terraces and a small restaurant. If you do not want to pay the somewhat expensive price for the four-minute ride, you can simply climb the mountain by foot.

#34   GRAZ

ITS OLD TOWN IS RENOWN AS AN ARCHITECTURAL JEWEL OF EUROPE – WITH ITS BEAUTIFULLY RESTORED LANDSCAPE OF WINDING STREETS AND SHINGLE ROOFS, BOURGEOIS HOUSES AND NOBLE PALACES FROM THE RENAISSANCE AND BAROQUE PERIODS. BUT THE STYRIAN PROVINCIAL METROPOLIS ON THE MUR WAS ONCE AN IMPORTANT BULWARK AGAINST THE OTTOMANS. TODAY WITH 250,000 INHABITANTS, IT IS THE SECOND LARGEST CITY IN AUSTRIA. IT IS NOT JUST THE BEAUTIFUL PANORAMA THAT MAKES THIS CITY FAMOUS. AT THE FOOT OF THE CLOCK TOWER, THE GRAZ LANDMARK ON THE SCHLOSS-BERG, THERE IS AN EXTREMELY LIVELY CULTURAL AND INTELLECTUAL LIFESTYLE. HIGH-RANKING UNIVERSITIES AND STAGE HOUSES, FESTIVALS SUCH AS THE "STYRIARTE" OR THE "STYRIAN AUTUMN", AND MUSEUMS SUCH AS THE KUNSTHAUS, THE JOANNEUM WITH ALTER (OLD) AND NEUER (NEW) GALLERY. ALL THOSE AND THE LANDESZEUGHAUS WITH ITS HISTORIC COLLECTIONS OF ARMOUR AND WEAPONS, ENSURE A SUCCESSFUL COEXISTENCE OF BOTH TRADITION AND MODERNITY.

Above: Created by Vito Acconci around 2003, the spectacular Mur Island has been floating in the river of the same name.

Left: A cable car has been running since 1894 on the Graz Schlossberg. You can enjoy the magnificent view of the Old Town during the ride.

○ OLD TOWN

Graz - the second largest city in Austria - has one of the best preserved historic old towns in Central Europe. The Old Town stretches from the southeast foot of Schlossberg, with its red-tiled roofs. Buildings from various centuries characterise this district, such as the Gothic St. Egidius Cathedral and the Kaiserburg with its late Gothic twin spiral staircase, dated back to the 15th century. Built in 1557–1567 by Domenico dell'Aglio for the Styrian Estates as a meeting house and now the seat of the State Parliament, the country house with its magnificent arcaded courtyard is one of the most important Renaissance buildings outside of Italy. The Landeszeughaus, built by Antonio Solari in 1643/44 as a weapon depot against the Turkish invaders, owns the world's largest collection of its kind with its complete arsenal of weapons. The university was founded in 1586 and it was from here that the Counter-Reformation began.

○ CATHEDRAL

The St. Agydius consecrated Graz Cathedral was mid-15th century built at the behest of Emperor Frederick III. according to the plans of the Swabia Hans Niesenberger. First only a Parish church, it was handed over to the Jesuits in 1577, and after the dissolution of the Order, two centuries later, it was upgraded to the Cathedral of the Bishops of the Bistums of Seckau. Its exterior is remarkably simple, instead of a tower, the cathedral is merely provided with a roof ridge, which, like the chapel and sacristy, was added during the Baroque period. In the interior of the church, the contrast between the relatively wide main nave and the towering, deep, but narrow choir, is very charming. In combination with the lighting, which makes the choir appear brighter than the nave, it gives the impression of a spatial structure leading to a kind of heavenly gate.

SCHLOSSBERG

The landmark of the city is the castle ruins built by the Slovenes around the year 800 on the Schlossberg. Now, only the clock tower of 1561 (the clock dates back to 1712) remains from the Renaissance fortress that was built here – which Napoleon almost completely destroyed later on.

SCHLOSS EGGENBERG

The entire layout of the Castle Schloss Eggenberg is based on astronomical symbolism taken from the – at that point in history – brand new Gregorian Calendar, by the builder, Prince Hans Ulrich von Eggen-

berg (1568-1634). The planetary hall was built in 1625 by the Palladio pupil, Pietro de Pomis. The result is the largest Baroque palace in Styria. Schloss Eggenberg in Graz accommodates 24 state rooms, each with their own magnificent ceiling paintings. The showpiece is the planetarium with large oil paintings on the ceiling and walls showing the planets. In the remaining rooms of the Beletage, which are arranged in a wreath style formation, scenes from the Old Testament as well as Greek mythology and European history are depicted.

SHOPPING

HOFBÄCKEREI EDEGGER-TAX

The carved and decorated entrance to Graz' oldest bakery is already a sight to behold but also outstanding are the Imperial and Royal delicacies inside with names like Kaiser zwieback, Pantertatzen, Rudolfstaler, Sissibusserl and "Hetschpetsche-Bäckerei".

// www.hofbaeckerei.at

MURGASSE

Fashion, jewellery, delicatessen - this alley in the Old Town of Graz has many exquisite shops with high-quality goods. It does not matter if you are just strolling around the alley or window shopping, it is certainly worth a visit.

WHERE TO STAY

Hotel zum Dom // Gorgeous accommodation in the heart of the UNESCO World Heritage city. There are 29 individual, comfortable guest rooms. The foundations of the city palace dated back to the 14th century.

// www.domhotel.co.at

Augarten Art Hotel // The Austrian architect, Günther Domenig, designed the plans for this elegant hotel, in which art and design play a major role. Over 200 works by contemporary artists are exhibited at the hotel. The rooms and suites are of the highest standard with modern amenities.

// www.augartenhotel.at

Gapsite Hotel // Perfect accommodation for a weekend trip. Located in the heart of the city, this trendy hotel is within easy reach to most attractions, including the Opera House. Even trips to Styria are easy from here. **// gapsitehotel.com**

GOING OUT

Gasthof Stainzerbauer // Delicious creative fashionable Styrian delicacies, excellent wines and refined hospitality, all can be enjoyed in the splendid Renaissance courtyard.

// www.stainzerbauer.at

NOT TO BE MISSED

CELEBRATE WITH THE STYRIAN AUTUMN

Theatre, performances, dance, fine arts, architecture, film, music, literature – the spectrum of the program of this international festival of contemporary art is diverse. Styrian Autumn is one of the oldest festivals for New Art. Annual highlights are the world premieres and commissioned works.

VISIT A SHOW IN THE HIN & WIDER

For almost 25 years, this has been one of the most important and well attended cabarets in the German-speaking countries. It is located in the theatre café, not far from the opera house, and is the venue of the Graz Small Art competition.

HAVE A LOOK AT THE ART HOUSE

This museum strives for a "living encounter with art". The Art House itself does not have its own collection, it belongs to the Universal Museum Joanneum and exhibits contemporary works. Just from the outside, the building is already worth seeing!

EXPERIENCE STYRIARTE

Since 1985, the Styrian Festival takes place in Graz and throughout Styria every summer. The unique ambience of this UNESCO World Heritage City, and, the European Capital of Culture 2003, make the 40 concerts (old style music, musical theatre, symphonic and religious works, chamber music, etc.) an exceptional unique experience.

ADMIRE THE GLASS WINDOWS IN THE SACRED HEART CHURCH

The glass windows are examples of Neo-Gothic glass art and form a self-contained ensemble. In addition, the tower of the church is the third highest in the country. Admission into the church is free.

#35   IBIZA

EVEN TODAY, THE NAME IBIZA IS INTIMATELY LINKED WITH THE IDEA OF ECCENTRIC PARTYGOERS WHO LOVE TO GROOVE TILL THE SUN COMES UP. AND INDEED, "PRIVILEGE", "PACHA" AND "CAFÉ DEL MAR" ARE SOME OF EUROPE'S BEST-KNOWN CLUBS ON THE ISLAND. BUT IBIZA IS NOT ONLY A PARTY NIGHTLIFE SCENE. ON THE NEARLY 600 SQUARE KILOMETRES OF ISLAND, DIFFERENT WORLDS MEET. WHILE SHEPHERDS AND FARMERS IN THE FIELDS START THEIR WORK IN THE MOUNTAINOUS NORTH OF IBIZA, EARLY RISERS IN IBIZA TOWN TAKE THEIR FIRST COFFEE, OLD OR NEO-HIPPIES DO THEIR FIRST MEDITATION EXERCISES AND TOURISTS SLEEP CONTENTEDLY IN THEIR HOTEL BEDS AND PARTY-GOERS ARE GETTING BACK TO THEIR OWN HOTELS. IN IBIZA, EVERYONE CAN FIND THEIR PLACE ON THE ISLAND.

Above: The Old Town of Eivissa, has been a UNESCO World Heritage Site since 1999.

Left: The small bay of Cala d'Hort in Ibiza offers a stunning view, especially from the offshore island of Es Vedrà.

○ EIVISSA
The capital of Ibiza is a Carthaginian Foundation, and is one of the oldest Mediterranean cities. Nested white houses surrounded by an ocher fortress wall, dominated by the cathedral which shapes the whole image of the Old Town. The town is divided in two sections: the upper town Dalt Vila lies within the fortress walls, and the lower town with the former fishing district of Sa Penya and the old harbour district of La Marina. Here, for many visitors, the city exploration begins – past the corsair monument in the Passeig des Moll, directly opposite the church of Sant Elm. Through the district of Sa Penya, the narrow Carrer de la Verge runs through all the boutiques that have made that playful neglected Ibiza look famous.

○ DALT VILA
The fortified Old Town of Ibiza is one of the reasons why Ibiza has been declared a UNESCO World Heritage Site. Strolling through the narrow streets, you will feel as if you have been time warped back to the Middle Ages.

○ CATHEDRAL OF SANTA MARIA
The Cathedral sits proudly in the middle of the Old Town of Ibiza and is visible from almost every point of the city. Originally built in the Gothic style, she was rebuilt in the Baroque style later on in the 18th century.

○ MUSEUM OF CONTEMPORARY ART
Located in Ibiza's capital, the museum showcases mainly works by local artists, and it changes its exhibitions quarterly.

○ NECROPOLIS DEL PUIG DES MOLINS
Ibiza's capital is home to one of the largest Punic cemeteries in the world. Nearly 3,500 well-preserved burial chambers and sarcophagi were discovered in the necropolis, "the city of the dead", and can be visited today.

WHY VISIT IN AUTUMN?

THERE IS NOWHERE LIKE IBIZA TO PARTY. AND AFTER EACH ENTERTAINING SUMMER OF SUN-DRENCHED DRINKS, DRUGS, DANCE AND DEBAUCHERY, THE BALEARIC ISLAND NIGHTCLUBS BLAST THEIR GLORY AND SAY GOODBYE TO SUMMER, IN THE BIGGEST AND GREATEST PARTY OF THEM ALL. IBIZA'S CLOSING PARTIES ARE LEGENDARY. CLUBS LIKE "ES PARADIS", "PACHA", "DC10" AND "SPACE" COMPETE FOR THE COOLEST ATMOSPHERE. THIS IS NORMALLY MORE FOR THE OLDER PARTY GOERS (AS THE TEENAGERS ARE ALL BACK IN SCHOOL), AND HARD CORE CLUBBERS, WHO WANT TO INDULGE IN THE SUMMER ONE LAST TIME IN THE DANCE MADNESS.

○ ARCHAEOLOGICAL MUSEUM

Already the exterior of the Archaeological Museum in Ibiza town takes its visitors back in time. Inside, exhibits from the prehistory of the island to Christianity are shown.

○ IGLESIA DE SANT RAFEL

Characteristic of the church of Sant Rafel is its pyramid-shaped bell tower and its small dome. The building is reminiscent of an Arabic building and is probably one of the most unusual churches on the island.

○ PUERTO DE IBIZA

Gigantic cruiseliners, small fishing boats or super yachts... In the swanky port of Ibiza town, seafaring friends can not get enough of such eclectic sights.

○ PLAYA D'EN BOSSA

Not only because it has the longest beach on the island, Playa d'en Bossa is the most popular resort on the island. The notorious nightlife offers by many clubs attracts party goers from all over the world.

○ NATURE RESERVE SES SALINES

This region has extensive seagrass fields next to salt extraction basins, and it is home to many rare indigenous species. With a little luck, you can even spot flamingos in this UNESCO World Heritage Site.

○ PLAYA DE LAS SALINAS

This beach is named after the salt fields, which you probably passed on the way here. The beautiful crystal-clear waters and the numerous beach bars make it the "in scene" of the island.

○ CAP JUEU

Driving southwest from Eivissa via Sant Josep de sa Talaia and Cala d'Hort, you will arrive at Cap Jueu, the southwestern tip of the island. After a short walk, you will reach high above the cliffs the 18th century Torre del Pirata.

○ MIRADOR DEL SAVINAR

Ibiza's most beautiful vantage point is at the southwestern tip of the island. The panoramic view over the offshore islands is spectacular in clear weather. Nearby is also an old watch tower that is really worth seeing.

Top left: Ibiza the famous party island. The end of the season party in September is one big climax to say farewell to summer and the annual party life.

Bottom left: Not only does Cap Jueu have a magnificent panorama of the island of Es Vedrà, but you can also explore the former Torre del Pirata watchtower, which stands dramatically on the cliffs.

○ CALA BASSA

Without a doubt, this bay near San Antonio is one of the most beautiful on the island. Turquoise waters, fine sand and quaint beach bars make the beach a popular destination for both locals and tourists alike.

○ SANT ANTONI DE PORTMANY

Sant Antoni is one of the major tourist centers of Ibiza with a very interesting old town center. Unfortunately, the view is largely obscured by more than 90 hotel buildings. This place is mostly frequented by younger crowds which creates a very lively, and often turbulent atmosphere. It is not only at night, but also during the day on the surrounding beaches along the bay of Badia de Sant Antoni, such as

Cala Tarida, Cala Comte, Cala Bassa, Cala Grassico, Cala Salada and Punta Sa Galera.

○ CALA DE SANT VICENT

Surrounded on both sides by forested cliffs, here you will find one of the most beautiful places on the island. Near the bay is also the stalactite cave Es Culleram.

○ SANTA EULÀRIA DES RIU

If you want to escape the hustle and bustle of Eivissa for at least a short while and explore the island, you should head back east to this much quieter area and the "catwalk" Passeig de S'Alamera. This town is dominated by the white walls of the 16th century church of Santa Eulária that sits at the top of a hill 52 metres high.

○ PONT VELL

Located near Santa Eulària, you will come across a small romantic bridge from the 16th century. Due to numerous myths and legends, the bridge, albeit seemingly romantic, is nicknamed the "Devil's Bridge".

○ AGUAS BLANCAS

Amazing blue turquoise waters, steep cliffs and unspoiled nature. This beach near San Carlos is a magnet for both tourists and locals. Some visitors will even smear themselves with the red clay from the cliffs, as it is believed to be good for the skin.

GOING OUT

Diskothek Pacha // Since 1973, this converted historic finca in Ibiza town has been holding the best and wildest parties. The Pacha has also become a worldwide brand with outlets around the world.

// pachaibiza.com

Diskothek Privilege // With room for over 14,000 people, Privilege locates near Sant Rafel is the largest club in the world. Dancing takes place here in the open air and around the clock. This spot will turn your night into day.

// privilegeibiza.com

Amante // Those who prefer a quieter evening to clubbing can order a drink here and enjoy a stunning panoramic sea view. The restaurant at the Cala Nova will spoil you with its first-class cuisine and is definitely worth a visit. You can also have lunch here in its lovely day-time atmosphere.

// www.amanteibiza.com

Right: You can find some peace and there is little of the commotion that prevails in some places in Ibiza. Fragrant lush bougainvillea trees hang over the small alleyway stone walls in the small villages of Ibiza - such as this spot in Santa Eulària des Riu.

SHOPPING

○ HIPPIE MARKET LAS DALIAS

Every Saturday between 10am to 8pm from June to October, you can experience the colourful hustle and bustle in the Hippie Market Las Dalias in San Carlos. Here not only are the fashion, jewellery and accessories vibrant, but also the owners and market visitors.

○ PASSEIG DE VARA DE REY

This magnificent boulevard of Ibiza town just invites you to go (window) shopping with its exclusive boutiques and shops. A visit to this area is worthwhile because of the regular concerts, and the myriad of cool, little street cafés.

○ FÁBRICA DE LICORES ANISETA

Since 1925, the famous Herbal Liqueur Hierbas has been produced in Ibiza town. More than 20 different types of herbs are used. Not only does it make a great souvenir, but it is fun tasting before buying.

○ ART CRAFT MARKET SANT RAFEL

This market is famous for its clay and ceramic craftsmanship in Sant Rafel. But you will also find fresh fruits, juices and sweets. The market is open every Thursday evening from June to September.

GOING OUT

○ ROCK ISLAND ES VEDRÀ

On just half a square kilometre, the striking rocks rise steeply up to 380 metres into the sky. The sight of this magical island is breathtaking. The easiest way to get around Es Vedrà is to take a sightseeing boat, where wonderful rare species of birds, such as the Eleonora hawk, can be seen breeding and making nests.

WHERE TO STAY

Agroturismo Can Jaume // Only 2 kilometres from Ibiza town and situated on the edge of the village of Puig d'en Valls, this hotel complex is a luxurious country estate that promises serenity and sublime rest in the countryside.

// canjaume.org

One Ibiza Suites // Situated right on the beach, this hotel is one of the best in Ibiza town. Infinity pool, whirlpool and a terrace with sea views – here you can relax to the max during the day before stepping out for a long evening in this party town.

// www.oneibizasuites.com

Hotel La Ventana // With the historic walls of Dalt Vila in front of you and countless restaurants and bars in the immediate vicinity, a stay in this colourful hotel is a unique experience. The 13 rooms are charmingly furnished. The hotel has a good bar and a relaxing roof terrace, although there is no restaurant.

// www.laventanaibiza.com

NOT TO BE MISSED

WATCH THE SUNSET ON CALA BENIRRAS BEACH

Feeling romantic? Then you do not want to miss the amazing sunset on this beautiful island. Take a good bottle of wine, some cheeses and Spanish ham, and make yourself comfortable for this natural colourful display on the beach of Cala Benirras.

ENJOY A COCKTAIL AT CAFÉ DEL MAR.

Sitting in the famous Café del Mar, chilling to the laid-back music and admiring the sunset.... This will be sure to bring any stressed workaholics to full relaxation.

WALK ALONG THE CLIFFS

Nowhere is the view more stunning than when being up high. Take a walk along the coastal cliffs to fully appreciate the natural wonders that Ibiza has to offer. Do allow yourself time for such a walk and plan your route so that you have a perfect ending at one of the dreamy beaches.

TRY DELICIOUS FISH DISHES

You will not find a fresher catch than at one of the numerous Balearic Island harbour restaurants. Whether shellfish, squid or dogfish, the menus are full of delicious Mediterranean delicacies.

TAKE A WALK IN THE OLD TOWN OF IBIZA

For those who prefer a quieter and more cultural experience, take time to walk through the picturesque Old Town of Eivissa. Amateur photographers will find especially beautiful motifs here. The Old Town is not only a highlight during the day; in the evening and later at night, you will find all the facades illuminated by spotlights, that just makes everything romantically enchanting.

#36   CORSICA

WHITE LIMESTONE AT BONIFACIO, RED GRANITE ROCKS IN THE CALANCHE AND THE GREEN WILDERNESS OF THE CASTAGNICCIA. IT IS NOT SURPRISING THEN THAT CORSICA WAS ONCE CALLED BY THE GREEKS KALLISTE - THE BEAUTIFUL ONE. THE ISLAND OFFERS SPECTACULAR COASTLINES, BUT ALSO HIGH MOUNTAINS AND GREEN FORESTS – AN INCREDIBLE LANDSCAPE SEEMINGLY UNTOUCHED EVEN IN MODERN TIMES. CORSICA IS AN OVERWHELMING PLAY OF COLOUR CONTRASTS AND THE CAPTIVATING SCENT OF THE MACCHIA - CONSISTING OF ROSEMARY, THYME, LAVENDER, WILD FENNEL AND BROOM.

○ BASTIA

The lively port city is the most important economic centre of Corsica, and is the second largest town on the island. Worth seeing is its landmark, the majestic Baroque church of St. Jean Baptiste (1636-1666). High up on the fortifications, built between 1480 and 1521, visitors can enjoy a sweeping view across the harbour to Cap Corse.

○ CAP CORSE

Like a finger pointing to the Gulf of Genoa, the peninsula extends out into the sea. Dreamy fishing villages line the coast of Cap Corse. Along the cliffs, travellers will continuously fall in love with the incredible views.

○ ERBALUNGA

A popular postcard motif is of the fishing village Erbalunga. Picturesquely setting of the old houses gather on the rocky peninsula by the water, dominated by a Genoese watchtower (1512). The place is also known for its Good Friday processions.

○ CENTURI-PORT

Just like a picture book, grey weathered, ocher and pink house facades with slated roofs line the only natural harbour at the north-western end of the Cap Corse, Centuri-Port peninsula. The Greeks and Romans adored this favourable location.

○ CALVI

Calvi, once a Genoese stronghold with a citadel towering far into the sea, would certainly have lost its importance after being taken over by the French, was it not for its charming location. The wide bay and the lively harbour district with its Mediterranean flair act as a powerful tourist magnet.

○ PORTO

Surrounded by bright red rocks on one side and a deep blue sea on the other side, the resort town of Porto with its massive Genuente tower lies on the rock in front of the harbour entrance. The mouth of the Porto River consists of two areas connected by an eucalyptus-trees-lined avenue: Porto and Marine de Porto. Numerous hotels, an enchanting landscape and the local beach make Porto a holiday destination with delightful excursions into the surrounding area.

○ AJACCIO

In 1811, Napoleon Bonaparte, the most famous of Corsicans, proclaimed "his" city the capital of the island. This claim has not been challenged to this day - Napoleon's birthplace, founded in 1492, is strongly influenced by the memory of this illustrious figure. Worth seeing is the 1582/1593 built cathedral with a simple facade but a rich interior design, and the visit can be followed up by a walk through the strongly Italian-influenced old town with its many restaurants, bars and pizzerias. The Rue Cardinal

Left: The upper town of Bonifacio extends over the high cliff walls; beneath the waves gnaw into the limestone coves.

Right: The most famous son of the port city in western Corsica is Napoleon Bonaparte, who was born here in 1769. In 1811 Ajaccio became the capital of Corsica.

WHY VISIT IN AUTUMN?

IT CAN BE A BIT WINDY OUT HERE IN THE MEDITERRANEAN AND ALL TOO EASY TO GET CARRIED AWAY BY THE ATMOSPHERE OF THE FESTIVAL DU VENT. THE GRACEFUL CALVI MAKES THE MOST OF THIS BREEZY CONDITION AND HOSTS A "FESTIVAL OF THE WIND". THE IS A CELEBRATION OF THE AIR, AND BY EVERY WAY POSSIBLE: HUNDREDS OF ARTISTS AND WIND FREAKS COME WITH THEIR KITES, BALLOONS, HANG GLIDERS (SOME ARE CUSTOM BUILDS) TO PAY HOMAGE TO THE FREEDOM OF THE SKIES. THE FOCUS IS ON SUSTAINABILITY WITH WINDMILL ART ON DISPLAY, A WINDSURFING COMPETITION, GRACEFUL HANG-GLIDING DEMONSTRATIONS AND ULTRALIGHT AIRCRAFT WHIRRING OVER THE SEA. A FUN OUTING FOR THE WHOLE FAMILY.

Fesch, the main street of the old harbour district Borgo, is also inviting for a stroll. For those who are interested, visit the Maison Bonaparte in Place Letizia – Napoleon's house and birthplace. Here, interesting documents, portraits and other memorabilia of the Bonaparte family can be seen. The Musée Fesch in Palais Fesch has a significant collection of Italian paintings.

○ FILITOSA

Filitosa is one of the most important prehistoric archaeological sites in the Mediterranean, with its numerous Menhirs statues and Torrean fortifications. Since 6000 BC the area must have been inhabited. The museum gives the visitor a chronological overview of the finds. Picturesque beaches can also be found on the Golfe de Valinco, which you'll pass to reach Sartène.

○ SARTÈNE

The "most Corsican of all Corsican cities" is Sartène, located above the Rizzanèse Valley. The city owes this reputation in part to its labyrinth of fortress-like granite houses and dark backyards in the historic district of Santa Anna, but also partly to its gloomy past as a former bandit stronghold. Due to its strategically favourable location, the whole area of the Sartenais was fought for fiercely and contested for many years.

Above: The Scali di Arreña, the "staircase of the King of Aragon," descends a total of 1,420 steps from the limestone cliff of Bonifacio down to the sea.

Left: Colourful variety of figures dance in the sky during the autumn kites festival.

Right: Many of the watchtowers in Corsica were built in the 16th century under the rule of the Bank of Saint George: Genoa had pledged the island to the financiers of that bank; the youngest date back to the 17th century, which includes the Tour de la Parata near Ajaccio.

○ BONIFACIO

On the 60-metre high chalk cliff lies the city of Bonifacio which looks across the strait that separates Corsica from Sardinia, 12 kilometres away. It is the southernmost and at the same time the most astonishing city on the island. It towers magnificently on the narrow rock, surrounded on three sides by water, which have hollowed out the cliffs from below by the centuries of waves. In the Bay of Bonifacio is the district La Marine with a yachting marina. In the Ville Haute, the Old Town, narrow streets and tower-like buildings tell a tale of a century-long history, which was characterised by sieges and lack of space. Most of the houses have their own wells and cisterns and even storage rooms for food. Steep, narrow wooden staircases, which could quickly be pulled up in case of danger, lead to the first floor of the houses.

○ CAPU PERTUSATO

It is easy to lose yourself in the narrow streets of Bonifiacio. If you want to wake up from the medieval dream and enjoy the vastness of the sea as a complete contrast, you should take a hike to Capu Pertusato. Along the cliffs on the "Promenade des Falaises", from Chapelle St. Roch, a 5-kilometre long path leads south to the headland of Pertusato. The beach, a lighthouse and the view of the chalk cliffs are great rewards for the rambler. Particularly stunning is the return to Bonifacio in the late afternoon, when the fading light of the setting sun falls on the Old Town over the cliffs.

○ PORTO-VECCHIO

With its own fishing port and a large marina, sitting on a hill on the rugged Gulf of Porto-Vecchio, this is the third largest city on the island. Settlers of the "Torrean culture" landed around 1600 BC in Porto-Vecchio and built these fortresses and villages. However, today's urban development dates back to Genoese defences since 1539. This was followed by numerous battles for the city, destruction and then renewed fortification. The greatest enemy of the city, however, was malaria for centuries. It was not until the 1950s that the disease could be contained, and from then on the city started to flourish. The finest sand, green pines and bright blue sea, Porto-Vecchio is a popular tourist destination, with its wonderful beaches in close vicinity. Not far from

GOING OUT

Porto-Vecchio: Via Notte // If you're a night owl, you will love Porto-Vecchio's outdoor discotheque, which is the largest in Europe. Here are only the best DJs, and party goers really get their money's worth!

// www.vianotte. com

Calvi: Chez Tao // This restaurant in Calvi is an institution. With music being played here since 1935. Tao Kerefoff opened the first nightclub of Corsica in the basement of a 16th century house. The motto of the club is as it was almost 100 years ago, "Be happy today because tomorrow will be too late".

// www.cheztao.com

Calvi: U Fanale // One of the best restaurants in Calvi for those who want to enjoy Mediterranean cuisine. Dinner is served with a wonderful view of the bay and the lighthouse.

// Route de Porto, 20260

Porto-Vecchio lies the largest cork oak forest of the island, which is still an important source of income for the population.

SHOPPING

○ TRADITIONAL MARKETS

In most towns, you can still find traditional markets where you will be able to buy local specialties: On Sundays there are markets in Porto Veccio or Bastia; Mondays in Sainte-Lucie-de-Tallano; and, Tuesdays in Bonifacio. One of the most beautiful though is the market of Ajaccio, which opens daily except on Mondays.

○ A CASETTA IN AJACCIO

Authentic food is served in the café, while the small shops sells local produce, including wine, ham, cheese, oil and anything your heart desires. If you are in Ajaccio, be sure to stop by!

// www.acasetta-produitscorses.com

WHERE TO STAY

Cala di Greco // Not far from Bonifacio, this romantic four-star resort boasts of two outdoor pools and several luxury suites. The panoramic sea view is spectacular. The Spérone golf course is also nearby.

// www.hotel-caladigreco.com

Bonifacio: Hotel Version Maquis Citadelle // The four-star boutique hotel with its ten suites is truly exceptionally beautiful. Surrounded by the evergreen maquis on the Gulf of Santa Manza, it offers guests on-site massage, a great outdoor pool and a fitness centre.
// http://www.hotel-versionmaquis.com

Ota: La Calypso // Its location on the pedestrian zone of Ota Harbour makes this property ideal for boat trips and outings to the surrounding areas. Many great reviews from guests on hotel's staff and their fantastic service, as well as reasonable room rate, make this a great place to stay.

// www.hotel-la-calypso.com

GOING OUT

○ GIROLATA

Boat trips can also be made from Porto: The Heritage Listed fishing village of Girolata is closed to cars, so it can only be reached on foot or by boat. Once upon a time, the bay was a pirate's hide-outs. Today, Girolata is appreciated for its seclusion that makes this village one of the most beautiful places in the Mediterranean.

○ GORGES DE LA RESTONICA

The valley with its gushing wild brook is surrounded by high rocky peaks. It narrows to the west and takes the form of a narrow gorge. The local fauna is characterised by chestnut trees, Corsican black pines, the so-called "Corte pines", are exclusively growing here. The classic hike through the valley starts behind the bridge that leads over the Timozza stream. It passes through several vegetation areas and ends after 4 to 5 hours. Refreshments are also taken care of – the numerous pools of Restonica just invite you to swim and splash.

NOT TO BE MISSED

TAKE A TRAIN RIDE ON THE U TRINICHELLU

It takes three and a half hours for the train from Ajaccio to Bastia. The 158-kilometre-long day trip with the "Trinichellu" is a journey from coast to coast via Corte, right through the heart of the island. In 1888, the railway line was opened; the route was considered a pioneering architectural achievement. A highlight is between Vivario and Venacoder, the viaduct over the Vecchio, built according to plans by Gustave Eiffel. The railway network of Corsica has a total length of over 230 kilometres, with 38 tunnels and 76 bridges - a great opportunity to enjoy the whole diversity of the island between the magnificent high mountain landscape and the fragrant scrublands.

DRIVE OVER THE COL DE BAVELLA

The 1,218-metre-high Col de Bavella is considered the most beautiful pass in Corsica. The view is spectacular of the 1,600-meter-high bizarre crags of the Aiguilles de Bavella, behind which rises Monte Incudine (2,134 metres). At the pass, there are some excursion places, where – with a little luck – you might see the "moufflons" (wild sheep).

WALK THROUGH LES CALANCHE

Between Porto and Piana lies Corsica's most impressive coastline - the Calanche, a 2-kilometre-long mass of red cliffs that is also a UNESCO World Heritage Site. It is advisable to visit the Calanche on foot to really enjoy the play of rock colours, blue sea and green vegetation. The charming Piana - a village high on the mountain with bright houses and a church from the 18th century - is another good starting point for a trip through the Calanche.

TAKE THE HIKING TRAIL

The lush green peaks and varied trails are ideal for hiking. Corsica's famous long-distance trail is the GR20, which meanders through the granite ridges of the interior over a distance of about 190 kilometres. If you like a shorter hike, you can walk the "Mare e Monti" (from the "Sea to the Mountains"), or the "Mare e Mare" (from the "Sea to Sea").

DIVING

The 1,000 kilometres of warm water coastline just invites you to dive. The dive sites of Corsica are among the best in the Mediterranean. Even under water, the landscape is rugged, but brightly carpets of yellow sea anemones and red precious corals are truly a beautiful sight.

#37 MILAN

MILAN HAS BECOME THE MOST IMPORTANT ECONOMIC CENTRE OF NORTHERN ITALY, WITH TRADITIONS THAT GO BACK CENTURIES AND A HISTORY THAT EXPRESSES ITSELF IN MAGNIFICENT CHURCHES AND PALACES. ART LOVERS, OPERA ENTHUSIASTS AND FRIENDS OF ELEGANT LIFESTYLE WILL BE THRILLED. FROM HERE, THE ROMAN EMPIRE WAS TEMPORARILY RULED IN LATE ANTIQUITY; IN THE MIDDLE AGES, THE CITY WAS THE CRYSTALLISATION POINT OF THE NEW ITALY. THE FIRST GOLDEN AGE BEGAN IN THE 11TH CENTURY. MILAN GAINED A LEADING POLITICAL POSITION IN THE LOMBARD CITIES ASSOCIATION. THE CITY BECAME THE CENTRE OF ART AND CULTURE UNDER THE VISCONTI AND SFORZA DUKES. THE EMINENCE ENDED IN 1500, WHEN THE INDEPENDENCE OF THE CITY-STATE ENDED.

Above: Milan Cathedral is one of the largest Gothic churches in the world. The construction took almost 500 years and was finally finished in 1858.

Left: The famous Galleria Vittorio Emanuele II, north of the cathedral, is Milan's most magnificent shopping mall that houses exclusive luxury shops, restaurants, bars and hotels. The "catwalk of the Milanese" was built from 1867 to the plans of the architect Giuseppe Mengoni in the form of a cross. It was completed in 1877.

○ MILAN CATHEDRAL

The third largest church in the world with all its small distinct angle towers, the Milan Cathedral is a classic masterpiece of Italian Gothic. There are no less than 2,245 individual statues decorating its façade of white marble. Even those who are not interested in churches will definitely appreciate the structure on the forecourt. The hustle and bustle just exudes an Italian flair.

○ PINACOTECA AMBROSIANA

The Pinacoteca Ambrosiana is custodian of the most important collections of paintings in Italy. In numerous halls, famous works by masters such as da Vinci, Botticelli, Titian and Caravaggio can be admired.

○ SAN BABILA

Probably the oldest church in Milan, the San Babila is located in the same district. The original Roman-esque structure is now located among dozens of famous fashion designer studios, making San Babila the fashion heart of the city.

○ GIUSEPPE-MEAZZA-STADION

Football fans will be particularly interested in the Giuseppe Meazza Stadium, home of clubs Inter Milan and AC Milan. Even outside match days, you can visit and walk on the legendary turf and inspect the cabins.

○ GIARDINI DI VILLA REALE

From its particularly picturesque side, Milan shows itself in the Giardini di Villa Reale, the city's oldest park. The well-kept lake and decorated statues invite you to take a break.

○ CASTELLO SFORZESCO

The magnificent Castello Sforzesco castle now houses several museums and exhibitions. Here you should

WHY VISIT IN AUTUMN?

FASHION IN FOCUS: WANT TO KNOW WHAT WILL BE WORN NEXT SEASON? THEN OFF TO FASHION WEEK. FROM THE BEGINNING OF SEPTEMBER, EVERY FASHION HOUSE AND DESIGNER, ALONG WITH THEIR MUSES AND MODELS, MOVIE STARS, MAGAZINE EDITORS AND FOLLOWERS MAKE THEIR ROUNDS THROUGH THE WORLD'S MAJOR FASHION CITIES FOR THE NEXT SPRING/SUMMER COLLECTIONS. THE FIRST WEEK IS HELD IN NEW YORK, THEN TO LONDON, AND FROM THERE ON TO MILAN, THEN PARIS. ACCESS TO THE LIKES OF CHANEL OR GIVENCHY SHOWS IS IMPOSSIBLE FOR MERE MORTALS, BUT THERE ARE ALSO SMALLER EVENTS FOR FASHION-LOVERS IN EVERY CITY. JUST DON'T FORGET: THE OUTFIT IS EVERYTHING!

not miss a stroll through the affiliated Simplonpark with its magnificent rose varieties.

○BAGATTI VALSECCHI MUSEUM

If you want to take a look into Italy's past, then this is the museum for you. The collections contain Renaissance art, but also furniture, tapestries and precious ivory table tops.

○TEATRO ALLA SCALA

For music-lovers, the opera house Teatro alla Scala is a must. After all, great composers such as Rossini, Bellini, Verdi, Donizetti and Puccini have all performed here.

○SANTA MARIA DELLE GRAZIE

Santa Maria delle Grazie is one of Milan's classics. The church, a foundation of Count Gaspare da Vimercate, was built from 1463 to 1490 as a Dominican monastery church. In the former dining room, Leonardo da Vinci painted by order of Ludovico il Moro from 1495 to 1497 his world famous painting "The Last Supper". It records the moment when Jesus spoke his prophetic words: "One of you will betray me."

○PIAZZA MERCANTI

Piazza Mercanti was considered the heart of Milan in the Middle Ages, with merchants and craftsmen going about their daily routine. Today, you can admire many unique imposing buildings and numerous sculptures.

○PALAZZO REALE

Despite being bombed in World War II, much was left intact from the former home of Maria Theresa, Napoleon and Ferdinand I. This makes the Royal Palace of Palazzo Reale one of the most beautiful sights in Milan.

○CIMITERO MONUMENTALE

One of Milan's most famous witnesses of the past is the monumental cemetery Cimitero Monumentale. On 250,000 square metres, you can view breathtaking sculptures and works of art, as well as famous tombs.

Left: Getting noticed at any price, that's the motto of Fashion Week in Milan. Here a model wears a creation by Vivienne Westwood.

○ TORRE BRANCA

There is a fantastic view of the city of Milan at 108 metres high from the observation tower Torre Branca, located in the Simplonpark.

○ GIARDINI PUBBLICI INDRO MONTANELLI

If you want to take a breather during all the sightseeing, this is best done in the green lung of Milan, the park Giardini Pubblici Indro Montanelli. The perfect place for a picnic on the manicured lawns.

○ BASILICA DI SANT'AMBROGIO

The church Basilica di Sant'Ambrogio shouldn't be missed. The church was started by the patron saint of the city, Bishop Ambrosius, and is dedicated to the martyrs Gervasius and Protasius, whose remains can be viewed here.

GOING OUT

Tartufotto Milano // Truffles in all variations. The Tartufotto with its casual beige-brown interior and soft inviting cushions, offers inspirational dishes using this luxurious tuber.

// tartufotto.it

Gianni e Dorina // Tuscan cuisine at its best, delicious dishes of wild boar and chestnut lasagne are served in this small restaurant.

// www.gianniedorina.com

Ristorante El Brellin // Lombard specialties such as beef stew, risotto or ossobuco alla milanese are on the menu. The restaurant is superbly located on the Naviglio Grande, with views of the canal. Good wine list.

// www.brellin.com

Top right: One of the most striking buildings in Milan - The Teatro alla Scala Opera House, with its magnificent hall.

Bottom right: World Heritage status Leonardo da Vinci's "The Last Supper" at the church of Santa Maria delle Grazie. The painting is 9 metres wide and 5 metres high.

○ NATIONAL MUSEUM OF SCIENCE AND TECHNOLOGY - LEONARDO DA VINCI

Milan has one of the most important science museums in the world, the National Museum of Science and Technology, which has many interactive exhibits - many that honor the great artist and inventor, Leonardo da Vinci. This place is a treasure vault to many of da Vinci's inventions and his drawings.

○ PINACOTECA DI BRERA

The Pinakothek in the Palazzo Brera was actually intended as a place of learning. Today, it is one of the most important art museums in Italy, showcasing significant paintings from the Renaissance and Baroque.

○ CAPELLA PORTINARI

Another one of Milan's most important buildings is the Capella Portinari. This magnificent church was designed by Vincenzo Foppa, the most important Lombard painter of the Renaissance.

SHOPPING

GOING OUT

○ MERCATONE DELL'ANTIQUARIATO
Always on the last Sunday of the month, the promenades of the Naviglio Grande turn into a large antique market. With over 400 stalls, you can buy antiques, jewellery, clothing and even furniture from the 1950s.

○ GALLERIA VITTORIO EMANUELLE II
A shopping palace of the highest nouveau, Galleria Vittorio Emanuelle II is next door to La Scala and Piazza Duomo, with artistic frescoes and more beautiful marble than one can ever imagine!

○ QUADRILATERO D'ORO
Great fashion houses and luxury brands are the focus here. Also perfect for window shopping, the Quadrilatero d'Oro is located on Milan's Golden Square. Where every imaginable high-end brands can be found in the four streets, which then connect as a square.

○ VIA MONTE NAPOLEONE
One of the streets of the Golden Quadrangle, the noblest and most expensive of all, is Via Monte Napoleone. This is the location for haute couture and majestic diamonds as well as high-profile glittering pieces.

○ CORSO BUENOS AIRES
High-street fashion, but by no means with less choice, is the Corso Buenos Aires. This is one of the largest shopping streets in Europe. Not only for fashion lovers, but also for electronic-geeks, book lovers and great furniture pieces.

○ FIERA DI SINIGAGLIA
On Saturday morning, many locals traditionally go to the Fiera di Sinigaglia, a flea market. This is a treasure chest. Here, you can find any second-hand luxury labels and vintage pieces at affordable prices. This place is also great for art and antiques.

○ MONZA
The circuit is famous mainly due to the Formula 1 Monza. But it also has historic churches, a fairy tale park and the Villa Reale. Above all, the cathedral with its impressive two-tone marble façade is a highlight.

WHERE TO STAY

Petit Palais // A former nunnery dated back to 17th century has been beautifully transformed into a chic boutique hotel, including silk wallpaper and Empire furniture, as well as a chalice.
//petit-palais-hotel-de-charme-milan.ibooked.ca

Straf // Puristic design with bare concrete walls, plus a pampering spa program in a class of its own. For those looking for stylish and luxurious accommodation, this centrally located Vincenzo De Cotiis house is the perfect choice.
// www.straf.it

Maison Borella // A boutique hotel located in the trendy area on the Naviglio Grande. A Palazzo from the 18th Century has been carefully modernized with charming detail. It has a beautiful banister courtyard, where you can relax and sooth in Milan's pleasant nights.
//www.hotelmaisonborella.com

NOT TO BE MISSED

GO OUT IN THE NAVIGLI AREA

Italy lives by its language, the mood and the enjoyment of good food. Wander the streets in the artisan quarter Navigliand and immerse yourself in the Italian flavours and feelings.

TRY OSSOBUCO ALLA MILANESE

Translated, this Milanese dish means something like "bone with a hole". What you will find on the plate though is namely a braised veal leg slice, up to five centimetres thick in a deliciously spiced sauce. Often added is the herbal spice mixture Gremolata. A must for all foodies.

ENJOY THE VIEW FROM THE MILAN CATHEDRAL ROOF

The best view can be experienced from the city's most magnificent landmark, the Milan Cathedral. You can climb up to the roof of the cathedral where you will be greeted with a stunning view of Milan.

TRY TORRONE AND AMARETTI

Italians are certainly true gourmet artists. Especially irresistible are their famous sweets. At the top of the list of amazing tastes is the white nougat, Torrone, and the small almond macaroons, Amaretti. Simply delicious!

ENJOY AN ESPRESSO ON THE PIAZZA

Now that you are in Milan - be the model in your own espresso advertisement! Sitting casually under Milan sun, Italian style with sunglasses on the nose, enjoying an espresso, or two, and appreciate the good life on a piazza.

#38

MUNICH

THE MOST BEAUTIFUL CITY IN THE WORLD? THE PROUD PEOPLE OF MUNICH MIGHT HAVE NEVER ACTUALLY SAID THAT ABOUT THEIR BELOVED CITY, AND THIS IS SOMETHING MAYBE EVERY VISITOR SHOULD DECIDE FOR THEMSELVES. MUNICH IS A CITY THAT APPEALS TO ALL THE SENSES: YOU CAN ENJOY THE RELAXING LIFE IN THE STREET CAFÉS, IN THE CHARMING BEER GARDENS OR DIRECTLY ON THE ISAR, AND THERE ARE EVEN ENGLISH GARDENS TO ENJOY. IMMERSE YOURSELF IN CULTURAL MUNICH WHEN YOU GO TO THE OPERA OR THE THEATRE OR VISIT THE WELL-KNOWN MUSEUMS SUCH AS THE THREE PINAKOTHEKEN OR THE DEUTSCHES MUSEUM. IN MUNICH, EVEN THE MODERN ARCHITECTURAL HIGHLIGHTS HAVE LONG BECOME FAMOUS LANDMARKS OF THE CITY, SUCH AS THE BMW WELT, THE ALLIANZ ARENA OR THE OLYMPIC STADIUM WITH ITS WORLD-FAMOUS TENT ROOF CONSTRUCTION. DURING THE OKTOBERFEST, THE CITY SHOWS A CHEERFUL AND FUN-LOVING SIDE, AND THE SLOGAN, WHICH MADE THE OLYMPIC CITY OF 1972 INTERNATIONALLY WELL-KNOWN SUMS IT ALL UP: "MUNICH, THE COSMOPOLITAN CITY WITH A HEART".

Left: Frauenkirche. The towers with the Welsh hoods are the true landmark of Munich. The "Stasi", which is the tallest being 100 metres higher than the "Blasi" that's only at a mere 99 metres. There is nothing higher as the city has set a 100-metre height limit on all buildings.

○ MARIENPLATZ

Munich's central square is lined with rows of civic houses as well as the New Town Hall and the Old Town Hall. The centre piece is the gold plated Marienplatz column with its pedestal surrounded by cupids. The Marienplatz was also the original starting point for Bavarian Land Surveying.

○ NEUES RATHAUS

The New Town Hall building was built in Flemish Gothic style in the 19th century. Famous for it, is the Carillon - a bell tower musical instrument with 43 bells and 32 mechanical figures. Tourists meet daily just before 12 pm midday to listen to the sounds of the Schäffler dance, or at 9 pm for the famous child of Munich performance.

○ FRAUENKIRCHE

Both onion domes of the Gothic cathedral and city parish church known as the Frauenkirche ("Liebfrauendom" or "Cathedral of Our Dear Lady") are unmistakable symbols of the city of Munich. Inside, there are pieces from the Gothic period, such as a huge bronze sarcophagus for Ludwigs of Bavaria, and the legendary footprint of the devil before the entrance to the nave.

○ ALTER PETER

The tower of the Parish Church of St. Peter, called Old Peter by the locals, takes 306 steps to a viewing platform. The exterior of the church, which is located on Petersbergl Hill, above the Viktualienmarkt, is in the Gothic style with a large baroque altar inside.

○ VIKTUALIENMARKT

The Viktualienmarkt is a daily food market. It is a square in the centre of Munich with mostly fixed stalls and a maypole in the middle, the outdoor shopping area for food looks more rural than most village markets. There is always something to discover here, from horse sausages, to the freshly-squeezed Dinkel grass juice.

○ RESIDENZ

A colossal Renaissance building with an impressive collection of Wittelsbacher treasures, including the Bavarian King's Crown. The building complex consists of several courtyards, with the Rococo-style Cuvilés Theatre and the Allerheiligen-Hofkirche. Inside the residence is an architectural highlight, the Antiquarium, which is a huge frescoed Renaissance vault.

○ FELDHERRNHALLE

The open hall, modeled after the Florentine Loggia dei Lanzi, was built by Friedrich von Gärtner in the mid-19th century, as a prelude to the magnificent Ludwigstrasse.

○ THEATINERKIRCHE

The Theatinerkirche is a Baroque church with its distinctive towers standing at the end of the actual Old Town. The exterior is painted in imperial yellow, while the interior is kept in more discreet colours. Under the two tower peaks, snail ornaments decorate the façade, making St. Kajetan (the official name) a key feature of the city landscape.

WHY VISIT IN AUTUMN?

IN 1810 A HORSE RACE WAS ORGAN-
IZED TO CELEBRATE THE WEDDING
OF THE BAVARIAN CROWN PRINCE
LUDWIG I. THIS LAVISH FESTIVAL
WAS SUCH A SUCCESS THAT IT WAS
REPEATED ANNUALLY, AND FINALLY
BECAME A MORE RUGGED PARTY
THAT IS KNOWN AS "OKTOBERFEST".
MORE THAN 6 MILLION BEER LOVERS
SIT AT LONG TABLES IN GIANT TENTS,
DOWNING MORE THAN 6.5 MILLION
LITRES OF THE AMBER LIQUID. THE
FESTIVAL MEAL PLAN INCLUDES HALF
A MILLION CHICKENS, 104 STEERS
AND MORE THAN 50,000 PORTIONS
OF PORK. THE ONLY BEER SERVED IS
THE SPECIALLY BREWED OKTOBER-
FEST BEER. AMONG THE HUSTLE AND
BUSTLE, THERE ARE A FEW NOSTAL-
GIC RETURNING FAVOURITES SUCH
AS THE LAST GERMAN FLEA CIRCUS,
WITHOUTWHICH SINCE THE 19TH CEN-
TURY THE OCTOBERFEST WOULD BE
UNTHINKABLE.

○ HOFGARTEN

A peaceful garden oasis between courtly architecture. The garden is formally laid out around two central footpaths that intersect at the Temple of Diana.
It is crowned by a female statue that symbolises
"Goddess of the Hunt" from the "Bavarian Earth"
fable.

○ TEMPLE OF ART

At the start of the Prinzregentenstraße directly at the
English Garden is an expressive Temple of Art (1937).
The contemporary exhibition is famous for its dark
past with "Degenerate Art".

○ NATIONAL THEATRE

At the Max-Joseph-Platz stands the National Theatre
with its stately entrance supported by grand Corin-
thian columns and a double gable.

○ VALENTIN-MUSÄUM

The Museum, housed in the Isartor, commemorates
the master of bizarre humor and son of the city of
Munich: Karl Valentin.

○ ASAMKIRCHE

This House of God, whose official name is St. Johann
Nepomuk, is like a jewellery box in a grotto. The
brothers Cosmas Damian and Egid Quirin Asam
created this enthusiastic overloaded legacy of their
art between 1733 and 1746.

○ JÜDISCHES KULTURZENTRUM, STADTMUSEUM

The building, shaped as a cube with a transparent
lower lobby topped with a massive windowless upper
level, provides an overview of Munich's Jewish history.
This open ensemble with a main synagogue opened
in 2006; the Jewish Museum and the Jewish
Community House creates a new promenade from
Viktualienmarkt to Oberanger. Also on Jakobsplatz is
the City Museum, which showcases exhibits from
Munich's cultural history.

○ ST. MICHAEL

The largest Renaissance church in Germany with its
mighty barrel-vaulted roof was a sign of solidarity for
the Counter-Reformation from William V, Duke of Bavaria. The impressive gable façade shelters standing
statues of his ancestors.

*Left: The Munich
Oktoberfest is one of the
wildest and the biggest
parties in the world. On
average, about 500,000
guests flock to the festival
every day, storming the
carnival rides and beer
tents that can take up to
6,000 people. With the
drinking song "Ein Prosit
der Gemütlichkeit",
meaning "A toast to
well-being", people from
all over the world
cheerfully sing and salute
each other.*

○ STACHUS/KARLSPLATZ

The open well attracts locals and tourists by the thousands in summer. Karlsplatz, as it is known by some locals, is the gateway to Neuhauser Straße.

○ DEUTSCHES MUSEUM

One of the largest scientific and technical museums in the world stands on an Isar island between Ludwigs and Corneliusbrücke. In the courtyard is a flight simulator, and there is also an astronomical clock which displays the constellations of each month.

○ KÖNIGSPLATZ

The Kings Square was designed by master builder Leo von Klenze for King Ludwig I. The mighty Propyläen gatehouse completes the Classicistic styled square layout to Brienner Straße.

○ GLYPTOTHEK

The building with its iconic portico porch houses a public collection of original antique statues and busts. The highlight is the "Barberini Faun", a Roman sculpture depicting a sleeping Greek mythological satyr.

○ LENBACHHAUS

The former residence of painter, Prince Franz von Lenbach, serves as exhibition space for the paintings of the artists group "Der Blaue Reiter" (The Blue Rider).

○ PINAKOTHEK DER MODERNE

The Pinakothek der Moderne was inaugurated in September 2002, after seven years of construction. It is one of the world's largest museums for modern and contemporary art. Since the 1950s, it exhibits works of classical modernism, contemporary art, and a delightful collection of New Media and Photography.

○ ALTE PINAKOTHEK

The free standing building houses a world renown gallery of old masters from Holbein to Rubens. Famous works include: Dürer's portrait of Oswolt Krel; Murillo's "Grape and Melon Eater"; Rembrandt's "Holy Family"; and, the portrait of Emperor Charles V of Titian.

○ NEUE PINAKOTHEK

From the French Impressionists to the German Expressionists; from the Nazarenes to Böcklin; Liebermann

Right: The Green Isar is Munich's most beautiful, natural lifeline. It was at the ford of this river with the Celtic name "The Tearing" that the settlement developed. Munich loves and appreciates the Isar, which comes from the Alps and flows into the Danube after 295 kilometres at Deggendorf. The people of Munich bathe, sunbathe, fish in the river, barbecuing, and even surfing on their tributary streams, such as on the Eisbach. The Isar is a beautiful piece of nature in the middle of this bustling city.

GOING OUT

Tantris // The Tantris has completely dominated the Munich's restaurant scene since 1971. The two-star Michelin chef Hans Haas is of course one of the best chefs in Germany.

// www.tantris.de/en

Emiko // This Japanese restaurant procures many of its produce daily from Munich's finest fresh food market, the Viktualienmarkt. These ingredients combine perfectly for the restaurant's modern Japanese dishes.

// https://www.louis-hotel.com/en/emiko-restaurant-bar/

Café Frischhut // This traditional café is also called "The lard noodle". Here, even in the early morning hours, you can feast on scrumptious lard-baked delicacies such as donuts and pastries. Pick a table outside so you can sit and chat with friends while enjoying the autumn sun.

// Prälat-Zistl-Straße 8

and Cézanne; in this museum you can indulge in famous art and architecture. The infamous painting "The Sunflowers" by van Gogh is housed here.

Left: Nymphenburg Palace is the highlight in the west of Munich. It is particularly impressive that this magnificent Baroque building stands in a big city and the horizon is not obscured by skyscrapers - today this a rare image in German urban planning.

○ ENGLISCHER GARTEN

This landscaped English Garden with its extensive green areas, groves, streams and lakes, are delightful showpieces in the park, among individual buildings such as the Monopteros and the Chinese Tower.

○ SCHLOSS NYMPHENBURG

The Electoral Prince Elector Ferdinand Maria gave his wife Henriette the start to this radiant Baroque creation. The interior of the palace is exuberantly decorated in the 18th century European style.

SHOPPING

○ SCHUHBECKS GEWÜRZLADEN

More than 100 spices and spice mixes from all over the world, ready packed decorative boxes, or you can create your own mixes. There are also delicious mustard and horseradish creations.

// www.schuhbeck.de

○ LUDWIG BECK

The "Store of the Senses", as the appropriately claimed, offers chic clothing, music, stationery and much more over five floors.

// www.ludwigbeck.de

○ DALLMAYR

One of the finest delicatessens with over 300 years of experience. A culinary history adventure with coffee, chocolate and wine from all over the world.

// www.dallmayr.com

○ HOHENZOLLERNSTRASSE

Typical of the district Schwabing! Here shopping locals and tourists will find exclusive shops and funky boutiques for which this area is well known for through Germany. A nice stroll peaking into the quieter side streets is also worthwhile.

WHERE TO STAY

Opéra // In a small urban palace in Lehel, this elegant hotel offers a magical atmosphere and a luxurious ambience. All sights of the city centre are within walking distance.

// www.hotel-opera.de/en

Bayerischer Hof // The first house on the square, with an endless list of prominent guests. On the roof is a modern and elegant spa area, which also offers day spa package (by appointment only).

// www.bayerischerhof.de/en

Torbräu // The oldest hotel in Munich (the house has been around since 1490), is located opposite the Isartor. There are 91 rooms - all are differently decorated. The hotel has an in-house restaurant.

// www.torbraeu.de

NOT TO BE MISSED

TAKE A VIKTUALIENMARKT DELICACY TOUR

The Viktualienmarkt was once meant for the daily groceries, but has now evolved into selling all sorts of luxury goods and delicacies available from this land of plenty. With this extraordinary guide, you will find so much sausages and cheeses, both sweet and hearty, that are a feast to the eyes as well as your stomach. You may find out some very interesting things about the history, customs and cultures of places you may not know existed!

A VISIT TO MÜLLER'SCHEN VOLKSBAD

You probably can't get any more "stylish" a pool than this one. The Art Nouveau indoor pool with Gargoyles and Baroque decor is probably one of the most beautiful bathing houses in Europe. There are two swimming pools that you can choose from - originally, one was only for women and the other for men - but, now both pools are accessible for all. There is also a delicious menu on offer in the café next door.

WATCH THE EISBACHSURFERN IN THE ENGLISH GARDEN

Despite being far away from the sea, the Eisbach wave is the centre for the surfer's scene. The best way to watch the surfing is from the bridge at the House of Art.

VISIT THE MÜNCHNER BIERGARTEN

Together with an ice-cold beer that goes perfectly well with chuncky grilled sausage, salad or filled meat rolls. There is a familiar atmosphere and self-service is not uncommon. Popular beer gardens are those around the Chinese Tower or in the Augustiner Brewery.

CLIMB THE HEAD OF THE BAVARIA ON THE THERESIENWIESE

The bronze lady is 18 metres high, perched in front of the Hall of Fame. From the top, you have a great view over the Theresienwiese, where the Oktoberfest and flea markets take place.

#39   SOUTH TIROL

BEAUTIFUL OLD TOWN STREETS WITH ROMANTIC ARCADES, MAGNIFICENT BAROQUE CHURCHES, IMPOSING FORTRESSES - SOUTH TYROL'S TOWN BEARS WITNESS TO THE IMPORTANCE THAT THE REGION HAS HAD AS A TRANSIT COUNTRY FOR CENTURIES. DUE TO ITS STRATEGIC LOCATION, THE ROMANS FOUNDED SETTLEMENTS HERE; IN THE MIDDLE AGES MERCHANTS USED THE LINK BETWEEN NORTHERN AND CENTRAL EUROPE AND THE MEDITERRANEAN. TODAY, TOURISM HAS REPLACED TRADE AS THE MOST IMPORTANT FORM OF INCOME FOR SOUTH TYROL. VISITORS FROM ALL OVER THE WORLD ENJOY THE WONDROUS BEAUTY OF THE CITY AND ITS TOWNS, AS WELL AS THE THERMAL SPRINGS.

Meran is almost too beautiful to work in, but it is even more stunning to walk through. Be it through the dreamy Old Town with its Lauben-gasse, or through the gardens of Trauttmans-dorff Castle (above), past longleaf speedwells, poppies and Geraniums, or around the Catholic Church of St. Nicholas, the landmark of the city with its 78-metre-high tower (left).

○ MERAN

St. Nicholas stands tall at the parish church and gestures with a raised finger through the Bolzano gate to the river Passer, as if to say: "Merano citizens, watch out for the floods!". Damage from earlier days has been long forgotten since reservoirs now regulate water flows. Now you can walk along the Passer, shop in the nearby stores, dance in the Kursaal and appreciate the Art Nouveau theatre. The pleasant Mediterranean climate delights the 37,000 visitors, which for centuries has enticed personalities, such as Empress Elisabeth, to visit.

○ LAUBENGASSE

The Laubengasse, which leads from Pfarrplatz to Kornplatz, is a perfect path to stroll through the city. There are beautiful houses, all of which have eye-catching facades and bay windows; an arcade which you can walk along the shop windows that will help you to stay dry if it rains. You will appreciate many archways as they give an interesting view into the pretty courtyards. The elegant arcades are from the period around 1420, when Meran was the capital of the country; their amusing secret being that they were originally cattle sheds.

○ KURHAUS

The oldest part of Kurhaus was opened in 1874. But today, the overall impression is dominated by the 1913/14 newly built wing, which also includes the Rotunda and the Great Kursaal. This new wing was designed by Friedrich Ohmann, a representative of the Vienna Secession and a master of Art Nouveau.

○ LANDESFÜRSTLICHE BURG

The relatively small Castle in the heart of the city was built by Archduke Sigmund of Austria, at the end of the 15th century. In the 16th century, a transformation took place. The interior seems to be both Gothic and Renaissance. There are collections of weapons and a collection of historical musical instruments to be admired.

WHY VISIT IN AUTUMN? SOUTH TYROLEAN AUTUMN IS FAMOUS FOR TÖRGGELEN. THE TERM COMES FROM "TORGGL" - THE ROOM IN WHICH THE WINE PRESS STOOD. IT IS ALSO WHERE WINEMAKERS INVITE THEIR HELPERS TO A JOYOUS FEAST AFTER THE HARVEST AND CELLARING, OF COURSE WITH THE WINE FROM THEIR ESTATES. THIS GIVES RISE TO THE CUSTOM TO HIKE FROM WEINHOF TO WEINHOF THROUGH THE AUTUMN VINEYARDS, AND TASTE THE NEW VINTAGE WINES TOGETHER WITH HOME-COOKED DISHES. DO NOT MISS THE ROASTED CHESTNUTS AS A FINISHING TOUCH! AN IDEAL TÖRGGELEN AREA IS THE MIDDLE EISACKTAL. EVERY YEAR IN NOVEMBER, MERANO OFFERS MANY CULINARY DELIGHTS WITH TREATS FROM OVER 100 DELICATESSEN SHOPS. HUNDREDS OF WINE PRODUCERS FROM ITALY AND ABROAD PRESENT THEIR EXQUISITE PRODUCTS IN THE KURSAAL. THE EVENT IS A FUN MIX OF LECTURES, TASTINGS, GLORIOUS FOOD AND MUSIC.

○ STADTPFARRKIRCHE ST. NIKOLAUS

The three-aisled Gothic church rises majestically at the end of Laubengasse. At 83 metres, the tower is one of the tallest church towers in South Tyrol. In its present form, the church was consecrated in 1465. The filigree interior (altars, choir stalls) are preserved in pure Gothic style.

○ HEILIGGEISTKIRCHE

Another Gothic church, built in 1271, as a chapel for a hospital (now-defunct) outside the city walls. In the 15th century, it was destroyed in a flood of the Passer, but was rebuilt soon after. Worth seeing is the Gothic portal with a statue of the Virgin with a child; inside, frescoes represent the dramatic flood.

○ SCHLOSS TRAUTTMANSDORFF

The castle is located to the southeast, just outside Meran. The highlight is the garden surrounding the castle, in which plants species from all over the world are grown. There are: a cypress swamp; an evergreen laurel forest; a bamboo forest; and, a garden with American crops. Of course, local flora is also represented.

○ ZENOBURG

The beginning of Zenoburg dates back to the late Roman period. It was built to control access to the Passeiertal. In the Middle Ages, pilgrimages took place to the chapel dedicated to St. Zeno. In the 13th century, Count Meinhard II had the grounds fortified, which was then the seat of the Tyrolean counts for almost 100 years.

○ BOZEN

Bolzano is more than South Tyrol. The provincial capital is also Bolzano - a cappuccino is enjoyed in the sunshine on Waltherplatz, where only the best outfits are worn for the evening stroll on the Talferpromenaden or through the arbors. You'll find the Dominicans celebrate in the Giottesque Chapel in Italian, and in the Franciscan Church predominantly in German.

○ DOM

On Waltherplatz is the Bozen Cathedral - also known as the Parish Church (full name is Parish Church of the Assumption of the Virgin Mary). Since the 1960s, this House of God has also been the Bishop's Church.

Left: Winegrowing in South Tyrol goes back well into the Rhaetian past. Later, the wines were shipped in barrels to Rome. Today, South Tyrolean wines, such as Sauvignon or Pinot Noir, are selling all over the world.

Construction started in the 14th century, beginning in the Gothic style but the completion of the Bell Tower was built in late Gothic form. This captivating building with a height of 62 metres was finally completed in 1517, and is now the landmark of the city.

○ WALTHERPLATZ MONUMENT

This Monument, unveiled in 1889, is dedicated to the most important German-language lyric poet of the Middle Ages, Walther von der Vogelweide (c. 1170-1230), in the square also named after him. Supposedly the poet was a son of Tyrol. The square is lined with many boutiques, bars and cafés - this makes for a nice stroll.

GOING OUT

Bozen: Restaurant Laurin // The Laurin is the flagship of a hotel in Bolzano, and the demand for Chef Manuel Astuto and his team in the kitchen is equally high. Old recipes are reinterpreted; great emphasis is placed on the best seasonal and regional products.

// www.laurin.it

Brixen: Finsterwirt // The restaurant is one of the city's most traditional establishments - the patio garden in the courtyard, or the stylish old dining rooms, just radiate charm and style.

// www.finsterwirt.com

Meran: Saxifraga // In this restaurant you can enjoy traditional South Tyrolean cuisine complemented by some international dishes. The restaurant is located just above Merano, so you have a gorgeous view of the city and a magnificent mountain scenery from its terrace.

// www.saxifraga.it

In Bolzano, an oasis of unexpected beauty can be found. The largest promenades are here on the banks of the Talfer, towards the Waltherplatz (top right). It is busy in the morning at Obstplatz, and leisurely in the evening at Gerbergasse (bottom right).

○ BOZNER LAUBEN

On the main shopping street, historical arcades stretch from east to west through the Old Town of Bolzano. The narrow town houses along the street are mostly from the late Gothic era. They are delightfully decorated with frescoes and stone carvings, and all have enchanting bay windows. Quaint boutiques and numerous shops will entice you to take a closer look. Some buildings are lavishly decorated, such as the Baroque house No. 46. The house No. 30 with its pointed Gothic arcades has on the eaves a gargoyle in the form of a dragon.

○ SOUTH TIROL ARCHAEOLOGICAL MUSEUM

The "Ötzi Museum" is home to the 5,000 year old "Man from the Ice", being the oldest and most famous "South Tyrolean" from the Copper Age. It also boasts many interesting facts about the early history of the country, as well as back to pre-historic times.

○ BRESSANONE

With its arbors and the cathedral visible from afar, the more than 1,000-year-old city of Bressanone, at the crossing of Eisack and Rienz, will immediately enchant

you. In the 16th century, it became the seat of an independent ecclesiastical principal which, in the following years, struggled for existence against the neighbouring county of Tyrol. The city is also the second campus of the Free University of Bozen-Bolzano.

○ **CATHEDRAL AND CLOISTER**

The cathedral - the full name is "The Assumption of Mary and St. Cassian" - is the largest church in the city. The Baroque three-nave building was constructed from 1745 to 1754 on the remains of a previous Romanesque building. The cloister adjoining the cathedral with its 20 arches is a place of silence, but also a masterpiece of historical art. Fifteen arcades are adorned with frescoes from the 14th and 15th centuries. A point of great curiousity here is the bizarre-looking representation of an elephant in the third arcade.

○ **HOFBURG**

The most impressive part of the Hofburg Palace, which was once the residence of the Bishop of Bressanone, is probably the south side courtyard with its three-storey Renaissance arcades. German Emperors stayed in the splendidly equipped Imperial Wing when their journey took them through South Tyrol. The Bishop's wind is conservative, but richly decorated.

SHOPPING

○ **FRUIT MARKET**

For more than 7 centuries, this green market in the Old Town has been providing Bozner with fresh produces and delicacies. It is also a meeting place for people from Bolzano, tourists and travellers. The market's hustle and bustle prevails in front of and behind the stalls, which are lushly laden with fruits, vegetables, a variety of sausages, and fresh flowers.

○ **RUNGGALDIER IN MERAN**

The Runggaldier family has been selling costumes, fabrics and accessories for more than 100 years.

// www.trachten-runggaldier.com

WHERE TO STAY

Meran: Villa Tivoli // A modern and very well-renovated house from the old Austrian glory days of Merans. Located on the western outskirt below the promenade Tappeinerweg, there are stylish rooms and suites; a large outdoor pool (rock lagoon), and a lush garden with Mediterranean flora. **// www.villativoli.it**

Bozen: Figl // Right in the heart of the Old Town, the house has been stylishly renovated and it has 22 comfortable rooms and suites. Parking is close by at the Walther underground car park.

// www.figl.net/en

Brixen: Hotel Elephant // The flagship of Brixen's hotels. This is a traditionally designed hotel with beautiful wood-panelled dining rooms, antique furniture in guestrooms, and a fine-cuisine restaurant for the guests to indulge in.

// www.hotelelephant.com

NOT TO BE MISSED

RELAX IN THE THERMAL WATER

If there is no thermal water, then it will be drilled for. As deep and costly as necessary, even if it reaches to the earths molten core, the healing water for the Spa Town of Merano is a must, and for South Tyrol's administration, money is not a concern. The place began here in 1837, after the suggestions of a Habsburg personal physician. The heart of the spa complex is enclosed by a huge glass cube, with a view extending to the imposing, snow-capped mountains in winter. The health resort is fed with Radon-rich water from the nearby mountains, and with a multitude of fitness and spa programs, spending some time here will certainly benefit both body and soul.

DRINK WHISKY

Who would have thought that Italy has a whiskey distillery? It has been in existence only since 2012. The South Tyrolean Highland Malt, which is being distilled in the PUNI distillery in Glurns in the Vinschgau, has already received some prizes for its quality!

ADMIRE MODERN ART IN MUSEION VON BOZEN

This museum displays contemporary international art from local artists. The collection focuses on works in the field of writing. Also impressive is the glass building, which connects the new and the old town via a bridge, and it lights up at night.

MARVEL AT THE SKY IN THE GUMMER OBSERVATORY

Near Bolzano, in Obergummer bei Steinegg, it can be spotted from afar placed on a hill between Eggental and Tierser Valley, and it is the largest public observatory in Italy. Particularly notable is also the Solar Observatory, which is equipped with state-of-the-art computer-controlled technology, including an 80-centimetre reflector telescope.

#40 SYLT

SYLT IS GERMANY'S MOST NORTHERN ISLAND AND THE SEASIDE RESORT LIST ON SYLT IS THE NORTHERNMOST MUNICIPALITY IN GERMANY. BUT SYLT IS NOT JUST AN ISLAND. IT IS ALSO A WAY OF LIFE. SYLT RECONNECTS YOU WITH MOTHER NATURE. IT HAS 40 KILOMETRES OF SANDY BEACHES, PLUS THE SOMETIMES UP TO 30-METRE-HIGH SAND DUNES BEHIND THE GREEN MARRAM GRASSES, AND TWELVE BEAUTIFUL LOCATIONS THAT YOU CAN VISIT. 8,000 YEARS AGO, THE ISLAND WAS SEPARATED DURING A FLOOD FROM THE MAINLAND, AND IN 1927 IT WAS CONNECTED AGAIN BY THE HINDENBURGDAMM. SINCE THEN, SYLT HAS WELCOMED UP TO 650,000 VISITORS EACH YEAR TO THE 38.5-KILOMETRE-LONG AND BETWEEN 350 AND 1,200 METRES WIDE ISLAND. WHILE THE WIND ON THE WEST COAST PROPELS THE NORTH SEA TO THE COAST, ON THE EASTERN SIDE MILLIONS OF SEA CREATURES LIVE PER SQUARE METER ON THE WADDEN SEA SOIL, ENJOYING THE QUIET SIDE OF THE NORTH SEA, KNOWN AS THE THE WADDEN SEA NATIONAL PARK.

Above: Sylt shows itself at its best when the sun is setting on the Red Cliff.

Left: Sometimes this landscape exudes great calm, and then again it is often literally whipped by the raging elements. While the seemingly endless panorama is already impressive, you will be captivated by its weather and wild wind. All this is Sylt and much more.

○ **ELLENBOGEN**

Sylt's northern tip is also Germany's most northern state. The peninsula, whose shape is reminiscent of an arm bent at the elbow, is perfect for a long leisurely walk. Between the dunes that are covered with billowing tall grasses rises two charming lighthouses, List Ost and List West, offering a great photo opportunity.

○ **WANDERING DUNES IN LISTLAND**

The last of the shifting sand dunes that make up the south and north of the island from the 19th century, are now protected and only accessible through hiking paths.

○ **ERLEBNISZENTRUM NATURGEWALTEN**

The Natural Forces Adventure Centre is a new, state-of-the-art museum in List on Sylt, which makes the natural forces that prevail in the national park come alive. In the "storm room", for example, you can brace yourself against the wind, create waves yourself, or watch mussels and crabs tunnel into the mud flats.

○ **BRADERUPER HEIDE**

A dream for nature lovers: in the huge heathland, which blooms beautifully in the summer months, grows numerous heather and rare plants such as Arnica and Marsh Gentian. Free-ranging flocks of sheep care for the protected landscape.

○ **DENGHOOG**

The burial chamber from the Stone Age is one of the most important of its kind in Northern Europe. It can be explored but you will need to grovel low to the ground to admire this burial site.

○ **ROTES KLIFF**

There is a hiking trail, which also leads past the "Red

WHY VISIT IN AUTUMN? WORLD CUP SYLT: AT THE END OF SEPTEMBER, THE BRANDENBURG BEACH IS AGAIN THE STAGE FOR THE WORLD'S TOP SURFERS. ON THE PENULTIMATE STAGE OF THE PWA WORLD TOUR, AROUND 100 ATHLETES WILL COMPETE IN THE SURF DISCIPLINES WAVE, FREESTYLE AND SLALOM. THE BEST VIEW OF THE SHOW IS FROM THE PROMENADE, WHERE YOU WILL ALSO FIND GASTRONOMIC DELIGHTS AND SIDE PROGRAMS.

Cliff" that you can follow. The path takes you all the way to the top of the up to 30-metre-high and four-kilometre-long cliff edge between Wenningstedt and Kampen. It shines surprisingly red due to its iron-rich clay. The small brick lighthouse at the top is one of Sylt's landmarks.

○ VOGELKOJE KAMPEN

What sounds so harmless was until 1921 a huge duck trap. Wild ducks fell into the trap, which were considered a delicacy in the 19th century. Today, the area is a fishing pond and a museum.

○ SYLT AQUARIUM IN WESTERLAND

Stingrays, cat sharks, octopuses and colourful corals can be admired in this aquarium with its 20-metre-long panorama tunnel. You are truly at eye level with these sea dwellers.

○ OLD FRISIAN HOUSE IN KEITUM

An experience in time warp. When you walk through the door of this captain's house built in 1739 in Keitum, you will find yourself transported to a bygone world. Furniture and household goods from the 18th and 19th centuries bring the old times back to life.

Above: Very pretty and in original form, the Frisian houses in the idyllic Keitum with their thatched roofs, brick walls and blue and white painted doors.

Top left: The North Sea island of Sylt is the German mecca of windsurfing. This location off Westerland is often used as a venue for international competitions.

Bottom left: In the aquarium of Westerland you can learn about the underwater world of the North Sea while keeping your feet dry.

CHURCH ST. SEVERIN IN KEITUM

The church tower used to serve as an orientation guide for the sailors and also as a prison for the Keitumers. Fortunately, these times are long gone. An important date for music lovers to visit the church is Wednesday for live music.

MORSUM-CLIFF

The imposing cliff on the east of the island is an important geological feature, because millions of years of strata are stored here not horizontally, but vertically. In addition, rare plants have been found in the area. You can discover these exciting facts via a guided tour.

SYLT LOCAL HISTORY MUSEUM

Whale bones as garden gate. Indeed, Keitum museum offers many exciting local historical facts and experiences of this island's life over the past centuries.

STONE AGE GRAVES HARHOOG AND TIPKENHOOG

The cemetery Harhoog from the Neolithic period was relocated twice. Now it is right next to the grave of the Giant Tipken, who guarded the island from here until a Dane struck him down.

RANTUMBECKEN

Created by the National Socialists as a water airport, the basin is today a unique bird sanctuary.

HÖRNUM-ODDE

Here you can go for a wonderful walk and enjoy the stunning landscape, but the constant erosion has endangered the southern tip of the island.

LIGHTHOUSE AND HARBOUR HÖRNUM

From Sylt's most southern town is where several excursions start. By boat you can reach numerous neighbouring islands from Hörnum Harbour; on foot it goes from Hörnum's Beach in the Odde. Moreover, Hörnum's picturesque lighthouse is open to visitors and guarantees a spectacular view of the island.

GOING OUT

Gosch Lister Fischhaus // If you are looking for a delicious fish roll, then you must visit the cult fish stalls of Gosch. In addition to the homely snacks, the on-site fish restaurant in List's Old Boats Hall offers fine delicacies with everything the sea has to offer.

// www.gosch.de

Sansibar in Rantum // Brunch in the middle of the sand dunes? Or, enjoy a romantic evening dining with wonderfully soft sand under your feet? That's possible at Sansibar.

// www.sansibar.de

Westerland: Alte Friesenstube // Authentic, comfortable, and warm atmosphere. Here you can enjoy roasted duck and typical Frisian dishes. The historic thatched house from 1648 just oozes pure Sylt charm.

// altefriesenstube.de

Right: The mecca for geologists is the Morsum Cliff. This 2-kilometre-long section of the Sylt cliff is in the east near the village Morsum. Here it is revealed how many and which layers of rock the base of Sylt Island sits on.

SHOPPING

○ **ALTE TONNENHALLE IN LIST**

The old warehouse has becomes a shopping mall – where buoys and boats used to be stored are now a variety of shops. You can find souvenirs, clothing, home accessories, books, and much more, luring tourists and locals to the north of the island.

○ **STRÖNWAI IN KAMPEN**

This is known as "Sylt's Luxury Mile" – many luxury, high-end brands such as Louis Vuitton and Chopard can be found here. Rows of luxury boutiques join the next. A well-deserved break is in Gogärtchen, which serves a delicious and affordable menu.

○ **FRIEDRICHSTRASSE IN WESTERLAND**

Westerland's main shopping street leads from the train station to the beach promenade. Clothes, souvenirs, delicacies, home accessories – here you will find everything your heart desires. Incidentally, Friedrichstrasse also has the island's oldest department store, H.B. Jensen, which has provided locals and tourists with everything necessary for more than 160 years.

○ **TEA HOUSE ERNST JANSSEN**

The Family Janssen from Westerland have specialized themselves in high-quality organic tea. The ingredients are harvest-fresh and the combinations are divine. A must buy from this shop is the "Sylt Frisian Mix" - to remind you of your time in Sylt or perfect as a gift.

GOING OUT

○ **AMRUM**

Sand as far as the eye can see! Amrum is a paradise for sandcastle building, beach jogging, sun worshipers and flying kites. The wide beach stretches along the entire west and south coast. For tea, it's time to visit Nebel. The oldest village of the island is enchanting with its thatched cottages and fascinating little streets.

Left: A lot of green, and ample white too – that's how you will recognize Amrum. In the centre, you'll find a glacial moraine ridge covered with forest and heathland. West of it sand dunes have settled over time with a much finer sand.

WHERE TO STAY

Keitum: Benen-Diken-Hof // Live in a Frisian country house with a family atmosphere and still have a lovely wellness program? If you want to spend a first-class night in Keitum, this privately-run holiday home is the right place for you.

// www.benen-diken-hof.de

Wenningstedt: Hotel Marcussen // Each apartment and bungalow has its own garden with beach chairs. The more than 100-year-old guesthouse in Wenningstedt-Braderup exudes real Sylt charm and leaves nothing to be desired.

// www.aparthotel-marcussen.de

Westerland: Alter Konsumverein // The apartments in this over 100 year old house are lovingly furnished. Each apartment has a kitchen and a living area with everything you need for a comfortable stay in Sylt.

// www.alterkonsumverein-sylt.de

NOT TO BE MISSED

INDULGE IN COFFEE AND CAKE IN THE KUPFERKANNE

This former bunker was found by refugee writer and turned into a cult café. This is the short version of the exciting story of the "Copper Can". The cakes here are delicious and their self-roasted coffee is legendary.

TAKE A WALK ON THE MUDFLATS

Of course, you can explore the mudflats on your own. But do not underestimate the dangers as there are sea fog, mud holes and strong currents. Therefore, joining a guided group is safer, and you will learn so much more about this area.

RELAX IN A BEACH CHAIR

Nowhere is it as easy to relax as in a beach chair (more sofa-like) and with the softest sand caressing your bare feet. There are 12,000 chairs available on the beach, but if you want to play it safe, make reservations before you get to Sylt. In October, decommissioned chairs will be auctioned off.

TRY THE SALT MEADOW LAMB

The Sylt's salt meadow lamb spends his entire life in the good salt sea air and feeds exclusively on natural herbs and grass - and this you can taste. Many good restaurants serve this delicious specialty.

TAKE A BIKE TOUR OVER THE ISLAND

If you want to feel the cool breeze gently hitting your face while admiring the stunning landscape, riding a bike from one end of the coast to another is a must. The bike tour will also allow you to cover more distance than walking.

#41   TALLINN

EXQUISITE CHURCHES AND NOBLE PATRICIAN HOUSES, THE FORTIFIED CITY WALLS AND THE IMPOSING TOWN HALL TESTIFY TO THE RICH HISTORY OF THE ESTONIAN CAPITAL LOCATED IN THE GULF OF FINLAND. THE HISTORIC CENTRE OF TALLINN, THE OLD REVAL (UNTIL 1918), IS CONSIDERED TO BE AN OUTSTANDING EXAMPLE OF A NORTHERN EUROPEAN TRADING AND PORT CITY OF THE MIDDLE AGES, AND THE ENTIRE OLD TOWN IS A UNESCO WORLD HERITAGE SITE. THE ORIGIN OF THIS CITY LEAD BACK TO 12TH/13TH CENTURY, WHEN ON DOMBERG FIRST A CHURCH AND THEN A CASTLE STOOD. THE SETTLEMENT BELOW DEVELOPED IN THE LATE MIDDLE AGES TO A LEADING HANSEATIC CITY, WHOSE UPPER CLASS WAS COMPOSED MAINLY OF GERMAN-BORN MERCHANTS. THE COMPLEX OF THE OLD TOWN WITH ITS SQUARES, STREETS AND WINDING ALLEYWAYS AS WELL AS NUMEROUS ARCHITECTURAL MONUMENTS STILL REMINDS OF THE CITY'S GOLDEN AGE OF COMMERCE.

Above: The centre of the Old Town of Tallinn is the sprawling Rathaus-Square with its numerous historical buildings.

Left: In the Middle Ages, the city founded by the Danes on the Baltic Sea became a centre of the Hanseatic League. Tallinn's former golden age still bears witness to many merchant houses and churches. Here you can see Karlskirche in the foreground.

○ OLD TOWN

Charming cobblestone streets meander through the Old Town and finish at the medieval marketplace. Narrow side lanes lead to many enchanting backyards, which are beautifully planted in the summer. Between brick walls and barns are left and right decorated restored gabled houses in white and cream. A good 80 percent of them are still in their original form from the 11th century. In the evening, historic street lamps give a very special atmosphere. Bars, restaurants and boutiques lure you to stroll and linger. The "White Nights" are magical in the summer, when life flourishes in the streets. The ancient, nearly 2 kilometres long city wall with 26 standing towers protects the city centre.

○ MARKET SQUARE AND TOWN HALL

For centuries, the Town Hall Square in the middle of the Old Town is a popular meeting place for locals. Surrounded by historical town houses, it is dominated by the Gothic style Town Hall (1404), which to-day still excudes the pride of the citizen, and also of the Hanseatic self-discipline. There is no glamour, but a confident simplicity, crowned by a striking tower. High up is the "Old Thomas", bearer of the weather vane and a landmark of the city. In the basement vaults, the history of the monument is documented. Another attraction is the historic town pharmacy "Ratsapotheke", which has been in operation since 1422 and is an inspiration with its display of ancient remedies. A reliable recommendation for a good restaurant in the city centre is "Silver Spoon" which constantly wins several gastronomic awards every year.

○ ALEXANDER-NEWSKI-KATHEDRALE

The Alexander Nevsky Cathedral sets a distinct accent in the city's landscape with its red and white façade and five onion-shaped domes. Tsar Alexander III ordered in 1894 to build the church in an area dedicated to Martin Luther. After the independence of Russia, all memories of the occupiers were to be removed, and the extravagant domed structure was to be demolished. But, luckily, it did not get to that point. The Russian Orthodox Church was named after the Prince of Novgorod, Alexander Yaroslavitz Nevsky, a Russian national hero who had defeated the German Knights in the Ice Battle of 1242. When the eleven bells ring, the whole city rings. The bells ensemble is the most powerful of all Tallinn's churches; the heaviest bell weighs 16 tons!

SHOPPING

○ OMA ASI

This is a budget accommodation located right in the city centre, and a great way to explore the Old Town: The National Opera is only 300 metres away, and the castle on the Domberg 500 metres from the hotel. The courtyard of the hotel is also excellent.

// www.omaasi.com

○ EESTI KÄSITÖÖ KODU

In this house of Estonian craftsmen, you can buy original handmade goods. Whether made of wood, textile or metal - the best of the local masters can be found here all in one place.

// folkart.ee/en

○ DEPOO

If you are hungry after all of your shopping, you should visit the Depoo in the creative centre Telliskivi. Here, in addition to fashion shops, are all kinds of delicious local street foods to try. A secret tip for coffee lovers is Café Renard.

WHERE TO STAY

The Three Sisters // This five-star boutique hotel is located in the middle of the Old Town of Tallinn. The medieval core of the house meets state-of-the-art equipment and design. The hotel has a gourmet restaurant.

// www.3s.ee

Boutique Hotel Schlössle // No one less than Queen Elisabeth II signed the guest book in 2006. The premises preserve the charm of a medieval residence, with the designer Jean Pierre Martel giving it the final modern touch.

// www.schloesslehotel.com

Villa Hortensia // This is a budget accommodation located right in the city centre, and a great way to explore the Old Town: The National Opera is only 300 metres, the castle on the Domberg 500 metres from the hotel. The courtyard of the hotel is also a nice place to relax.

// www.hoov.ee/villa-hortensia

GOING OUT

Sauna-Straße in the old Town // This street has some of the best cocktail bars in the city. Go for a drinks or two at the "Sigmund Freud", the "Frank", or the "Sazerac".

Rataskaevu 16 // Although it is located direct in the Old Town, this restaurant is not overly crowded with tourists, and you actually dine with many locals. The home-made bread is a hit. In summer, you can sit outside on the terrace.

// rataskaevu16.ee

NOT TO BE MISSED

WATCH THE MIGRATORY BIRDS GATHERING

It is estimated that 50 million migratory birds migrate annually through Estonia, on their way to the Arctic and back. Many of them rest along the enchanting coastline with its bays, estuaries and islands. Most tourists travel to the Matsalu National Park, southwest of Tallinn, which attracts 10,000 to 20,000 Gray Cranes and houses seven watchtowers. You can also go east on your own and travel to the Lahemaa National Park on the Parispea Peninsula. The park is one of the best places in Northern Europe to spot migrating Arctic waterbirds, counting up to 100,000 geese; 250,000 ducks; and, tens of thousands of Pochards and Scoters. Other great places to watch are the harbour of Virtsu, the Bay at Kurressaare and Ristna on the Island of Hiiumaa.

STROLL THROUGH KALAMAJA

Typical colourful wooden houses, but yet trendy with a special artististic flair. These are former factory buildings converted into cool cafés. This former fishing district has become a hip area and is definitely worth a visit.

ADMIRE ART IN KUMU

The Art Museum was opened in 2006 and mainly exhibits Estonian works from the 18th century to the present day. Modern works of art from all over the world can be seen in various exhibitions. The museum building alone is a work of art in itself - the seven-storey semi-circular glass building blends harmoniously into its surroundings.

VISIT THE CREATIVE CENTRE TELLISKIVI

What can become of an old factory site? The Telliskivi is considered one of the hippest addresses in the city. There are workshops, studios and offices. Cultural programs are held regularly and there is a flea market every Saturday.

WINTER

*The cold weather creates peculiar structures on the shores of Lake Geneva, allowing
the city skyline of Geneva to shine in the cosy glow of the lights.*

#42   BERLIN

THE GERMAN CAPITAL HAS ALWAYS BEEN A MAGNET FOR TOURISTS AND, SINCE THE REUNIFICATION, IT HAS DEVELOPED INTO AN ABSOLUTE HOTSPOT FOR VISITORS. YOU'LL BE ATTRACTED BY THE VAST COLLECTIONS OF ART, THE NEW BUILDINGS IN THE GOVERNMENT DISTRICT AROUND THE REICHSTAG OR IN OLD URBAN AREAS SUCH AS THE POTSDAMER SQUARE, AS WELL AS BY THE PARKS IN THE CITY CENTRE AND, LAST BUT NOT LEAST, BY THE CREATIVE YOUNG SCENE IN DISTRICTS SUCH AS THE CENTRE, PRENZLAUER BERG, FRIEDRICHSAIN AND KREUZBERG.

Left: Since the 3rd of October 1969, Berlin's tallest structure at 368 metres, has been located in the centre of the city. Planned as a national transmitter, the central location is said to have been decided on by the State Council Chairman Walter Ulbricht: as an unmistakable symbol of socialist will to build. In only 40 seconds, an elevator brings visitors to the rotating café, situated at 207.5 metres height.

Right: The Reichstag Building, in the Republic Square: since 1999, it has been the seat of the German Parliament. With its glass dome, the fundamentally redesigned building has quickly become one of the main attractions Berlin has to offer.

○ BRANDENBURGER TOR

It is the emblem of Berlin, it was the symbol of the division and, today, it stands as a symbol for the unity of Germany: the 26-metre high and 65-metre wide Brandenburg Gate, which completes the grand boulevard Unter den Linden with five passages to the west. For the older generation, it is still amazing that it is possible to behold the gate from both sides. The only surviving city gate is today the focus of Berlin's party mile.

○ REICHSTAG

As early as the German Empire and during the Weimar Republic, today's seat of government was a centre of power. For a guided tour that includes the visiting of the glass dome, it is for the best to register. Obviously, you have the best view from up high – and so became the Reichstag dome, which was placed on an existent building by the star architect, Norman Foster, one of the most beloved touristic attractions of Berlin.

○ MUSEUM ISLAND

A concentration of high-class museums can be found on the headland of the Spree River: Pergamon Museum, Old and New Museum, Collection of Classical Antiquities, Museum of Pre- and Early History and other institutions are located in five magnificent buildings.

○ EAST SIDE GALLERY

A few months after the fall of the Berlin Wall, 118 artists from 21 countries painted a section of the wall in Berlin's Friedrichshain. Thus, the biggest open air gallery of the world came into being.

○ CHECKPOINT CHARLIE

A checkpoint replica reminds of the former border location, between the American and the Soviet sectors of the city, on Friedrichstraße.

○ JEWISH MUSEUM BERLIN

This museum is worth visiting simply because of the new construction designed by Daniel Libeskind. The permanent exhibition is dedicated to the two thousand years of German-Jewish history.

○ HOLOCAUST MEMORIAL

Not far from the Brandenburg Gate, there is an always accessible field of pillars, commemorating the Jews killed throughout Europe. The centre below the pillars is informative and moving.

○ POTSDAMER SQUARE

It is more than a square – it is a gigantic area filled with new buildings, full of splendour and glass. Architects compete here for the boldest buildings, and thus, you get to see numerous ambitious, transparent buildings, from which perhaps the most impressive is the Sony Centre with its tented roof construction.

WHY VISIT IN WINTER? THE COLD IS PART OF IT. BUT MAYBE NOTHING ILLUSTRATES THE VALUE OF THE BERLIN FILM FESTIVAL BETTER THAN WHEN THE FILM STARS, DESPITE ICY TEMPERATURES, POSE IN EXCITING EVENING CLOTHES IN FRONT OF THE BERLIN PALACE IN THE POTSDAM SQUARE AND GREET THE FANS THAT HAVE COME, PATIENTLY WAITING FOR HOURS IN THE LONG LINES AT THE TICKET OFFICES. THE BERLIN FILM FESTIVAL IS, LIKE THE ONES IN CANNES AND VENICE, ONE OF THE MOST IMPORTANT ONES WORLDWIDE. WITH AROUND HALF A MILLION SPECTATORS, IT IS THE WORLD'S LARGEST PUBLIC FESTIVAL. NUMEROUS CINEMAS TAKE PART AROUND THE CITY, ALTHOUGH THE MAIN FOCUS IS THE CENTRE, AROUND THE POTSDAM SQUARE. TICKETS ARE AVAILABLE THREE DAYS IN ADVANCE AT NUMEROUS CENTRALIZED SALE OFFICES.

○ CULTURE FORUM

A collection of cultural institutions has evolved at the Potsdam Square, many of which are housed in architecturally interesting buildings, such as the philharmonic or the new national gallery.

○ CHARLOTTENBURG CASTLE

The largest, most beautiful castle in Berlin has a yellow façade of a record-breaking width of 505 metres, with a centrepiece crowned by a multi-level tower with a decorative copper dome. The castle is the work of several architects and has been expanded many times, yet its architecture is very uniform. Inside, you can visit various rooms of the palace as well as the Museum of Pre- and Early History. In front of the castle stands the imposing equestrian statue of the Great Electoral Prince, created by Andreas Schlüter.

○ KURFÜRSTENDAMM

Tourists know the so-called Ku'damm as a promenade. But the street, which was built in 1542, was once the connecting route of the electors from the town to the hunting castle.

○ MEMORIAL CHURCH

One of Berlin's landmarks is the Memorial Church of Emperor Wilhelm, which was built at the end of the 19th century and bombed in 1943. It was not rebuilt, but an altar was added in 1961, which shines a magical blue light on the inside due to the thousands of small windows that ornate it, thus making it a quite soothing place to rest in the otherwise hectic Breitscheid Square.

○ UNTER DEN LINDEN

The gorgeous boulevard leads to numerous important sights. These include the Brandenburg Gate, the State Opera, the Museum Island, the cathedral and the armoury.

○ PRENZLAUER BERG

The neighbourhood in the north of Berlin is mainly known for its international restaurants and bars. The cultural life, from music to theatre, is also important.

○ BERLIN WALL MEMORIAL

The border right through the centre of the Bernauer Street. The Berlin Wall memorial reminds us of its

Left: for the opening of the Film Festival, the Musical Theatre in the Potsdam Square is turned into a Berlinale Palace every year. As is the case with film screenings for visitors from all over the world, the arrival of the actors at the opening of the Berlinale causes a major gathering of the public.

story with films, an exhibition and a documentation centre.

○ THE NIKOLAI DISTRICT

The Nikolai district presents itself as pretty and old – it was largely rebuilt in 1987 for the 750th anniversary of the city of Berlin. Old houses from other places were brought here, and new ones were added, made to look old with gables and oriel windows – a beautiful illusion of an old town and a pleasant district for a stroll. In the centre, there are also authentic old buildings, cafés and restaurants, as well as the two-tower Nikolai Church.

○ TELEVISION TOWER AND ALEXANDER SQUARE

The "Alex" is located in the middle of the capital. The world clock is a popular photo subject. The sec-

ond highlight is the television tower, Germany's highest building, 368-metres tall.

○ GENDARMENMARKT

With its ensemble of classicist buildings such as the Theatre, the German and the French Cathedral, the Gendarmenmarkt is probably the most beautiful square in Berlin. At its centre, facing the theatre, is the statue of Friedrich Schiller, surrounded by allegorical figures from poetry, drama, philosophy and history.

○ HACKESCHE COURTYARDS

The largest and most beautiful courtyard complex in the centre of Berlin: A huge building complex with

Top right: Like Siamese twins: you can recognize the area named after it by the unusual towers of the Nikolai Church. Berlin's oldest religious building originated from a roman stone basilica that was consecrated in 1230 by Saint Nicolaus, the patron saint of sailors and merchants.

Lower right: The Gendarmenmarkt is dominated by three imposing buildings: the German Cathedral, the former Royal Theatre (centre), which is now used as a concert hall, and the French Cathedral (on the right).

GOING OUT

Jedermann's // Just a stone's throw away from the Museum Island, this place lures in the locals with lavish breakfasts and its home-style kitchen.

// **jedermanns.berlin**

Facil // Gourmet restaurant in the Potsdam Square, housed on the 5th floor of the Mandala Hotel. The special highlight, in addition to the excellent French cuisine: during the summer, the glass roof of the restaurant can be easily pushed aside

// **www.facil.de**

Fischschuppen // "Fresh on the table" is the motto of the Friedrichshain fish shop and restaurant. Whether for cooking at home or consuming freshly prepared in the guest room with its wood panelling and maritime touch – fresh fish is the trump card here

// **www.fischschuppen-berlin.de**

apartments, studios, boutiques, shops, restaurants, cinemas and galleries that are grouped around a total of eight courtyards. Al were built at the beginning of the 20th century, decorated with beautiful Art Nouveau elements and adorned with colourful glazed tiles, and have since been restored lovingly and lavishly.

○ THE BEBEL SQUARE

In the middle of the architecturally charming square, the underground memorial to the book burnings can be seen through a glass plate.

Left: Nothing can be seen from the outside, the stucco façade was already taken down in 1961, but those who enter the Hackesche Courtyards enjoy a sparkling reception: golden, blue and green glazed bricks, burned in the traditional manner, arranged in dynamic patterns, along with high windows and the curved roof lines which draw people to the yard.

SHOPPING

○ LAFAYETTE GALLERIES

Parisian shopping in the middle of Berlin: five floors built around a dazzling cone of light. And the products on offer: elegant French fashion and accessories, international cosmetics, a French bookstore and, of course, an excellent food department can be found here.

// www.galerieslafayette.de

○ KADEWE

The Kaufhaus Des Westens, that was opened in 1907 has always been a shopping temple in a class of its own. Every Berlin tourist should visit the gourmet floor and one of the four champagne bars.

// www.kadewe.de

○ GROBER UNFUG (GREAT MISCHIEF)

Probably the best sorted comic shop in Germany. Current series from all over the world, as well as old treasures can be found here.

// www.groberunfug.de

○ FLEA MARKET AT THE ZOO

The largest, most popular and best visited flea market in Berlin. It also has an attached market for handicrafts.

WHERE TO STAY

Art Luise Kunsthotel // Friends of art are attracted by the restored, classicist city palace from 1825, which first started receiving guests in 1995 as the "Luise Home for Artists". Over 50 artists gave the rooms their personal artistic touch and created a habitable work of art.

// **www.luise-berlin.com**

Hotel Adlon Kempinski // A luxury hotel in a class of its own and certainly one of the best-known hotels in Germany. The Adlon, one of the first addresses of Berlin, lies directly in the Paris Square

// **www.hotel-adlon.de**

Art Nouveau // A mix of old and modern in a Art Nouveau building near the Kurfürstendamm. Individual and colourfully designed interiors.

// **www.hotelartnouveau.de**

NOT TO BE MISSED

PLUNGING INTO BERLIN'S NIGHTLIFE, WHETHER IN PUBS, BEER GARDENS OR CELLAR CLUBS

The Berlin nightlife is as diverse as the city itself. Venture to the East Harbour with the Watergate techno temple or to the Savigny Square where you'll find the Quasimodo jazz club! The latest nightlife spot is Kreuzkölln between Kreuzberg and Neukölln.

GOING UP INTO THE TELEVISION TOWER AND SEEING THE WHOLE OF BERLIN FROM ABOVE

The Sphere restaurant is found at a height of 207 meters. It revolves around its own axis in one hour. Haute cuisine garnished with a dream view and piano background music starting at 19 o'clock.

EAT AN ORIGINAL BERLINER CURRYWURST

The Berliner currywurst is fried in oil without the skin. The best one can be enjoyed at the traditional Konnopke's Imbiss on the Schönhauser Avenue, at Curry36 in the Bahnhof Zoo or try the organic version at Witty's in Witenberg Square.

GO ON A TRABI SAFARI AND FEEL YOURSELF TRANSPORTED BACK IN TIME

You can drive the iconic Trabant yourself and feel yourself transported back to the time of East Germany, while following the guide. You will get a lot of information about the experience along the way. A number of tours are offered.

DRINKING A BERLINER WEISSE IN THE BEER GARDEN OF THE ZOO

In reality, the Berliner Weisse is a white beer type, but it is, however, mainly ordered mixed, with raspberry or woodruff lemonade. You can try one in the greenery of the zoo, in the Schleusenkrug or in the café in Neuen See.

#43   GENEVA

"GENEVA IS THE FIRST AND RICHEST CITY IN SWITZERLAND, WITH THE CHARACTER OF AN AUTHENTIC METROPOLIS". THIS WAS HOW GENEVA WAS DESCRIBED BY THE GERMAN PEDAGOGUE AND WRITER AUGUST WILHELM GRUBE, IN HIS GEOGRAPHY BOOK FROM 1868. EVEN AT THAT TIME, GENEVA STOOD OUT FROM THE REST OF THE WORLD WITH ITS EXCEPTIONAL OPENNESS. TODAY, GENEVA IS THE CULTURAL AND ECONOMIC CENTRE OF WESTERN SWITZERLAND, WITH OVER 200 INTERNATIONAL ORGANIZATIONS BEING ACTIVE HERE. NEVERTHELESS, THE CITÉ, AS THE HISTORIC CENTRE IS CALLED, HAS MANAGED TO PRESERVE A LOT OF ITS ORIGINALITY. THE SYMBOL OF THE CITY IS THE 140-METRE HIGH JET D'EAU, THE WATER FOUNTAIN IN THE YACHT HARBOUR. DESPITE ITS SURPRISINGLY SCENIC LANDSCAPE, THE GENOVESE COUNTRY BACKDROP IS RELATIVELY UNKNOWN, DESPITE IT BEING THE THIRD BIGGEST WINE-GROWING DISTRICT IN SWITZERLAND AFTER VALAIS AND VAUD.

Above: The buildings of renowned hotels and financial institutions border Quai street in the yacht harbour. In the past decades, the historic centre (cité) has been restored and, today, it awaits its visitors with numerous restaurants and bistros.

Left: The landmark of the city is the famous Jet d'Eau

Right: The interior of the Genovese Cathedral is rather straighforward and uncomplicated.

○ ST. PIERRE CATHEDRAL

The three-aisled pillar basilica in Geneva, that was built between 1150 and 1232, was, until 1536, the seat of the Catholic Church. In the Reformation period, it was turned into Jean Calvin's Maintenance Centre and main church for the Protestants, who took out the Catholic decor. During the Calvinist period of austerity, the majestic wonder first shone in the Romanesque style, later on, completed, in the early Gothic style. Both of the unfinished main towers were added in the 13th century, the classicistic pillared portico in 1750, the metallic steeple in 1895. The seat of Calvin is worth seeing, also the carved choir stalls and the tomb of the Huguenots chief, Henri de Rohan (1579 -1638). A steep spiral staircase leads to the north tower, which offers a splendid view from above. In a museum under the cathedral, you will find many local archaeological findings.

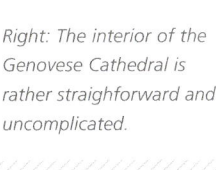

WHY VISIT IN WINTER? PERHAPS JUST TO HAVE A GOOD REASON TO EAT CHOCOLATE BEFORE CHRISTMAS? AT THE BIGGEST CITY FESTIVAL IN GENEVA, L'ESCALADE, PEOPLE GATHERS TO SMASH A MARZIPAN-FILLED "CHOCOLATE MARMITE" (CHOCOLATE CAULDRON) TO COMMEMORATE THE DEFENCE OF THE CITY AGAINST THE ATTACK LED BY THE DUKE OF SAVOY ON 11TH OF DECEMBER 1602. THE LEGEND IS THAT THE INVASION WAS AVERTED WHEN A HOUSEWIFE UPENDED A "L'ESCALADE MARMITE" (A CAULDRON FILLED WITH HOT CHOCOLATE) ON AN INVADING SOLDIER AND THEN RAISED THE ALARM. THERE IS ALSO A TORCH-LIGHT PROCESSION, AN EIGHT-KILO-METRE WALK THROUGH THE HISTORIC PART OF THE OLD TOWN, AS WELL AS A COSTUME PROCESSION.

Left: The Fête de l'Escalade, the historic public festival taking place in December, is all about chocolate.

Above top: A sculpture of a celestial globe stands in front of the Palace of Nations, the People's Palace.

Above: Deeply frozen is this pier of Lake Geneva, standing as an impressive testimony of winter beauty.

○ HISTORICAL BUILDINGS OF THE LEAGUE OF NATIONS AND THE UNITED NATIONS

When the League of Nations was founded in 1919 in London, it was decided that its main seat should be relocated to Geneva, as the city had already been used for the conciliation of international conflicts. At the end of the 1930s, the Palace of Nations, was completed as a building in the Art Déco style. Today, it is possible to visit the palace, where most of it is dedicated to the seat of the European UN Mission.

○ PLACE DU BOURG-DE-FOUR

This is the oldest square in Geneva and a beloved meeting point for the young and old alike. Since the 11th century, the square stands as the centre of the city, with all streets leading to it. Where once busy markets prevailed, today, the guests can sit serenely in one of the inviting cafés or on the terraces of the different venues. So, where better to relax for a little while than here?

○ MUSEUM FOR ART AND HISTORY

The well stocked museum offers many treasures. The fact that Geneva is also an alpine town was confirmed by Konrad Witz as early as 1444 in his Petrus Altar, which can now be seen in the Art museum: The "Miraculous Draft of Fishes" shows Lake Geneva in front of Mont Blanc.

○ LAKE GENEVA

"Normally, it is smooth and without an obvious colour, with frolicking shades of grey or silvery-white, but sometimes, when the breeze blows, it darkens and it ripples and it suddenly turns into a big, blue, freshly-ploughed field." So, described the writer Charles Ferdinand Ramuz the sickle-shaped water surface of Lake Geneva, overshadowed by the peaks of Dents du Midi and the majestic Savoy Alps, adjoined by the Jura hills in the vicinity of Geneva. After the Hungarian Lake Balaton, Lake Geneva is the second-largest body of water in Middle Europe, and a beloved location for those who enjoy water sports. It is mainly fed by the Rhône. For centuries, viticulture has been practiced on its shores, and today, Vaud is the second-largest growing region of Switzerland. In Lausanne, the vineyard terraces of Lavaux create a unique cultivated landscape.

GOING OUT

Restaurant Bains des Pâquis // Students, workers, employees of international organizations and bankers all swear by this lakeshore restaurant. The self-service lunch is especially popular, given its affordable price.

// www.bains-des-paquis.ch

Brasserie de l'Hôtel de Ville // Not only long-established Genovese come to this venue, with its markedly old-fashioned interior design, but also representatives of the urban art scene and businessmen are attracted by its flair. In addition to fish-based dishes, one can commit to the little-known specialty Longeole du Val d'Arve, a sausage (wurst) delicacy seasoned with caraway or, optionally, Provençal delicacies.

// www.hdvglozu.ch

SHOPPING

○ **MANOR**

This tradition-steeped store, which fortunately is also available in other Swiss cities, beckons in the vicinity of the Cornavin Train Station, with its comestible goods department (edibles) and a well-stocked wine cellar.

// www.manor.ch

○ **CHOCOLATERIES**

Those who love chocolate should go to at least one of the many chocolate stores in the city; there are several, for example, between Rue de Rive and Rue du Rhône.

○ **RUE DU RHÔNE**

Exclusive shops and boutiques lie side-by-side on this street as pearls on a string. Watches and jewels sparkle, and fashion labels are vying for the best spot in the shop window.

DAY TRIPS

○ **LAUSANNE**

Earlier, travellers have praised the picturesque Vaud's capital city, located on three hills, as the "True queen of Lake Geneva". Today, the smallest of the Swiss metropolises stands as a dynamic business, congress and banking centre, with a truly youthful flair. Its small, carefully maintained historic centre offers during the summer an ideal backstage for festivals, during which it feels truly medieval. Lausanne has a renowned university as well as a lively culture scene, which was shaped by the late choreographer Maurice Béjart. Furthermore, since 1915, the town has been home to the International Olympic Committee. Lausanne is an ideal starting point for excursions to the surrounding region. Recently, the town has added a small metro, modelled over the Parisian system.

Left: The cathedral from Lausanne is classified as a significant edifice of the Early Gothic style on Swiss territory. It is the only Swiss place of worship, as renown as the biggest cathedrals of Europe. It is estimated that the construction of the church began in 1150.

WHERE TO STAY

Four Seasons Hotel des Bergues Geneva // Can hardly be topped: located on the shore of Lake Geneva, with a Michelin-starred restaurant and an excellent spa area. Since 1834, this hotel has been one of the finest addresses of the city.

// www.fourseasons.com/geneva

Hôtel Restaurant Edelweiss // A short distance from Lake Geneva you can find this enchanting hotel with a cosy atmosphere. The restaurant serves traditional fondue, and it also offers other Swiss delicacies. The rustic but classic furnishings looks a bit like a mountain cabin, including the feel-good factor.

// www.hoteledelweissgeneva.com

Les Arcades // Not far from the Genovese Main Train Station you can find this affordable hotel. The functionally-designed, bright rooms sometimes have, for contrast, baroque overloaded mirrors and cheerful secretaries in the style of Louis XV.

// www.hotel-arcades.ch/de

NOT TO BE MISSED

TAKE AN EXCURSION ON THE LAKE

While the passenger liners do not operate during the cold season on the majority of the Swiss lakes, the Compagnie Générale de Navigation sur le Lac Léman operates year-round. Aboard this veteran, you can enjoy a tasty meal and take delight in the lakeside and mountain scenery, while feeling quite relaxed. From the vessel, you can reach the world-renowned Château de Chillon and many others.

START THE NIGHTLIFE IN „ARTHUR'S RIVE GAUCHE"

„Arthur's Rive Gauche", on the Rue du Rhône, is chic, international and glamorous. During the week, the American bar, with its amazing view of Lake Geneva, stands as a meeting point for a little drink after work. On weekends, the venue changes into one frequented with pleasure by the bohemians and night owls, before plunging into the exciting nightlife of Geneva.

SIP ON A COCKTAIL

If there is something that this city can do, it is mixing Fondue cocktails. Far from the tourist mile in the centre and around Lake Geneva there are numerous, truly excellent bars in Eaux-Vives, Carouge or Plainpalais.

TAKE A SELFIE IN FRONT OF THE WATERFOUNTAIN

You will have the best view of the Lake Geneva fountain that shoots water 140 metres into the air, from Pont du Mont-Blanc and the Promenade du Lac. If you want to go even closer, take a boat trip. The iconic Jet d'eau must be pinned in any case!

TRY A FONDUE IN GENEVA

Dunking bread cubes in gooey cheese is one of the things that you should try at least once while in Geneva. Recommended places include Café du Soleil, Bains des Pâquis and Le Gruyérien.

#44   INNSBRUCK

INNSBRUCK'S SCENIC LOCATION INSPIRED GOETHE. AT FIRST, HOWEVER, THE GREAT POET DID NOT WANT TO STAY UNTIL HE WAS FINALLY TRAPPED BY THE CITY - "SPLENDID IN A BROAD, RICH VALLEY BETWEEN HIGH ROCKS AND MOUNTAINS." BUT IT WAS NOT SO MUCH THE BEAUTIFUL SURROUNDINGS AS THE LOCATION ON ONE OF THE MAIN TRAFFIC ARTERIES OF EUROPE THAT MADE INNSBRUCK BLOSSOM FROM A ROMAN CAMP TO THE PRESENT STATE CAPITAL OF TYROL. A MAN SHAPED THE FORTUNES OF THE CITY IN PARTICULAR: EMPEROR MAXIMILIAN I. THE HABSBURG RULED FROM 1490 TO 1590 OVER THE HOLY ROMAN EMPIRE OF THE GERMAN NATION AND MADE INNSBRUCK NOT ONLY TO HIS FAVOURITE CITY, BUT ALSO - AND AS AN EMPEROR HE HAD A LARGE SELECTION - TO HIS MAIN RESIDENCE. AS USUAL FOR A RULER AT THAT TIME, HE IMMEDIATELY BEGAN TO DEVELOP THE CITY MAGNIFICENTLY.

○ GOLDEN ROOF

The most notable legacy of Emperor Maximilian – at least from a touristic point of view – is the Golden Roof, the landmark of the city. The most famous oriel house in Europe is decorated with 2,657 gold-plated copper panels. The balcony and the window frames are adorned with a carved relief that remains mysterious to the present day. The purpose of the alcove balcony – stylistically, it belongs to the late Gothic style – was definitely profane. The emperor revealed himself here to the city folk or used it to watch festivals or tournaments.

○ INNUFER

Before Innsbruck visitors dedicate themselves to visiting the historic centre, with its multitude of attractions, they should cast a glance to the opposite north shore. The colourful houses which are lined up along the river stand out in a very appealing manner, with the mountain panorama behind them. The north district, accessed through the bridge over the Inn, is no less ancient than its southern counterpart. The Walter Park, next to the bridge, is the place to compare the city silhouette with the one from the 15th century – a steel model of the old city makes this possible.

○ ALPINE ZOO

The Alpine Zoo offers a distraction from the broad art history. On the way to the zoo, one should cast a glance to the wonderful Baroque castle Büchsenhausen. At the zoo, visitors will discover otters, brown bears and also golden eagles and the tousled hermit ibis. The zoo is known as one of the highest-located animal parks in Europe.

○ ST. JACOB'S CATHEDRAL

The inward-swaying double tower façade of the Innsbruck Dome rises elegantly in front of its astonished visitors. The high corral crowning the chancel is no less impressive. At the beginning of the 18th century, the dome was erected on the site of a late Gothic church. The stucco and painting come from the hands of the renowned brothers Asam, Cosmas Damian and Egid Quirin. Even though the richly-decorated organ draws quite a lot of attention – the most famous art treasure of the dome is the painting "Maria Hilf" (painting with miraculous powers), the work of Lucas Cranach the Elder. Made around the middle of the 16th century, for Saxon electors, it took a lot of detours before reaching Innsbruck. The tender devotion of the Holy Virgin to the Child Jesus, who clings to her lovingly, has become a model for many other representations of this kind.

Left: the historic centre of Innsbruck is known not only for the Golden Roof, baroque house facades and arcades but also for the traditional stores that complete the urban image.

Right: The luxurious construction style of St. Jacob's Cathedral (Innsbruck Dome) is clearly baroque by nature: wonderful stucco work and splendid paintings on the ceiling adorn the interior of this beautiful church from the early 18th century.

WHY VISIT IN WINTER? PERHAPS TO CELEBRATE CHRISTMAS IN THE MOUNTAINOUS LANDSCAPE OF INNSBRUCK: AT CHRISTMAS TIME, TIROL IS PARTICULARLY SPECIAL. BEGIN BY VISITING THE MARKETPLACES AND TAKING IN THE SMELL OF ROASTED ALMONDS AND CHECK OUT THE ROWS OF HOUSES RADIATING IN THE WARM BLAZE OF LIGHTS. THE CHRISTMAS SPECIALTIES ARE NOT ONLY THE LOVELY CARVED CHRISTMAS NATIVITY SCENE; THE BENEVOLENT SAINT NICHOLAS OR THE TRADITIONAL CAROLERS WHO WILL GO FROM DOOR TO DOOR SINGING, BUT ALSO THE CHRISTMAS MARKETS. IN INNSBRUCK, THESE ARE FREQUENT; THERE ARE SIX MARKETS COURTING THE VISITORS. IN THE HISTORIC CENTRE, THE GOLDEN ROOF SHINES UNDER THE LIGHT OF THE BIG CHRISTMAS TREE, IN THE MARKET SQUARE THERE IS A 14-METRE HIGH CRYSTAL TREE, FROM THE HUNGERBURG MARKET YOU CAN ENJOY A WONDERFUL VIEW OVER THE FESTIVELY DECORATED CITY.

○ IMPERIAL COURT CHURCH

Bronze monuments, called "Schwarzmander", surround the tomb of Maximilian I in the Imperial Court Church. Here, there are 28 important rulers, from the legendary Artus King to Friedrich III of the Habsburg, the emperor's father. The main grave, which the tomb guards with so much dignity, is however empty, as the emperor was buried in Vienna. The Imperial Court Church from Innsbruck was built in the 16th century, with the purpose of accommodating the tomb, however not as a burial site but rather as a monument to the emperor. The most important pilgrimage site of the church is today the tomb of Andreas Hofer.

○ THE IMPERIAL PALACE

Various regal personalities contributed to the building of Hofburg, starting with Sigmund "the one rich in coins" and continuing with Emperor Maximilian I and Maria Theresa. The Empress gave the palace complex the rococo appearance we see today: here her beloved husband died, the room in which he passed away having been turned into a court chapel. The most important ceremonial room is the Giants' Hall. Its name, however, is not related to its stately dimensions but rather to the original murals. Instead of mythical giants, Maria Theresa had family portraits and the eulogistic ceiling paintings of her dynasty displayed here.

○ MARIA-THERESA-STREET

The numerous shopping opportunities along Maria Theresa Street, which was partially turned into a pedestrian area, should not distract the tourists from the buildings and monuments worth seeing here. Above everything, the animated street is dominated by St. Anna's Column. The statue shows, without doubt, the Virgin Mary; the name refers to it being donated on St. Anne's Day. The magnificent old country house is also worth checking out. The baroque palace impresses with its expensively designed façade. Today, the State Parliament of Tirol meets here under the ceiling frescos of Cosmas Damian Asam. Maria Theresa Street ends with the Triumphal Arch, which commemorates the wedding of the empress' son.

○ AMBRAS CASTLE

Jewellery and white, the castle stands out from the surrounding mountain panorama. The idyllic park

Left: those who travel to Tirol in order to experience the right Christmas market atmosphere, have quite a multitude of choices available. In many cities of the region there are different Christmas markets; one of the most beautiful, however, is in Innsbruck.

sets the corresponding green colour accents. Castle Ambras comes suspiciously close to a fairy-tale castle. Even the story could have come from a fairy tale: Archduke Ferdinand secretly married the not befitting merchant daughter Philippine Welser and signed her over the castle. The duke brought along his art chamber and his weapons collection, both of which can still be visited here today. The most impressive is the Spanish Hall, an early example of renaissance room art in German-speaking countries.

○ WILTEN ABBEY

In the beginning, there was a murder: the giant Haymon slew another of his kind and grieved so much, that he founded a church in the same spot, but only after he was warned by a monk of the abomination of his crime. The first documentation of the church is, however, known only from the beginning of the 12th century. The abbey was continuously rebuilt so that today it exhibits a baroque appearance. The reason for the renewed reconstruction was the falling of one of the towers, which was never rebuilt.

○ BERGISEL SKI JUMP

Normally, no one with a healthy, pronounced instinct of self-preservation would want to catapult himself after a 70-metre long racy descent on skis and into the air. How crazy ski jumpers must be, becomes evident when you stand next to the ski jumping hill. In 1964 and 1976, Bergisel was even a venue for the Olympic competition. The star architect Zaha Hadid, who also re-designed the northern funicular, completely re-designed the ski jump area in 2001. From the breathtakingly-shaped head of the jumping tower, it is possible to enjoy a wonderful view of the Innsbruck landscape. Bergisel is not only the city of sports history and annually one of the venues for the Four Hills Tournament; here, the people of Tirol also fought four battles for their freedom under the lead of Andreas Hofer. An enormous panorama painting is reminiscent of this part of history.

GOING OUT

Bergisel – Tower Cafe // The modern café on the viewing platform of the Bergisel ski jump, designed by Zaha Hadid, offers meals at affordable prices and a top-class panoramic view of the mountains. It is one of the best attractions the city has to offer.

// **www.bergisel.info**

M+M Bar // Before diving into the Innsbruck nightlife, you should enjoy a drink or two here. The cocktails are really good, the bartender mixes classic creations with his own. In the lounge area, in the back area of the bar, you can feel truly comfortable.

// **www.mm-bar.at**

Top right: The 28 bronze figures surrounding the tomb of Emperor Maximilian I represent the central focal point inside the Court Church.

Bottom right: The newly-designed Bergisel ski jump stands almost vertically atop Innsbruck.

SHOPPING

○ **KAUFHAUS TYROL**

First, you'll see the façade. It was created by the architecture star David Chipperfield. Beyond the surprisingly-modern exterior, there is a veritable shopping mall with mostly modern stores and cafés.

// www.kaufhaus-tyrol.at

○ **KUNSTRAUM INNSBRUCK**

In the premises of the non-profit association there are exhibitions and vernissages with exciting contemporary art.

// www.kunstraum-innsbruck.at

○ **TIROLER HEIMATWERK**

„I would prefer to buy a Tyrolean hat"… In accordance with the adage of this hit song, here, in the vicinity of Maria-Theresa Street, it is possible to purchase real regional costumes. A nice dirndl and a chic cardigan are truly authentic souvenirs.

// www.tiroler.heimatwerk.at

DAY TRIPS

○ **STAMS ABBEY**

The double towers of the Stams Abbey stand massively in their white-yellowish baroque splendour in stark contrast to the landscape. The abbey church is a baroque jewel. Upon entering it, connoisseurs notice immediately that the church, re-designed in the baroque style, still exhibits its original Romanesque floor plan. The interior space presents itself in white magnificence with wonderful ceiling frescos, made by the painter Johann Georg Wolcker and fine stucco work, made by the Munich stucco artist Franz Xaver Feuchmayr. The carved high altar is especially notable, representing the tree of life. In the abbey shop, you can also enjoy the fruits of the abbey's schnapps distillery as well as homemade marmalade or honey.

Left: The illuminated Maria-Theresa Street appears as a small „shopping mile.

WHERE TO STAY

Goldener Adler // The oldest restaurant in the city is located in this traditional house. The history of the oldest European hotel, maintained to the present day in its original style, goes back more than 625 years, having been mentioned as early as 1390.

// www.bestwestern.at/hotels/ Innsbruck

NALA individuellhotel // Each of the 55 rooms of this hotel are different: designers created completely individual sleeping rooms, which have names like Zen, Garden or Nightingale. Regardless of the room booked, it is guaranteed that you will be pleasantly surprised.

// www.nala-hotel.at

Hotel Zach // In the hotel's 39 stylishly-furnished rooms, both businessmen and families feel quite comfortable. The central location is practical, if you wish to visit the attractions of the Olympic city.

// www.hotel-zach.at

NOT TO BE MISSED

TAKE A RIDE IN THE NORTHERN FUNICULAR

Those who want to see Innsbruck from above, have to take a ride with the northern funicular to the Hafelekar peak, which is 2,334 metres high. The railway has three sections covering the Karwendel mountain range. The first section is covered by the "Hungerburg funicular", travelling to the corresponding district of Innsbruck. All stations are examples of modern architecture. British star architect Zaha Hadid, who passed away early in 2016, won the competition organized in 2004 for the re-design of the northern funicular. On the ride, you will be able to enjoy a wonderful view of the regional capital, as well as, on the way towards the peak, see the finest modern architecture.

ADMIRING THE "EAGLES" DURING FLIGHT

Every year, between the end of the December and the Epiphany, the whole world is concentrated on the "Eagles" (German. "Adler"), who measure their strength in Oberstdorf in Allgäu, in Garmisch-Partenkirchen, in Innsbruck and in Bischofshofen. The international Four Hills Tournament is a ski jumping world event, which has been organized since 1952.

VISIT THE KULTURGASTHAUS BIERSTINDL

Emerging from the Pradler Knights Games ("The villainous Kuno"), the Kulturgasthaus Bierstindl is now an institution in Innsbruck. From the boulevard to the knight's game to the cabaret, from literature reading to jazz brunch, the range of the program reaches far beyond Innsbruck's borders.

STROLLING ON MARIA-THERESA STREET

The most frequented street of the city is today a shopping paradise and a promenade. A long time ago, craftsmen and businessmen settled into this new town and, in the 17th and 18th century, baroque and renaissance houses of those prosperous burghers were built here. Since 2009, the northern part has been a pedestrian zone. Those who visit Innsbruck in December should not miss the Christmas market!

#45 COLOGNE

„COLOGNE ALREADY EXISTS BUT IT IS A DREAM ", HEINRICH BÖLL ONCE SAID ABOUT HIS HOMETOWN, AND BY THAT HE MEANT THAT COLOGNE COULD ELUDE ANY CLASSIFICATION. THE CITY COMBINES A NUMBER OF CONTRASTS: IT IS THE SECOND-OLDEST CITY IN GERMANY AND A MODERN METROPOLIS. IT IS THE HOLY COLOGNE WITH THE DOME CLASSIFIED AS A UNESCO WORLD HERITAGE, A DOZEN ROMANESQUE CHURCHES AND AN ARCHBISHOP, BUT, AT THE SAME TIME, ALSO A TRANSGRESSING AND CHEERFUL CARNIVAL HOTSPOT. DESPITE ALL THE CONTRADICTIONS - ONE THING IS CERTAIN IN COLOGNE: THE CENTRE, THE PULSATING HEART OF THE CITY, THE STARTING POINT FOR ALL - THAT IS THE DOME.

Above: At the beginning of the 20th century, a 170-metre long storehouse was built in the Rhine harbour, receiving the name of Siebengebirge, after the number of gables. One century later, the harbour has changed into a district, in which one can work, live and spend his free time. The futuristic crane houses in the Rhine harbour now accommodate offices and apartments.

Left: Emperor Wilhelm II inaugurated the Hohenzollern Bridge in 1911, which was blown up in the Second World War and broadened after its re-construction at the end of the 1980s. The bridge today serves not only the trains; it is also used by pedestrians who wish to savour the breath-taking panorama of the dome.

○ COLOGNE CATHEDRAL

The biggest church of Germany, and also the biggest gothic cathedral in the world: truly, there are hardly sufficient superlatives that could be attributed to the Cologne Cathedral. The landmark and centre of Cologne draws visitors and pilgrims from all over the world.

○ HOHENZOLLERN BRIDGE

The Hohenzollern Bridge points directly towards the axis of the Cologne Cathedral – it was how the Prussian kings, who built the bridge initially, combined technological wonders of the early 20th century with the Middle Ages. The structure, which is today exclusively used as a railway bridge, measures 409 metres.

○ LUDWIG MUSEUM

A cultural temple of the finest quality hides under the grey zinc shed roof: the Ludwig collection, which presents modern and contemporary art, was founded in 1976, with the donation of 350 works of art. The Cologne Philharmonic Orchestra with its concert hall is found under the same roof.

○ ROMANO-GERMANIC MUSEUM

Between 1970 and 1974, the Romano-Germanic Museum was built around the Dionysus mosaic, which once decorated a Roman villa, reminiscing of the day-to-day life in the Roman city Colonia Claudia Ara Agrippinensium.

○ CITY HALL

The most remarkable part of the city hall is its late gothic tower decorated with sculptures of 130 meritorious Cologne personalities. Using a pair of binoculars, you can see some of them: for example, Stephan Lochner, Heinrich Böll or Konrad Adenauer. The high-gothic Hansasaal and the balcony dating from the Renaissance era are also worth checking out.

○ OLD MARKET

The biggest and liveliest spot in the historic Old Town, as well as its focal point, is the "Old Market" lined with some of the most wonderful traditional town houses of the past centuries. In the middle, you'll find the Jan-von-Werth fountain, which was erected in 1884 in the honour of the cavalry general to the

pleasure of Protestant Prussians, it was deliberately placed without a Marian column. Directly opposite, you can admire the oldest pharmacy in Cologne.

○ GREAT ST. MARTIN CHURCH

From the outside, it is large, imposing and massive; inside, however, it is surprisingly simple and bright – thus presents the Great St. Martin Church, which was completed in the middle of the 13th century, with a Romanesque architecture which already revealed clear signs of the emerging Gothic style.

○ WALLRAF-RICHARTZ-MUSEUM

The Wallraf-Richartz Museum belongs to one of the biggest classic collection of paintings in Germany and shows, predominantly, European art from the 13th century to the end of the 19th century, with numerous works signed by famous artists, such as Lochner, Dürer, Rubens and Renoir.

○ ALT ST. ALBAN

The church, built in the 11th century and destroyed in the Second World War serves today as a memorial to those who were killed in both World Wars.

○ GÜRZENICH

The largest gothic secular building in Cologne, after the City Hall, was built in the 15th century as an ceremonial house for Cologne's citizens – today, it still serves to this purpose, and, among other things, the exuberant Rhenish carnival balls are celebrated here.

○ ST. MARIA IM KAPITOL

Built on the foundation of a Roman temple dedicated to the Capitoline gods Jupiter, Juno and Minerva, the complex is one of the biggest Romanesque churches in Cologne. There was a precursor building completed around 690, with the construction of the contemporary building being finished in the 11th century. The three apses or the cloverleaf chancel, was used here for the first time in all of Germany.

○ OVERSTOLZENHAUS

Wine trading made the family Overstolz rich in the 13th century, and so they decided to build a new, representative patrician house between 1225 and 1230 – the only residential building in Cologne dating from the Romanesque period, which is almost completely preserved today.

Left: Hurray Cologne! Colourful and strident is everything in the fifth season, when the carnival lures the people of Cologne to the streets.

○ THE CHOCOLATE MUSEUM

All that is worth knowing about the cultivation and processing of cocoa is conveyed here – however, not only in dry facts and diagrams. One can satisfy his or her sweet tooth, as there is enough for everyone to have a test, among others, a chocolate fountain in the foyer, from which liquid chocolate runs, or also in the Chocó shop.

○ THE SPORTS AND OLYMPIC MUSEUM

From the antique Olympic Games to the modern professional sport, the museum is the best place to find out interesting facts on the development of competitive sports, about the highlights, great athletes, triumphal victories and bitter defeats.

○ THE RAUTENSTRAUCH-JOEST MUSEUM

The ethnology museum in Cologne is very cramped where space is concerned, but quite still exciting: it houses important collections of Indian art and the way of living in North and South America, as well as of art and culture from Africa and Oceania.

○ SEVERINSTORBURG

In Chlodwig Square, one can find Severinstorburg, the southern most of the medieval city gates, which dates back to the 12th century. The upper part of the basement dates from the 13th century, the other construction parts were later rebuilt. Today, the halls of diverse sizes are rented out for festivities and also for private functions.

○ ST. SEVERIN

The „cathedral in the southern part of the city" is a mixture of numerous stylistic periods. The re-buildings and additions from various centuries have mainly transformed the originally Romanesque basilica, dating from the 10th century, into a gothic one. St. Severin is the patron saint of the church, whose bones are resting here. The carnival, which is a special point of attraction in the southern part of the city, leaves its impression on the church as well: in the lower part of the window on the western façade, a small carnival clown can be seen.

GOING OUT

Brauhaus Sion // In this large brewery, tradition is all that matters. Several brewing casks are inviting you to savour a cold beer.

// www.brauhaus-sion.de

Em Streckstrump // In the oldest jazz club of Germany, it is possible to enjoy live music every night. Over 14,000 performances have taken place here over the years.

// www.papajoes.de/strickstrumpf

Le Moissonnier // A casual, premium restaurant, where you can have a nice meal without having to don any fancy clothes. The menu includes creations from the French chef. The décor of the bistro-style restaurant makes you think you are in Paris rather than in the middle of Cologne.

// www.lemoissonnier.de

Haifischclub // Those who come here are truly spoiled, as there are over 100 drinks to choose from.

// www.haifischclub.de

Right: Those who want to see how the football shoes of Franz Becken-bauer looked after their continuous use, has arrived at the right address in the former customs hall in the Rhine harbour. The German Sports and Olympic Museum covers 2,000 square meters, with over 3,000 exhibits of national, international and Olympic sports.

SHOPPING

○ **DUMONT-CARRÉ**

Shopping arcade on Breite Street with everything your heart desires; from fashion to drugstores.

○ **APOSTELNMARKT WEEKLY MARKET**

With a central location in the historic northern centre, the market is rich in pretty stands, with the best foods and flowers. Thursday and Friday before noon.

WHERE TO STAY

Hotel Ahl Meerkatzen vun 1264 // This hotel offers modern comfort and cosiness to all guests, in one of the oldest buildings of the entire city. The cathedral is only a stone's throw away.

// www.novum-hotels.com

Hopper Hotel et cetera // The four-star hotel combines art, decent comfort and a historic structure with the contemporary hotel culture – the successful Renaissance of a former 19th century monastery.

// www.hopper.de

Hotel Viktoria // The hotel Viktoria, built as a music history museum in 1906, is one of the most imposing and noble grand villas in Cologne, housing within its walls is an innovative private hotel. The exterior and interior come together to form a stylistic unity, with bay windows, marble walls, stucco work and column niches.

// hotelviktoria.com

○ **THE NEUMARKT GALLERY**

The shopping centre is located straight after the renowned Schildergasse. The upside-down ice cream cone on the corner of the building is quite striking.

// www.neumarktgalerie.com

○ **HOSS AN DER OPER**

Delicatessen shop since 1900. In addition to wine, spices and international specialties, one can find frozen gourmet meals.

// www.hoss-delikatessen.de

○ **NIPPES WEEKLY MARKET**

A particularity of the market located in the Nippes district: all days except Sundays, you can find fruits and vegetables, meat, cheese and many other products – only before noon, though.

○ **THE KARNEVALSWIERTS**

The specialty store has everything, especially when it comes to clothing and make-up. You can also find wigs, fabrics and accessories for do-it-yourself projects.

// www.karnevalswierts.com/de

DAY TRIPS

○ **ZONS**

A trip to Zons, north of Cologne, is like a journey back in time, as the city appears to have arisen from the Middle Ages, with its town walls, mill and castle.

○ **AHR VALLEY**

The Ahr is a tributary river of the Rhine, with a length of just 90 kilometres. The valley is a point of attraction for hikers and bike riders, with its ravines, vineyards and meadows.

○ **SIEBENGEBIRGE**

The low mountain range, with a maximum height of 460 meters, is located on the right side of the Rhine. The best-known town is Königswinter. The Drachenfels Castle is a magnet for visitors, with its castle ruins and scenic plateau.

NOT TO BE MISSED

ATTEND A CHORAL CONCERT OF THE COLOGNE DOMMUSIK

The choir of the cathedral was consecrated in 1322, 74 years after being founded – so, it now has a proud history of almost 700 years. With 104 seats, the choir stalls from the early 14th century are the largest in Germany. Due to the surroundings and the acoustics, a concert in Cologne's cathedral is an extraordinary experience. The concert with its sacred music is particularly recommended at the Epiphany Shrine with the dome ensemble and guest choirs.

SAVORING A KÖBES BEER AFTER WORK AT THE PÄFFGNE BREWERY

The Päffgne is a traditional brewery in Cologne. As in many pubs in the city, the top-fermented Kölsch is brought by the waiter, known as Köbes, in generous quantities and without having to ask for more.

ATTEND A PERFORMANCE OF THE „COLOGNE PUPPET SHOW"

Since 1802, the Hänneschen Theatre has been situated here with only a short interruption. Instead of people, there are stick puppets coming on stage. There is even a carnival session, the puppet session. Knowing the Cologne dialect is an advantage.

VISIT THE ZOO

The zoo was founded in 1860. Next to the ones in Berlin and Frankfurt am Main, this is the third-oldest zoo in Germany. It has come a long way from the original concept with cages. The elephant house has been preserved, but today the animals live in the large elephant park of over 20,000 square metres. The tropical house, with fruit bats that fly freely, is also modern in its style.

A GUIDED TOUR OF THE ARCHAEOLOGICAL AREA IN THE CITY HALL DISTRICT

History has left its mark around the city hall, from the Roman to the Jewish district. The excavations represent an impressive underground museum.

#46   LAPPLAND

AN ARCTIC BREEZE BLOWS THROUGH LAPLAND, AND YOU CAN SEE THE MARKING OF THE POLAR CIRCLE IN THE MOORS. THIS IS A LANDSCAPE FOR OUTDOOR FANS, WHO ALSO SEEK SOLITUTIDE, AS, WITH APPROXIMATELY TWO INHABITANTS FOR EVERY SQUARE KILOMETER, YOU'LL RARELY MEET ANYONE OUTSIDE OF THE TOWNS. SKIING AND SNOWSHOE HIKING ARE PART OF THE WINTER SCHEDULE. ICE-SKATING ON FROZEN LAKES, SNOWMOBILE TOURS AND ICE CLIMBING ARE ALSO PART OF THE VARIOUS ACTIVITIES THAT THE WILDERNESS OF LAPLAND HAS TO OFFER. AND, WHEN THE WEATHER IS CLEAR, YOU CAN SEE THE POLAR LIGHTS DANCING IN THE SKY!

Above: North of the Polar circle, travellers are enchanted by the winter wonderland. Even if the sun sets early, the sky shines for hours with delicate dusk colours.

Left: The northern lights dance on the tip of the island in such a precise manner, as if the small rocky island, off the coast of Norway, emits green smoke. The polar lights can assume various forms, most commonly they are in the form of ribbons, bows and waves.

○ ROVANIEMI

The Finnish city of Rovaniemi is closely located to the Polar circle and to the Fins, it is known as the hometown of Santa Claus. Here, you can find a tourist centre dedicated to Santa Claus, the amusement park "Santa Park", the Santa Claus repair shop/village (between the last two, there is a reindeer sleigh), and a school for the helpers of Santa Claus. Even the Rovaniemi airport has been recognized by the international Civil Aviation Organizations as the official Santa Claus airport. Those who have had enough of the corpulent man in the red suit, can discover that Rovaniemi is also a good starting point for all kind of winter sport activities. The fact that Lapland has polar nights during winter (expect about four hours of dim light per day) fortunately does not hinder the fun.

○ JOKKMOKK

The Jokkmokk municipality, with its 5,500 inhabitants, is a cultural centre of the Swedish Sami. Here, the pupils learn the traditional craftsmanship techniques at school. The nature is equally impressive.

Those who aren't acquainted with the northern regions of the territory, can visit the botanical garden of the museum and inform themselves about the diverse habitats of Lapland.

○ GÄLLIVARE

There are approximately 20,000 people living in Gällivare, with Sami tradition eveident everywhere. The open-air museum Hembygdsområdet, in the eastern part of the city shows, among others, the northern windmills of Sweden, a warehouse with pantry rooms, "Härbren", as well as the Sami dwellings. An old wooden church, dating from 1755, is located close to the centre. Once, the church was located in the wilderness, being one of the first buildings of the former Gällivare-Malmberget village. The church was initially used as a place of worship by the Sami, being known as the "Lap chapel". Since 1882, there has been a new, bigger church – it is located close to the city centre. A point of attraction is the local mountain. The 820-meter high Dundret is a beloved excursion destination, especially during the summer. The

WHY VISIT IN WINTER? THE FINNS CALL IT "REVONTULI" (FOX'S FIRE) AND BELIEVE THAT THE PHENOMEN IS REPRESENTED BY SNOW PARTICLES, WHICH WERE STIRRED UP BY THE TAIL OF A MAGICAL CREATURE. THE NORWEGIANS CONSIDER THEM TO BE THE SPIRITS OF OLD MAIDS, WHO ARE PERFORMING A DANCE. ACCORDING TO THE SAMI BELIEF OF LAPLAND, THEY ARE ENERGIES PRODUCED BY THE SOULS OF THOSE DEAD. THE SCIENTIFIC EXPLANATION IS SUBSTANTIALLY MORE CLARIFYING. THE POLAR LIGHTS MATERIALIZE FROM SOLAR WIND PARTICLES, WHICH WERE EJECTED BY THE SUN IN OUTER SPACE. THESE PARTICLES ARE DRAWN TO THE POLES, GIVEN THE MAGNETIC FIELD OF THE EARTH, WHERE THEY COLLIDE WITH AIR PARTICLES, THUS EMITTING PHOTONS IN VARIOUS COLOURS AND FORMS. GREEN IS THE MOST COMMON, BUT ALSO RED, YELLOW AND VIOLET LIGHT REFLECTIONS CAN BE SEEN. THEIR MOVEMENTS ARE HYPNOTISING.

Left and above: During winter, Lapland is a beloved objective for fans of the Northern Lights. There are only a few larger towns, which disturb the night sky with their street lights. Top above: A view of the tunnelled island of Tromsø, which can be reached via two bridges, has a very nice city centre with shopping streets.

Right: The 35-metre high Arctic Cathedral in Tromsø, made from glass, concrete and aluminium, is also definitely worth seeing from the inside: the spectacular glass mosaic windows, which occupy the whole back wall (140 square metres), making it the largest church with mosaic windows in Europe.

sun can be enjoyed from its peak from the beginning of June until the middle of July, for 24 hours per day.

○ KIRUNA

With an area spanning 20,000 square kilometres, Kiruna is just as big as The Netherlands Today, it has around 23,000 inhabitants; those who are seeking solitude can certainly find it here. Kiruna exists only because of the ore mines: the workers transport the ore piece by piece, above ground, as well as underground. Visitors can travel via the tram and bus into one of the largest pits in the world, finding themselves deep inside the mine, at 540 meters below the surface. In the warm, humid tunnels, there is not only mining but also growth: Shiitake, a Japanese mushroom, is a true delicacy.

○ TROMSØ

The university city of Tromsø, regional capital of the Troms province, is, with its 62,000 inhabitants, the biggest city in the north of Norway and reputed as the "Paris of the north". A cable railway can take you to the closely-located Hausberg Storsteinen (420-metre high). From there, you will find a magnificent view of the city, in the midst of the island world belonging to the most extreme north-western part of Norway, with an appealing climate favoured by the warmth of the Gulf Stream. The moment the settlement, which numbered only 80 souls, was turned into a city in 1794, it quickly developed into a trading and cathedral city, as well as the capital of the Arctic Sea: Tromsø was legendary, as a point of departure for Arctic expeditions, with the Polar Museum documenting undertakings such as the ones of Fridtjof Nansen. From an economic point of view, universities and research institutions dominate here. The Universitary Hospital is the largest employer in Northern Norway.

ARCTIC CATHEDRAL

The renowned landmark of Tromsø is built on the mainland and can be reached from Tromsøya through the Tromsø Bridge: the "Arctic Cathedral" was built in 1965. Formally, it was only a simple Protestant-Lutheran church, although it quickly became a tourist attraction. Actually, another cathedral is the second house of worship in the city, which is the classically-looking Tromsø Cathedral from 1861 – and, also, the only Norwegian cathedral built entirely from

GOING OUT

Tromsø: Fiskekompaniet // This restaurant is located in the harbour, with the freshest fish landing on the plate. Selected products and a top-class service impel the customer to choose this restaurant.

// fiskekompani.no

Rovaniemi: Café Bar 21 // Daily, you can enjoy amazing pasta dishes and salads or coffee and cakes, while guests are drawn in the evening to cocktails and drinks. The Finnish design decorates the interior of the Café Bar 21. Reservations are recommended.

// www.cafebar21.fi

Tromsø: Rorbua Pub // For more than 40 years, it has been possible to savour local beer and wine. It is well-known, among others, for being a filming location of a Norwegian TV series.

// www.rorbuapub.no

Glada Gocken // Located just outside Gällivare, the restaurant offers local specialties such as reinder or Arctic char.

// glada-kocken.se

wood. A favourite of the visitors remains the top-gabled white building designed by the Norwegian architect Jan Inge Hovig, which impresses with its architecturally-striking design. From afar, it resembles a tent, but it is actually intended to represent ice floes coming together, as they pile up on some coasts during harsh winters, or of the jagged mountaintops of the nearby Håja Island.

ALTA

The biggest city of Finnmark is located on the estuary of one of the richest salmon rivers in the world, the 200-kilometer long Altaelva, protected at the end of a fjord. Thanks to the North Atlantic current, it is not glaciated, but, in fact, habitable throughout its entire length. In 1973, by accident, more than 3,000 petroglyphs have been discovered here, spread over more than 40 sites. It has been estimated that the drawings date between 4200 and 500 BC. The drawings are carved several centimetres deep into the stone and, in addition to elks, reindeers and bears, they depict scenes from everyday life: people catching fish and navigating boats, hunting scenes, religious rituals and ceremonies. The representations offer an impression of the life of the prehistoric man in the northern Europe, his relationship with nature and the world of the gods.

○ KIRKENES

The port city of Kirkenes in the Sør-Varanger municipality, on the border between Russia, is the end point of the E6 and the "express route" of an iconic site. It stood, as a symbol for the development and end of a blooming mining industry (1906-1996), it was one of the most bombed cities of Europe during the Second World War with a total of 320 air strikes, and then a frontline town during the Cold War, with a direct border between NATO and the Warsaw Pact. In 1996 it became known as the "capital city of unemployment" of the Finnmark province, after the ending of the Erzära. Now, it positions itself as a service centre and waits for the establishment of the much-discussed "Barents Sea Region" in the "Europe of Regions": migration, demographic decline and the unemployment rate, which is high by Norwegian standards, led to the idea of bringing together the Finnmark, Troms and Nordland provinces.

Left: Since 1985 part of the UNESCO World Heritage: the petroglyphs of Alta present humans and animals, including fishermen on a boat.

NOT TO BE MISSED

WINTER FUN IN ROVANIEMI

From Rovaniemi, you can go to the huts in the wilderness, where you can go reindeer sleighing or skiing, take a hike while wearing snowshoes or try ice fishing. You can go hunting with a lively husky team in the sparkling white snow, or speed over a frozen lake on a snowmobile. Do not forget: this dark winter sky represents the perfect background for the magical Northern Lights – the most beautiful Christmas lights ever.

VISIT THE MUSEUM OF THE SAMI CULTURE IN JOKKMOKK

The „Fjälloch Samemuseum Ájtte" opened in 1989. Its floor plan corresponds to a reindeer enclosure, and visitors can discover here the Sami tradition of keeping reindeer, from its history to its culture. The exhibition is interactively designed, with films, slide shows and animation techniques. And if you want something special, you can try the Sami specialties at the restaurant.

TAKE A RIDE WITH THE HURTIGRUTEN

Originally intended as a quick connection for the postal ships and as supply route for the remote settlements in the far north of Norway, since the expansion of the road network, Hurtigruten has become a beloved cruise route, from Bergen on the south-west coast to the North Cape and Kirkenes. One-day guests can also travel a partial section without booking a cabin. There is space for cars as well.

EXPERIENCE THE POLAR HISTORY IN THE POLAR MUSEUM OF TROMSØ

Located immediately in the vicinity of the harbour, the Polar Museum is housed in the austere former customs buildings. Above all, it provides information about the history of polar research, the Northwest Passage and Arctic hunting. Fridjof Nansen and Roald Amundsen are the focus of the exhibition. You can also find out interesting facts on famous polar bear hunters of the country and the way trappers lived. Not far away, you'll find the interactive polar research exhibition of the Adventure Museum "Polaria". The award-winning construction reminds you of the "Arctic Cathedral", with the ice-floes that seem pushed together.

#47 NÜRNBERG

THE CHRISTMAS MARKET, GINGERBREAD, BRATWURSTS, MEDIEVAL IMPERIAL GLORY, HANS SACHS AND ALBRECHT DÜRER: THE BIGGEST FRACONIAN CITY HAS MANY CLICHES, WITH WHICH ALL MIGHT BE RIGHT, ALTHOUGH NOT ALL ARE. IT IS NO COINCIDENCE THAT THE FRANCONIAN METROPOLIS HAS A MEDIEVAL FLAIR. IN THE EARLY GERMAN HISTORY, NUREMBERG WAS, AS AN IMPERIAL CITY, ONE OF THE MOST IMPORTANT CITIES OF THE KINGDOM AND ESPECIALLY, UNDER KARL IV, THE LOCATION OF IMPORTANT IMPERIAL DECISIONS. BUT NUREMBERG'S HISTORY IS ALSO ONE OF SUCCESSFUL ENTREPENEURSHIP. THIS BEGAN WITH THE RICH PATRICIANS OF THE MEDIEVAL AGE, WHO BESTOWED MANY OF THEIR MAGNIFICENT BUILDINGS TO THE CITY, CONTINUING WITH THE INDUSTRIAL REVOLUTION, WITH THE FIRST RAILWAY FUNCTIONING HERE AND ALSO MODEL TRAINS AND OTHER TOYS BECOMING EXPORT HITS, AND THEN CAME THE ECONOMIC MIRACLE PERIOD.

Above: The Christmas market in Nuremberg is considered to be one of the oldest and most beautiful of its kind in the world. Accordingly, every year, on the last Friday before the first Advent, the Christkindl is chosen and the Christmas Market opens.

Left: The Nuremberg Imperial Castle was initially built as a Salian Royal Castle around the middle of the 11th century. The Sinnwell Tower rises in front of the south entrance (in Middle High German, sinnwell means "all round"). In the middle of the 16th century it was fitted with a tent roof and a pointed spire tower.

○ OLD TOWN

The "historic mile" is, with its signage system, one of the most important structures in the Old Town and offers an overview of Nuremberg's past. The rich history of the city was always connected with its convenient location at the crossroads of important roads, which led from the Franconian wine country upon Main, towards south on one side, and from the Swabian markets across Bohemia on the other side. An inspiring walk leads, among other things, from the Fembohaus (today, City Museum) to the Town Hall Square, with the Town Hall from 1622, to the St. Sebaldus Church (13th century) with the Sebald grave of Peter Vischer as well as to the main market.

○ KAISERBURG (NUREMBERG CASTLE)

The castle from Nuremberg was, during the Middle Ages, one of the most important imperial palaces, being regularly visited by each reigning emperor. It has one of the most significant weir systems of Europe. The historical rooms of the palace can be visited on their own or in combination with the Castle Museum in the bower. The courtyard and the imperial garden can be visited free-of-charge.

○ ST. SEBALDUS CHURCH

The former church of the town council, above the grave of the City Patron Sebaldus, is a Gothic masterpiece, which contains many medieval works of art, as well as the Sebaldus tomb of Peter Vischer, the apostle figure of Veit Stoß and the colourful glass windows, partly designed by Dürer.

○ ALBRECHT-DÜRER-HAUS

In the former home and studio of the famous artist, nearly all roms are in original condition, or they have been renovated in the original style, conveying a vivid image of his work. In the old workshop, historic print-

ing technologies, such as copperplate engravings and wood engravings are presented. Moreover, as part of the temporary exhibitions, visitors can see graphic representations or copies of his works.

○ ST. LORENZ

Built some time later than the St. Sebaldus in the south part of the Old Town, the Lorenz Church stood from the beginning somewhat in the shadow of its big sister, which, however, did not impede the rich inhabitants of the South City to decorate it in a particularly valuable style. Inside, one can find a somewhat imposing ambry by Adam Kraft, an Annunciation Scene created in the form of an enormous, suspended medallion by Veit Stoß, many valuable altars and old glass windows.

○ CHURCH OF OUR LADY

The cathedral from the 14th century has an unusual square layout. It was conceived by Emperor Karl IV for the storage of the imperial regalia. A particular point of interest is the musical mechanism of the clock, above the main portal. At every 12 o'clock, the seven electors bow to the emperor. Inside, a Star of David reminds of a synagogue that once stood in this place, which was destroyed during the pogrom.

Above: Upon seeing the mighty pillars of St. Sebaldus, which seem to merge seamlessly with the vaulted ceiling, you'll feel like being in a gigantic forest of pillars.

Left: The stall city is open until Christmas Eve, promising a cozy attunement, respectively culinary delicacies and all sorts of trinkets can be purchased.

○ BEAUTIFUL FOUNTAIN

The design of the 19-metre high fountain in the main square reminds of a Gothic Church spire. Its four levels are decorated with colourfully painted figurines, representing the Nine Virtues, the seven liberal arts, the seven electors, seven prophets, the four evangelists and the four church fathers.

○ OLD TOWN HALL WITH DUNGEONS

The town hall of Nuremberg was built in the early 17th century in the style of late renaissance. The most valuable part, from a cultural-historic point of view, however, is the integrated gothic hall of the former town hall on the south side. The medieval dungeons represent a tourist attraction, as you can visit them as part of the guided tours.

○ HENKERSTEG UND WEINSTADEL

From the picturesque old Weinstadel (wine repository), which today is a residence for students, Henkersteg leads to the hangman's tower on the flea market island in Pegnitz. Once, the hangman lived here, away from the ordinary folk. Today, the island is an idyllic neighbourhood for going out, being filled with small shops and restaurants. The tower, the bridge and repository are beloved points of interest for photographs.

○ JOHANNIS CHURCH CEMETERY

The scenic cemetery, located next to the town wall, is often known as the cemetery of roses, because of its many rose bushes. There are many beautiful, historically-interesting gravestones that make it worth visiting. This cemetery is the resting place for a multitude of important people, including Albrecht Dürer, Hans Sachs, Veit Stoß and Anselm Feuerbach.

○ HOSPICE OF THE HOLY SPIRIT

The hospital was donated in the 14th century by a rich Nuremberg resident, caring for the old and the sick, being used today as a senior residence. It is built on one of the arms of Pegnitz, and is often photographed by tourists.

○ HANDWERKERHOF

The ensemble of picturesque timbered houses and stalls is not original but it was created, on the 500th birthday anniversary of Albrecht Dürer, in a converted courtyard, near the King's Gate. Since then, the arts and crafts booths, the toy makers, gingerbread delicacies, wine taverns and the historic grilled sausage kitchen have turned it into a first-class tourist magnet.

GOING OUT

Essigbrätlein // In the oldest, originally-maintained inn of the city, you can discover creative and exquisite cuisine.
// www.essigbraetlein.de

Zum Albrecht-Dürer-Haus // This wonderfully located timbered house with a view of the Albrecht Dürer House. Even before 1800, there was a restaurant here, today, you can enjoy Franconian dishes and beverages
// www.zum-albrecht-duerer-haus.net

Zum Gulden Stern – Historische Bratwurstküche // Those who would like to eat an original Nuremberg grilled sausage or Saure Zipfel (traditional meal, grilled sausage cooked in vinegar), has arrived to the right place. There is also an exhibition here, which proves that this grilled sausage kitchen is the oldest in the world.
// www.bratwurstkueche.de

Right: The Handwerkerhof is decorated quite beautifully during the Advent season, .

○ GERMAN TRAIN MUSEUM

Dating from 1899, the Transport Museum is the oldest railway museum in the world. The collection includes, among other items, the oldest preserved German steam locomotive and a replica of the "Adler", the very first locomotive of Germany.

○ TOY MUSEUM

In an old Patrician house, on Karl Street, there is an extraordinary collection of historic toys, as a clear proof of the Nuremberg's tradition as a city of toy makers.

Left: You can admire the historic toys in the Toy Museum.

SHOPPING

○ GREEN MARKET

Especially farmers from the garlic country - located in the middle of the triangle Nuremberg-Fürth-Erlangen - offer every weekday their products from farm and fields at the largest weekly market in the city.

○ LANDBIERPARADIES

A 350-m2 beverage business with a knack for beer coming from the Franconian microbreweries. Approximately 85 different beer varieties are offered here. Organic beers represent the latest trend.

// www.landbierparadies.com

○ LEBKUCHEN SCHMIDT

Just one of the numerous opportunities in the Franconian metropolis, the world-renowned Nuremberg specialty can be bought as a sweet souvenir for you or your loved ones – regardless of the season!

// www.lebkuchen-schmidt.com

○ PRAGER KUNSTSALON

The gallery of Vera and Verena Hinze, located in the main market, presents international fashion, design and jewellery as well as extraordinary Czech commercial and contemporary art of top quality.

// www.prager-kunstsalon.de

WHERE TO STAY

Drei Raben // A themed hotel of high standards, located in the vicinity of the train station. The brightly-coloured lounge already resembles a theatre production. The junior suites "Legend and Bathtub Enchantment" are particulary appealing to guests, with a wonderful bathtub in the room, as well as numerous other charming details. **// www.hoteldreiraben.de**

Dürer Hotel // Further down from the Imperial Castle and only a stone's throw from the Dürer House, you can find this top-class hotel with 106 rooms, underground parking, bistro bar, fitness room with sauna and steam bath.

// www.duerer-hotel.de

Le Méridien Grand Hotel // Tradition-rich and stylish building on the edge of the Old Town, which has been successfully restored to its old Art Nouveau charm. The brasserie and also the hotel bar are definitely worth checking out! **// www.lemeridiennuernberg.com**

NOT TO BE MISSED

WALK THROUGH THE GERMAN NATIONAL MUSEUM

This is one of the biggest museums of art and cultural history in the German-speaking countries. The sculptures of Adam Krafft and Veit Stoß or the globe of Martin Behaim are among the most valuable pieces. The affiliated library is a valuable collection of works, with 3,380 manuscripts, 1,000 early printed books and 3,000 prints from the 16th century.

VISITING THE DOCUMENTATION CENTRE OF THE NAZI PARTY RALLY GROUNDS

On the former Nazi Party rally grounds, panels inform about this dark part of history. There is a permanent exhibition in the documentation centre, which is dedicated, first and foremost, to the mass meetings of the NS propaganda, being presented under the title "Fascination and Force".

VISIT THE ZOO

The spacious, landscaped zoo has numerous enclosures for mammals, a tropical house, a water park, as well as a dolphinarium and a manatee house to captivate visitors of the zoo.

DISCOVERING THE STONE PASSAGE

In the past, there was a network of stone passages under the city that was used by the breweries, in order to cool their beer stocks. These passages can be visited as part of the guided tours by the association of "Nürnberger Felsengänge" (Nuremberg Stone Passages), as well as the castle casemates and the war bunkers.

TRY THE "DREI IM WECKLE" AT THE CHRISTMAS MARKET

A must in November/December! World-renowned and absolutely original are the Nuremberg grilled sausages, which can be purchased here only around Christmas time. For over 700 years, everything in the city has been about the sausage (Wurst).

#48

PORTO

THE SECOND-LARGEST CITY OF PORTUGAL IS LOCATED ON A STEEP SLOPE ABOVE THE RIO DOURO, SHORTLY BEFORE ITS ESTUARY TO THE ATLANTIC. RULED BY THE MOORS BETWEEN 716 AND 997, THE SETTLEMENT KNOWN IN ANCIENT TIMES AS "PORTUS CALE" WAS MADE CAPITAL OF PORTUCALIA COUNTY, THE ORIGIN OF THE LATER PORTUGUESE EMPIRE, IN THE 11TH CENTURY. THIS IS A GREAT CITY FOR HERITAGE WITH ITS TERRACED HOUSES, LOCATED NEAR THE ROCKY WALLS. EVEN THOUGH THE ECONOMIC DYNAMICS OF THE METROPOLIS ARE DISTINCTLY DOMINATED BY THE WINE TRADE, AS IN THE PORT NEAR MATOSINHOS, THE REVENUES ARE GENERALLY NOT ENOUGH, IN ORDER TO FINANCIALLY SUPPORT ALL THE NECESSARY RESTORATION. THE CITY RECEIVES SUPPORT FROM UNESCO, WHICH HAS DECLARED THE HISTORIC CENTRE AS A WORLD HERITAGE SITE IN 1996.

Above: Porto, already known as Portus Cale in ancient times, distinguishes itself through the wonderfully-preserved Old Town and numerous Baroque churches. The picture is dominated by the terraces located on the steep cliffs. The centre of the Old Town Portos is the shore promenade Cais de Ribeira am Douro.

Left: There is something special about the Dom Luís I Bridge: It has two levels, the upper one is reserved for the tram, while the lower one for the road transport. Both levels are accessible for pedestrians, the upper one offers however the best views.

○ PONTE DOM LUÍS I

Upon looking at this steel construction, many are reminded of the Eiffel Tower – and this association almost hits the mark: the planning and supervision of the construction were handled by Théophile Seyrig, a former associate of Gustave Eiffel. The construction is a masterpiece of the finest engineering that existed at that time. There are 3,000 tons of steel placed in the double, freely-tensioned construction of Ponte Dom Luís I. The tram goes above the arch and thereby connects both shores of the Douro; Porto and Vila Nova de Gaia. Cars drive on the lower, suspended road. Pedestrians can walk on both levels.

○ CAIS DA RIBEIRA

The quays on Douro, in which the trading ships berthed once and goods were unloaded, are attractions for tourists today. The former storage rooms have been turned into cafes or restaurants; the tables in the open outdoors and in the dim backyards are always full. The

neighbourhood between Praça da Ribeira and the Ponte Dom Louís I Bridge is one of the oldest in Porto, and, up to recent times, also one of the poorest. Today, many of the former residents have gone into the field of tourism; others cling defiantly to their every-day lives in the winding narrow streets, with the laundry fluttering on lines suspended between buildings.

○ SÉ CATEDRAL

The massive cathedral construction, dating from the 12th century, appears like a fortress in the Ribeira neighbourhood. Two imposing towers frame the transept building with Romanesque rosettes and pinnacles. In the interior, the fortified church resembles more a tomb than a place of worship. However, in the 18th century, Nicolau Nasoni, a very busy builder of that time, added a few exciting touches, using several tricks: he created a radiant high altar, covered in gold, beneath a bright coffered ceiling made of marble and granite and placed another exquisite al-

WHY VISIT IN WINTER? FIRST, YOU WILL DISCOVER MODERATE TEMPERATURES, BETWEEN 6 AND 10 °C. AND THE FAMOUS FRANCESINHA (LITTLE FRENCHIE), A BIFANA (SANDWICH WITH PORK MEAT) OR A CALDO VERDE (GREEN BROTH) TASTES TRULY BETTER THAN IN THE SUMMER, AS THE BODY IS THANKFUL FOR A WARM MEAL. AND DON'T FORGET THE DELICIOUS BACALHAU (CODFISH FRITTERS). MOREOVER, THERE ARE NUMEROUS FESTIVALS TAKING PLACE, SUCH AS THE FILM FESTIVAL IN FEBRUARY/MARCH. AND WHEN IT RAINS OR IT IS TOO COLD OUTSIDE, THE PEOPLE ARE DRAWN TO THE INSIDE, FOR EXAMPLE, TO BOOKSHOPS LIKE LIVRARIA LELLO, ONE OF THE MOST BEAUTIFUL IN THE ENTIRE CITY.

tar made of 800 kilos of pure silver in the sacrament chapel of the left transept.

○ IGREJA DE SANTA CLARA

Those who are looking at Igreja de Santa Clara only from the outside, might have the impression that this is only another church building, one of the many Porto has to offer. However, the interior promises an explosion of forms to those who visit it: "luxurious" is not sufficient to describe the diversity of ornaments and decorations! The religious wood carvings are true works of art made in the Baroque and Rococo styles. In addition to the Azulejos, the gilded wood carving, the Talha dourada, is a particular feature of the Portuguese art.

○ IGREJA DE SÃO LOURENÇO

The foundation of the Church and Monastery built by the Jesuits in the 16th century, was laid despite vocal protests. The citizens of Porto fought especially against the establishment of a college, as they feared that they would lose their privileges: aristocrats, at that time, were not allowed to stay in Porto for more than three days. The school, the concern was, would lead to noble-born children and their parents to settle in the city – this is what actually happened, despite the protests. The Monastery no longer exists, but the Church, with architectural styles – from mannerism to baroque and classicism – dominates the square located opposite from the Sé. Inside, one can revel in the Azulejos and Talha dourada.

○ PALÁCIO DA BOLSA

Money is earned in Porto and spent in Lisbon – this is how Porto sees the relationship between the two cities, which have traditionally competed with one another throughout the times. Is there a better symbol for the great importance of trade other than the pompous stock market building? The Stock Exchange Palace was commissioned in 1842 as the seat of Porto's Trade Association and was completed as late as in 1910. As a result of the long construction period, it combined all of the styles of the 19th century, exhibiting an eclectic décor. Beneath the classicist façade, there are rooms decorated in the style of Louis XVI, empire salons, a neo-renaissance courtroom and a library in the best British tradition.

Left: Food warms the body and the soul, and there are a number of delicacies to be enjoyed by hungry visitors in Porto, such as the Croquetas de bacalo (fried pieces of dried codfish) and the Calo verde, a potato soup with Chouriço and Couve Galega, a Portuguese version of kale.

○ IGREJA MONUMENTO DE SÃO FRANCISCO

The church was founded by Franciscans in the 13th century. In the 1720s, architects and sculptors removed the gothic furnishings and replaced them with a cover from Talha dourada, which covered almost all the chapels. The gilded carving soars to fantastic altars, such as the one of Nossa Senhora da Rosa.

○ IGREJA DO CARMO

The double façade of the two Churches built next to one another, Igreja do Carmo and Ingreja dos Carmelitas, is the most noticeable landmark of Porto's highly-located Praça de Carlos Alberto, the very

centre of the university district. The two houses of worship took a little bit more than 100 years to be completed.

○ ESTAÇÃO SÃO BENTO

The train station of Porto, which without any doubt is the most popular railway station in the country, was built at the beginning of the 20th century. Its huge station concourse is completely lined with Azulejo paintings: they conjure important moments in the Portuguese history such as the knight tournament of Batalha de Arcos de Valdevez from 1141 or the conquering of Ceuta by Infante Dom Henrique in 1415.

○ AVENIDA DOS ALIADOS/PRAÇA DA LIBERDADE

It is as if a Parisian avenue has sneaked its way into the northern Portuguese metropolis: the Avenida dos Aliados with its neoclassical magnificent buildings could have been just as easily in the beautified the French capital. At the beginning of the 20th century, the prosperity of Porto was reflected in the development of this street, when an old neighbourhood was demolished in order to make way for the representative promenade. It leads to the town hall, which was built in 1920 and has a 70-metre high tower, made to resemble the Torre dos Clerigos. Several monuments and the equestrian statue of King Dom Pedros IV, in the adjacent Praça da Liberdade, decorate the Avenida.

○ MERCADO DO BOLHÃO

The imposing structure impressive food market dates from the beginning of the 20th century. The main

GOING OUT

Botequim Nostalgic // Sitting on the Douro, sipping a cocktail and eating delicious tapas – one of the best locations for all of that is the Botequim Nostalgic.

// Praça Ribeira

Bonaparte // A classic among the bars of Porto. It was founded at the end of the 1970s by a German, and even today, German beers are served here.

// Av. do Brasil 130

O Paparico // The O Paparico is not a cheap restaurant, however regional cuisine is prepared here at the highest level of quality; of course, one should not miss out on the seafood.   **// www.opaparico.com**

essência // As a vegetarian, you can easily get the impression that there are only a few vegetarian restaurants in Porto, while fish and meat are omnipresent. The essência reveals a very different picture.

// www.essenciarestaurante vegetariano.com

Right: Two houses of worship under one roof and having a lot of things in common: the Igreja do Carmo and the Igreja dos Carmelitas accommodate in their interior wonderful Talha dourada altars.

focus of the two-storey building, which is located at the heart of the city between the pedestrian area Rua Sáda Bandeir and the parallel-running Rua de Santa Catarina, is the covered inner courtyard, where vegetable and fruit sellers have their stands. Butchers and fish sellers, food stalls and cafés are grouped along the galleries which are decorated with wrought-iron balustrades. When the gates of the market open in the morning, housewives flock to the marble counters in order to grab the freshest fish, the most aromatic herbs and the sweetest oranges. In 2006, the building was declared a Heritage Site. Sellers and inhabitants have protested vehemently against the imminent transformation into a modern shopping centre.

WHERE TO STAY

Hotel Infante Sagres // This luxurious traditional hotel was completely renovated and opened with a new lustre, albeit without its stylistic origin from the Belle Époque having been forgotten. The central location and its own restaurant "BOOK" are pluses to take into consideration.
// www.infantesagres.com

Hotel Torel Avantgarde // Art is here not only simply for decoration, but as a program on its own! Each of the 47 rooms has the name of an artist from the Avantgarde period and are correspondingly decorated. The result is an exquisite boutique hotel located close to the Palacio de Cristal.
// www.torelavantgarde.com

Baumhaus Serviced Apartements // Big, decorated with attention to detail, and offering a good starting point for those looking to explore the city and is a good choice for the flexible self-catering traveller.
// www.baumhaus.pt

SHOPPING

○ **RUA DE SANTA CATARINA**

The most important shopping street of Porto begins at the train station and goes in the north-east direction, as a pedestrian street, until reaching the outskirts of the city centre. It has chic boutiques, outlets of major fashion houses, cafés, restaurants and also many shops, which, given their somewhat antiquated assortment, such as buttons or corsetry, might seem outdated.

○ **MERCADO BOM SUCESSO**

Regional or from all over the world, sweet or savoury, for special occasions or the daily meal – the choice of food products is quite versatile. If you are interested, you can feast at one of the many stalls inside the hall.

○ **SHOPPING CIDADE DO PORTO**

A modern shopping temple made of stone, steel and glass. Inside, those eager to buy can find up to 100 stores.

DAY TRIPS

○ **VILA NOVA DE GAIA**

This city, located opposite from Porto, smells of its most important product: the delicate aroma of the Porto wine hovers over the trading houses. Vila Nova de Gaia was founded in the middle of the 13th century by King Alfons III as an alternative port, after a fight with the bishop of Porto for toll paid by docking ships; only later, did he agree to share the receipts. Up to the present day, Vila Nova de Gaia has remained an important storage and trading centre for the wine. Over a relatively short section of the river it is possible to cross the Douro by one of the three bridges.

NOT TO BE MISSED

BROWSE THE LIVRARIA LELLO

Livraria Lello e Irmão on the Rua das Carmelitas 144 in the centre of Porto, is an unforgettable tourist attraction and not only for bibliophiles, as it is one of the most beautiful bookshops in the world. The elaborately-decorated façade of the attractive Art Nouveau building, dating from 1906, is impressive. Inside the "cathedral of books", you'll be impressed by the busts of famous authors, created by the sculptor Romão Júnior, and the arched wooden steps that lead to the wood-panelled, open upper floors. In addition to a diversity of Portuguese and foreign literature, you can find a wide range of tourist guides and postcards. In the small cafeteria under the stained-glass ceiling on the upper floor, you can – amongst other things - enjoy a glass of Port wine.

VISIT A PORT WINE CELLAR

All around the city, you will find the most important growing regions for the exquisite grapes of Porto, so a visit to a wine cellar – tasting included! – is a must. The biggest selection is available on the other side of the river in Vila Nova de Gaia.

ENJOY A COFFEE AT CAFÉ MAJESTIC

A juxtaposition of the old and the new contribute to the particular charm of Rua de Santa Catarina, and it is especially evident in the Art Nouveau ambience of the nostalgic Café Majestic. Since its opening in 1916, intellectuals and artists have enjoyed their time here, and, believe it or not, J. K. Rowling wrote the first chapter of the Harry Potter saga under a chandelier in this plush ambience. Today, the café is one of the most beloved touristic contact points in Porto – the old style is, however, still intact.

TAKE A RIDE WITH THE HISTORIC TRAM

The old trams make their rounds via three lines. By taking a tram, you can enjoy not only a tour of the city but also a journey back in time. Those who would like to find out more, should visit the Museu do Carro Eléctrico.

#49   STOCKHOLM

THE SWEDISH CAPITAL IS KNOWN AS ONE OF THE MOST BEAUTIFUL CITIES IN THE WORLD, NOT LEAST BECAUSE OF ITS UNIQUE POSITION. IT IS EMBEDDED BETWEEN LAKE MALAR, AN INLAND BODY OF WATER WHICH STRETCHES OVER 115 KM FROM WEST TO EAST, AND THE BALTIC SEA. THE "VENICE OF THE NORTH" SPREADS OVER 14 ISLANDS, BEING PROTECTED FROM THE OPEN SEA BY A MYRIAD OF ISLETS, KNOWN AS THE SWEDISH ARHIPELAGO. THE CITY IS RICH IN HISTORIC TOURISTIC ATTRACTIONS AND PRESENTS ITSELF AS A MODERN, COSMOPOLITAN METROPOLIS. RESTAURANTS OFFER SPECIALTIES BELONGING TO THE INTERNATIONAL CUISINE, ENSURING A METROPOLITAN FLAIR. DOZENS OF MUSEUMS ARE LOCATED IN STOCKHOLM, MAKING THE CITY A TRUE MECCA FOR ART LOVERS.

Above: Narrow alleys are representative for the Old Town of Gamla Stan. The Stortorget (public square) is an absolute tourist spot.

Left: Water is omnipresent in the capital of the Swedish kingdom, which is spread over numerous islands, peninsulas and the mainland. As it has many bridges, it has often been described as the "Venice of the north".

○ GAMLA STAN

The actual centre of the Swedish capital has moved to other parts of the city long ago; however, the Old Town on the Stadsholmen Island is still a major tourist attraction. The maze of streets and alleys invite for flâneurs to go for a stroll. The neighbourhood, which has grown over the centuries, has buildings from all periods of the city's history. Inside of the old walls you can find numerous cafés, restaurants and galleries.

VÄSTERLÅNGGATAN

The Västerlånggatan is the main shopping street in Gamla Stan. Here, as everywhere in the Old Town, not much has changed since the 16th century. Only the houses that border the narrow alleys date from the 18th and 19th centuries. Today, you can find numerous boutiques, souvenir shops, pubs and restaurants here. On its south end, the Mårten Trotzigs-Gränd branches off from the Västerlånggatan – with a width of only 90 cm, it is the narrowest alley in all of Stockholm.

○ ROYAL PALACE

The Royal Palace is located at the northeast end of Gamla Stan – with 608 rooms, it is one of the biggest Palaces in the world. This magnificent building was erected in the first half of the 18th century on the site of a medieval royal residence, which had been destroyed in a fire, and it represents an excellent example of architectural transitioning from baroque to rococo. The Palace is rarely used by the Swedish king, who resides today at Drottningholm Palace. Therefore, many rooms have been opened to the public. A particular moment of interest is the daily changing of the guards in the palace courtyard, which takes place at 12 o'clock.

○ STORKYRKAN

Millions of people from all over the world followed how the Crown Princess Victoria and Daniel Westling exchanged their wedding vows on 19th of June 2010 in Stockholm's Catehdral, the Storkyrka. The wedding and the Coronation Church of the Swedish monarchs

WHY VISIT IN WINTER?

STOCKHOLM IS A PREFERRED LOCA-
TION FOR ICE SKATERS. AS SOON AS
THE ICE IS THICK ENOUGH, THE BIG
LAKE OF STOCKHOLM AND ITS CA-
NALS ARE FLOODED BY ENTHUSIASTIC
ICE SKATERS TRYING TO SKATE THE
FARTHEST THROUGH THE CAPITAL.
MALAR LAKE, WEST OF STOCKHOLM,
IS THE THIRD-BIGGEST LAKE IN THE
COUNTRY AND THE MAIN VENUE FOR
NORDIC SKATING EVENTS. BY GOING
LESS THAN 100 KILOMETRES, YOU
CAN SKATE ON FROZEN FRESHWA-
TER, AND STOP ON THE WAY IN THE
OLD VIKING CITY BIRKA, WHERE YOU
WILL FIND THE BIGGEST VIKING CEM-
ETERY IN ALL OF SCANDINAVIA. SINCE
1999, ON THE MALAR LAKE, THE
"VIKINGARÄNNET" (THE VIKING RUN)
HAS BEEN ORGANIZED; A SKATING
MARATHON COVERING A DISTANCE
OF 80 KILOMETERS FROM UPPSALA
TO STOCKHOLM; THE RECORD IS 2
HOURS AND 44 MINUTES. WHEN THE
BALTIC FREEZES COMPLETELY, WHICH
HAPPENS ONCE OR TWICE EVERY TEN
YEARS, IT IS EASY TO TOUR THE IS-
LANDS AROUND STOCKHOLM.

is the oldest house of worship in the City, located a
short distance from the Stortorget and the Nobel Museum at the end of steep ramp of Slottsbacken. Its
beautiful baroque façade deceives initially with regard
to its interior: inside, you will find that the entire construction is more like a late-gothic hall church. It is
open to visitors all year long, and during winter the
admission is free-of-charge.

○ NOBELMUSEUM

Not far from the Royal Residence, you can find the
stock exchange building. It was built in the 18th century, and today it houses the Nobel Museum. The exhibition informs about Alfred Nobel as well as about
famous laureates.

○ TYSKA KYRKA

The construction of the German Church in the south
part of Gamla Stan was originally meant to accommodate a branch of the Hanseatic League, but was
converted into a church in the 16th century. Its tower, with a heigh of 96 metres, is the highest in the
Old Town.

○ NORRMALM

Wide streets and a busy life: in the 1950s, in Norrmalm, hardly a single stone was left unturned. The
reason for that was the construction of the metro.
High-rise buildings and modern, somewhat cold-look-
ing glass façades of the buildings give this neighbourhood its own appearance. Life is vibrant here now
and there are many large and luxurious stores on the
shopping street. In the evening, there is a lot going
on: at night Kungsgatan, Sveavägen and Birger Jarls-
gatan come to life, turning into real promenades. Restaurants, bars, cinemas – locals and visitors can find
here a lot of entertainment prospects. There are cultural opportunities as well: the Kulturhuset (cultural
centre) serves as a forum for exhibitions and as state
theatre; it also has a library and several cafés.

○ RIDDARHUSET

The House of Nobility, which was erected between
1641 and 1674, west of the Royal Residence, is also
worth seeing. Up to the present day, the Swedish
knighthood meets here every three years. The magnificent building impresses with its baroque interior.

*Left: Ice skating in the
middle of the city – this is
only possible during the
cold winter days, when
the lake and the canals of
Stockholm are frozen
solid.*

○ RIDDARHOLMEN

The delicate Riddarholm Church, located on the island with the same name, west of Stadsholmen has, over the centuries, been the burial Church of the Swedish kings. The last monarch, who was buried here, was King Gustav V. (1858-1950).

○ DJURGÅRDEN

The island located to the east is part of the National City Park, which was established in 1995 as a protected area, which is dedicated to the maintenance of the cultural and natural heritage of the region. Some of the most important museums of Sweden can be found here.

SKANSEN

Skansen, which was inaugurated in 1891, became a model for the open-air museums of the world. In

Top Right: the Sergelstorg in the Norrmalm district has a 37-metre high glass column, the "crystal vertical accent" of Edvin Öhrström.

Bottom Right: The metro of Stockholm is known as the "longest art gallery in the world". The artistic design is present in 90 percent of the train stations, such as the station Solna centrum, which reminds of the entrance to a dragon's lair with its blood-red ceiling.

GOING OUT

Lux Dag för Dag // In an old light bulb factory, a unique concept has been established: Not until after the morning delivery of regional vegetables, fresh fish and the best meat, will the menu be determined.

// **www.luxdagfordag.se**

Wedholms Fisk // This restaurant is all about fish and seafood. The preparation of these dishes is varied, but very traditional. The restaurant is closed on Sundays and on holidays.

// **wedholmsfisk.se/**

Pet Sounds Bar // The youth of Stockholm venture to this beloved bar in Södermalm, where local artists and DJs always play true independent sounds. The cocktails have a good reputation here as well.

// **www.psb.bar**

the museum area, there are historical buildings from the 19th century, including farms, workers' housing and workshops from all parts of Sweden. A traditional Sami storage area, with a reindeer enclosure, was brought here from Lappland.

VASA MUSEUM

The Vasa Museum is named after the famous warship which sunk on its maiden voyage in 1628 and wasn't recovered until 1961. The meticulously restored three-masted vessel can be seen in a large hall that was expressly built for this purpose.

○ STADSHUSET

The Stockholm City Hall was built between 1911 and 1923 on Riddarholm, exactly opposite from the southeast point of the Kungholmen Island. Inside the brick building, a huge banquet is organized every year in the honour of Nobel Prize winners. Some halls and rooms are open to the public. A beautiful panoramic view can be enjoyed from the town hall tower.

SHOPPING

○ **HÖTORGET (HAYMARKET)**

The traditional market for fruits, vegetables and flowers. From here, it is only a stone's throw to the market hall Hötorgshallen, where you can find specialties from all over the world; since 1958, this has been located underground.

○ **ÅHLÉNS**

Here, you can buy almost everything that the heart desires: in addition to fashion, make-up, modern living designs and a huge selection of music and movies, the department store also has a supermarket and even a spa area.

○ **CAJSA WARG**

The store, named after a Swedish cookbook author, offers everything from lunch to take away, and all will delight your palate. All products have been carefully selected, and you'll find them in individual pretty stores, which combined will remind you of a small market.

○ **CHOKLADFABRIKEN**

The name is true to what it says: food lovers will find distributed amongst the branches a wide range of pralines, deserts and cakes to be enjoyed.

○ **ÖSTERMALMS MARKTHALLE**

This remarkable red brick building, which is reminiscent of an old railway station, has served as a market hall since 1888.

DAY TRIPS

○ **SANDHAMN**

The archipelago represents the perfect dream of Sweden with its wooden houses and waterfronts. With its yacht port, it is a beloved location for weekend-sailors. Perfect for relaxation after long hours in the city.

Left: Wooden houses in the city of Falunrot confirm the image of the small archipelago island of Sandhamm, where you can enjoy a relaxing day trip away from Stockholm.

ÜBERNACHTEN

M/S Monika Hotell // Welcome on board! The M/S Monika is an old ship, which now serves as a permanent hotel on the Kungsholm beachfront, offering comfortable rooms to guests below deck.
// www.msmonika.se/

Hotel Sven Vintappare // You cannot get any closer to the tourist attractions of Stockholm. The hotel is particularly impressive with its Swedish charm and a touch of luxury, and located right in Gamla Stan.
// www.hotelsvenvintappare.se

Hobo Hotel //The still-young designer hotel wants to convey the feeling of uncomplicated freedom, as if you were on the perfect road trip with friends. It belongs to the pure urban style, with a lively atmosphere and you can borrow useful things such as umbrellas and city maps for your trips around the city.
// www.hobo.se

NOT TO BE MISSED

VISIT DROTTINGHOLM PALACE

The residence of the Royal Family: built after the French and Dutch counterparts in 1690, several wings with Rococo rooms were later added by Crown Princess Lovisa Ulrika. Drottningholm has been considered UNESCO World Heritage since 1991. It is the best-preserved Palace in the country, and located only eleven kilometres west of Stockholm on the small island of Lovön on the Malar Lake. The majority of the property can be visited, with the exception of the private rooms of Queen Silvia and Carl Gustav XVI. You can take an elegant ride with a historic steamship from Stockholm to the Palace.

TRADITIONAL SWEDISH MEATBALLS

The famous Swedish meatballs are particularly good at the Pelikan in Blekingegatan, a traditional restaurant with a beer hall charm. If you prefer a cosier atmosphere try the Operakällerns "The Hip Pocket".

MARVEL AT THE IMPERIAL LIBRARY COLLECTION

Those who love books, prints and handwritten documents, come here for all of the right reasons. On 100 kilometres of shelves, you can find everything that has been printed in Sweden, or in the Swedish language, since 1661.

STROLL THROUGH THE KUNGSTRÄDGÅRDEN

When you hear the locals saying Kungsan, you know they are referring to this park in the heart of the City. Until the 18th century, the area was reserved for the blue-blooded, who cultivated their vegetables here and also relaxed. Today, it is the "antechamber" of Stockholm.

RIDE THE KATARINA PASSENGER ELEVATOR AND SEEING THE CITY PANORAMA FROM ABOVE

The elevator goes up along the Katarina Mountain. However, many only use it to enjoy the fantastic views of Stockholm from above. The platform can also be reached by foot, using the wooden steps.

#50 STRASBOURG

AS THE SEAT OF THE EUROPEAN PARLIAMENT, STRASBOURG IS THE METROPOLIS OF POLITICS IN EUROPE. THE OLD CAPITAL OF THE ALSACE, CHARACTERIZED BY THE TURBULENT HISTORY BETWEEN FRANCE AND GERMANY, HAS, SINCE THE MIDDLE AGES, BEEN ONE OF THE MOST PROSPEROUS CITIES OF EUROPE, WITH A VIBRANT ART AND SCIENCE SCENE. TODAY, VISITORS ENJOY THE GRANDE ÎLE WITH THE STRASBOURG CATHEDRAL AND THE NARROW STREETS OF THE OLD TOWN, WHICH ARE LINED WITH NEAT TIMBERED HOUSES DATING FROM THE 16TH AND 17TH CENTURIES. ESPECIALLY ON PLACE DU MARCHÉ-AUX-COCHONS-DE-LAIT, YOU CAN ADMIRE THE ALSACIAN HALF-TIMBERED HOUSES IN ALL OF THEIR GLORY. LA PETITE FRANCE – THIS IS HOW THE TANNER QUARTER IS CALLED, STILL HAS THE FOUR TOWERS OF THE MEDIEVAL TOWN FORTIFICATION AT ITS EDGE, AS WELL AS THE PONTS COUVERTS, THE WOODEN BRIDGE OVER THE ARMS OF THE RIVER ILL.

Above: La Petite France and the contorted Old Town of Strasbourg begin with Ponts Couverts.

Left: ALong the small river of Ill and its tributaries, there are rows of timbered houses of La Petite France. Along the canals, there are narrow, romantic cobblestone alleys as well as small squares to linger, and a beloved pedestrian area that is busy in all seasons. Historically, the quarter has successfully managed to find the balance between renovations and historical charm.

○ GRANDE ÎLE

The medieval Old Town of Strasbourg is located on an island – Grande Île – in the river Ill. Important historic constructions and neighbourhoods are concentrated in a very confined space. The landmark of the city is the Cathedral, one of the most important sacred buildings of the Middle Ages. The Cathedral square is lined with half-timbered houses, which have up to five storeys, such as the Haus Kammerzell and Palais Rohan, which was built in 1740 in the Louis-quinze style.

CATHEDRAL OF OUR LADY OF STRASBOURG

The Cathedral of Our Lady of Strasbourg was erected in the 8th century on the premise of a former Roman castle. The Romanesque Church was destroyed in a fire, being replaced in the 11th century with an imposing three-isled Basilica. Since the beginning of the 12th century, this Church has gone through numerous expansions. It reflects the differ-

ent styles of developments in a unique manner, from the Staufian High Romanesque period to the French High Gothic period. The sculptural décor, dating from the 13th century, is of exceptional quality. The Cathedral, which was erected in red sandstone, was greatly admired by – among others – Johann Wolfgang von Goethe, who wrote about it, in 1772, in an essay entitled "About the German Architecture". The Gothic tower with a height of 142 metres, was the highest Church tower in the world until the late 19th century.

PALAIS ROHAN

Built in a classicist style, the imposing Rohan Palace rises from the cityscape of Alsace. It was erected for the Prince Bishop of Strasbourg between 1732 and 1742. After the French Revolution, it has also been used by rulers, such as Ludwig XV and Emperor Napoleon. At the end of the 19th century, the Palace was used as a university. In 1944, the complex was destroyed by American and English bombs, and the reconstruction wasn't completely finished until in the 1990s. Today, the magnificent building is one of the most beautiful pieces that belong to the 18th century architecture, housing three different Museums: the Archaeology Museum, the Arts and Crafts Museum as well as the Fine Arts Museum with works belonging to old masters.

LA PETITE FRANCE

What appears so peaceful and picturesque today, must have seemed like an ill-famed neighbourhood in the Middle Ages: in the half-timbered houses, dating from the 16th and 17th centuries, fishermen, millers and tanners used to live. The latter used to hang the hides of their animals on the streets to dry and, thus, caused the presence of a particularly strong odour. It also had the reputation of being a poor neighbourhood. Today, the neighbourhood, which is also known as "La Petite France", meaning "the small France", is like an island of history between the canals, and it represents a beloved point of interest for tourists.

SHOPPING

○ **MAISON DES TANNEURS**

The tanner house in La Petite France is one of the best-preserved houses of the city. Restaurants, small cafés and creative boutiques have settled in the small rooms of the half-timbered house in the meantime.

GOING OUT

Restaurant Au Crocodile // A restaurant of the highest class with an exquisite wine list, located at the edge of the Old Town.
// **www.au-crocodile.com**

WHERE TO STAY

Le Bouclier d'Or Hôtel & Spa // Not only the location in Petit France makes this hotel ideal for romantics, but also the furnishings of each room. A huge breakfast buffet can help you start the day in a perfect manner.
// **www.lebouclierdor.com**

Les Haras Hôtel // Once, it was the imperial stud farm, today it is a noble hotel with an interior from wood and leather that takes you back in time. Centrally located in Petit France.
// **www.les-haras-hotel.com**

Ciarus // The Ciarus, with its rooms for two to six people, represents the perfect choice for anyone: families with children, singles who want to turn the City upside down, couples on city breaks, groups of friends who want to enjoy their freedom. It is based on a flexible concept, oscillating between the concepts of "hostel" and "hotel".
// **www.ciarus.com**

NOT TO BE MISSED

TAKING A STROLL THROUGH THE CHRISTMAS MARKET

When people talk about the Christmas market in Strasbourg, they should actually refer to it in plural. During the Advent season, stands are built all over town, where delicacies, decorations and presents are sold to punters. The most traditional and popular is the Christkindelsmärik on Place Broglie. But you can also find wonderfully-illuminated stands near the Cathedral or on Place d'Austerlitz. You should definitely make a detour to the Place Kléber, where a giant Christmas tree is erected every year.

EMBARK ON A COZY BOAT TOUR

A lot of people might consider that a City tour by boat is a good idea only for the summer, without even thinking about exploring Strasbourg in this manner during the winter. However, in winter, the boats are covered and heated, and, thus, the ride on the Ill is really cozy. The tour takes you to Petit France and, if you embark on one of the longer tours, all the way to the European Parliament.

EATING TARTE FLAMBÉE

For the majority, tarte flambée represents the first association that they make with Alsace. When visiting Strasbourg, of course, you must taste this specialty in its original version. It is traditionally covered with onion and bacon but, for vegetarians, there are a few places in the city where you can find a suitable alternative.

COUNTING STEPS AND ENJOYING THE VIEW

Those who have feasted on the culinary side of Strasbourg, with its ring cake and tarte flambée, may be interested in the possibility of burning some calories, without waiving sightseeing. The Cathedral of Our Lady Strasbourg offers a wonderful solution. A narrow staircase leads to the tower platform at an impressive 66 metres high – an exciting task for children or the less motivated is to count the steps. The view of the city from above is quite "formidable".

EXPERIENCING POLITICS

Strasbourg is rightfully called the Capital of Europe. Here, you will find more than the European Parliament; It is, however, probably the main attraction in the so-called European quarter. By the way, if the plenary meets here, you may take part as a visitor and experience politics in action.

#51   VENICE

THE MAGIC OF VENICE - IT ALL ADDS UP: NARROW STREETS AND SERENE CANALS, PIAZZA SAN MARCO WITH THE MAGNIFICENT BASILICA, CANAL GRANDE AND THE PARADE OF PALACES, THE TRADITIONAL CAMPI IN DORDODURO AND THE AMAZING VIEW FROM THE TOWER OF SAN GIORGIO MAGGIORE CHURCH. AND, OF COURSE: ALL THE PEOPLE WITH THEIR LIVELINESS, THE ELEGANCE OF THEIR FASHION, THE TRADITIONAL MASKS OF THE CARNIVAL, THE LIVELY BARS, THE BUSTLING MARKETS AND THE NOBLE HOTELS. AND THOSE WHO WANT TO GET AWAY FROM ALL THE BUSTLE, CAN TAKE A BOAT TO ONE OF THE ISLANDS AND DISCOVER THE LAGOONS WITH THE WORLD OF THE GLASS BLOWERS OR LACEMAKERS.

Left: St. Mark's Square is the heart of the Serenissima. Those who arrive by water, can enter it via the piazzetta, which opens into the lagoon, where you'll find the Doge's Palace and the the Biblioteca Marciana at the opposite end

Right: The richly decorated façade of Basilica di San Marco with its golden shining mosaics, pillared portals, Gothic tabernacles and statues draws all the attention in St. Mark's Square. The former Chapel of the Doge and the State Church of the Republic is the most important medieval construction of Venice.

○ PIAZZA SAN MARCO

This is the heart of the city and apparently, Napoleon called it the "most beautiful salon in the world". Here pigeons fly, the Viennese Coffee house music enchants and two giant figurines strike the hour on the clock tower. The square is surrounded by the Arcades of the Procuratie, the old seat of the city administration. Towards the lagoon, you can find a smaller piazzetta with its two pillars (one the Lion of Venice and the other Saint Theodore of Amasea) completing the whole area.

○ SAN MARCO

The Church, which was founded in the early Middle Ages, owes its styling to the connection of Venice to Constantinople. Just as in former times, the marble-clad Cathedral with its five domes is decorated with mosaics. The mosaics in the right entrance hall dome are particularly beautiful. The domes themselves, and also the Pala d'Oro, a Byzantine altar piece from gold, enamel and gemstones, are among the special treasures you can find here.

○ CAMPANILE UND LOGGETTA

The tower of San Marco offers a spectacular view over the city. The 95-metre high construction collapsed on 14th of July 1902, but was later re-built. The Loggetta, built by Jacopo Sansovino, lying at the foot of the Campanile, was badly affected by the collapse but it was faithfully re-built as well. Originally, it was as a representative building and used as a backdrop for the ceremonies of the Serenissima; later on, the Palace guard moved here. Rich sculpture-like decorations show the power and importance of Venice: you can see the ancient Gods Minerva, Apollo and Mercury, who stood for science, art and commerce, as well as an allegory of peace carved in stone.

○ BIBLIOTECA MARCIANA

Built by Jacopo Sansovino and later extended to the lagoon, it is one of the most representative examples of Renaissance building in the city. The sculpturally-embodied style, however, has its roots in Rome, where Jacopo Sansovino completed his education. Nevertheless, the preference for small-scale decorative forms and the uniformity of the long front are characteristic for the lagoon city of Venice. You will also find the Archaeological Museum inside. Today, the library is located near Zecca, which was the former mint.

○ THE DOGE'S PALACE

Initially, it was the seat of the Venetian City Republic, a Castle surrounded by water – however, in the 12th century, it already looked more like a Palace than a Castle. Its façade, which can be traced back to the Gothic period, is light and delicately adorned. Inside, you can visit the giant steps in the yard, on which the Doges were crowned, and in the Palace itself, the golden steps. Additionally, there are the representative rooms, the council chambers with their coffered ceilings, paintings (among others, by Tizian, Tintoret-

WHY VISIT IN WINTER? THE MOST POPULAR BAROQUE COSTUME PARTY IN THE WORLD, THE CARNIVAL OF VENICE IS AS EXTRAVAGANT AS THE ONE IN RIO. THE VENEZIANS HAVE CELEBRATED THEIR CARNIVAL AT LEAST SINCE THE 15TH CENTURY. IT OFFICIALLY OPENS TWO WEEKS BEFORE ASH WEDNESDAY, WHEN THE PARADE OF MASKS LEAVES FROM ST. MARK'S SQUARE AROUND 16 O'CLOCK. THE HIGHLIGHTS INCLUDE THE DOGE BALL (FOR THE DANCING EXPERTS WEARING ELABORATE COSTUMES) AND THE PARADE OF THE DECORATED BOATS AND GONDOLAS ON CANAL GRANDE. ASIDE FROM THE MAIN EVENTS, THERE IS A LOT HAPPENING. STREET ARTISTS EXHIBIT THEIR TALENTS IN THE SQUARES, SOMETIMES THERE IS ALSO A SKATING RINK IN CAMPO SAN POLO. SO, LET THE FUN START: FIND YOURSELF A MASK AND CHECK OUT THE CARNIVAL ATMOSPHERE!

to and Paolo Veronese), the residence of the Doges and the notorious prisons behind the Bridge of Sighs.

○ SAN GIORGIO MAGGIORE

A vaporetto (a water bus) leaves for the San Giorgio Maggiore Island from the pier of St. Mark's Square. The Monastery Church (1566-1610) stands out with its façade, scaling the succeeding two antique temple fronts. Two paintings of Tintoretto are worth seeing inside. The view of Venice from Campanile is magnificent.

○ VENETIAN ARSENAL

The Arsenal, which was already founded in 1104, was initially a shipyard protected by walls, as part of the dreaded Venetian maritime fleet. In 1420, as many as 16,000 people worked there. The Venetian ship hard biscuits are also produced here in the Arsenal.

○ IL REDENTORE

The Church of the Redeemer, completed in 1592, a later work of Andrea Palladios, was commissioned in 1576, just as the plague conquered Venice. Each year, as gratitude for overcoming the distress, a large procession of the Doge and his cortege came to San Marco over the boat bridge. The Redeemer Festival is still celebrated on the third Sunday in July. The Church façade shows the characteristic successive gable motifs of Palladio, while bright white dominates the interior.

○ GRANDE CANAL

The main – wet – street of Venice is lined with magnificent Palaces and a few Churches, but only four bridges traverse it: directly next to the train station of Ponte Scalzi and the new Calatrava Bridge, and further along, in the direction of the centre, the Ponte Rialto and the Accademia Bridge. Gondolas and vaporetti represent the major means of transportation covering the distance of almost four kilometres and, on average, only five metres deep waterway.

○ CA' PESARO

The massive construction, erected by Baldassare Longhena, with its heavy column decoration, placed in front of a row of windows and with many sculptural accents is representative for the baroque style. Inside the palace, you will find the Gallery of Modern Art (among others, with works by De Chirico, Boccioni,

Left: The game with masks and costumes: there are no limits to the imagination at the Carnival of Venice. The carnival was officially opened by a disguised civil servant in the 18th century. The wearing of the masks was allowed for two months until Ash Wednesday. Venice was once considered the most amusing city in Europe: The authorities believed that "Those who amuse themselves, will not start a revolution".

Bonnard, Chagall, Rouault and Matisse, Klimt, Kandinsky and Klee) as well as the Museum for the Oriental – mainly Japanese Art (with lacquer work, weaponry, porcelain) dating from the 17th to 19th centuries.

○ CA' D'ORO

The famous Gothic Palace of the city once had a gilded façade, after which it was named. The contracting authority was the trader Marino Contarini, the main architect was the Venetian Bartolomeo Bon. Filigree tracery with quatrefoils and ogee arches define the asymmetrically structured marble façade. Inside, you will find Galleria Franchetti, a museum. It presents artworks from the 14th to 18th centuries many of them bearing the signatures of Venetian artists.

GOING OUT

Caffè Florian // The "Florian" is one of Venice's original cafes that still exist. Stucco, mirrors and mural paintings are responsible for the characteristic coffee house atmosphere that you'll find inside. This comes, of course, with its price, in the form of a considerable surcharge on the bill. An espresso at the bar is considerably cheaper.

// www.caffeflorian.com

Algiubagio // The modern bar, located in an old building just opposite from the vaporetto station Fondamente Nuove, represents an ideal stop for a refreshment or a snack. There is also a nice view from the terrace.

// www.algiubagio.net

Trattoria Sottoprova // Although this Trattoria lies off the beaten track, even the locals enjoy the pizza here.

// Via Giuseppe Garibaldi, 1698

Top right: The Historic Barques show themselves magnificently in front of the Rialto Bridge, which are here for the Regata Storica. The origins of the competition date back to the 13th century.

Bottom Right: The San Giorgio Maggiore Monastery Church (1566-1610) impresses with its façade, with two antique temple fronts scaling it.

○ GALLERIA DELL'ACCADEMIA

Here, you can find the works of many Venetian masters from the early Middle Ages to the Rococo. Particular points of interest include the fairytale painting of Giorgione "The Thunderstorm" (around 1507), the Polyptych of Paolo Veneziano with the Coronation of the Virgin, and the eight-part cycle of life of St. Ursula, a work by Vittore Carpaccio (1490-1500).

○ RIALTO BRIDGE

The best-known bridge of Venice with its huge bridge arches, the steps, perspectives and souvenir shops, was built by Antonio da Ponte, from 1588 to 1591 and, up to the 19th century, it was the only way to cross the Canal Grande. At that time, the old commercial area spread to this part of the town. The beautiful Rialto Market still reminds a little bit of it today.

○ PALAZZO CORNER (CA' GRANDE)

The Palace built in 1537 by Jacopo Sansovino is an example of High Renaissance style. Opposite, on the right side of the canal, you will find the collection of Peggy Guggenheim, with its magnificent modern art.

SANTA MARIA DELLA SALUTE

This wonderful sacred building is, like Il Redentore, a Votive Church, donated against the background of a plague. With regards to the urban development, it is meticulously placed and is one of the landmarks of Venice. The Baroque Church, with its cupola and the rich sculptural decorations of Baldassare Longhena, was erected in 1631. The founding purpose can be seen at the high altar: an allegorical figure, Venezia, kneeling in front of the Madonna, who helps her, and the plague – in the form of an old woman – is chased away.

WHERE TO STAY

Concordia // There is no other location for overnight stays positioned as close to the St. Mark's Basilica as this particular one. In this comfort hotel, with good service and top-quality standards, you can enjoy the scenery of St. Mark's Square while having your breakfast.

// www.hotelconcordia.com

Antica Locanda Sturion // This three-star hotel is found in a Renaissance Palace, centrally located in Rialto and with a view of the Grand Canal. In earlier times, the house accommodated merchants, sailors, ambassadors and artists.

// www.locandasturion.com/de

Bauer Venezia // This luxury hotel boasts a unique location directly on the Grand Canal, which can be enjoyed from one of its 91 rooms and 18 suites. The hotel offers, of course, fitness, wellness, and, with the gourmet restaurant, "De Pisis", a very good cuisine.

// www.bauervenezia.com

SHOPPING

MERCERIE

A shopping district stretches between Rialto and St. Mark's Square, which is known as the Mercerie. Here, you will find both shopping streets and promenades. Expensive boutiques are the focus, with Venice being rather expensive overall. You can find pretty much all of the Italian designers here. Eager-to-buy visitors can shop for jewellry, carnival masks, costumes, souvenirs and food products. The Mercerie is best reached from the north over the Rialto Bridge.

ALIANI

A long-established delicatessen shop and a dream for enthusiasts of good Italian cheese, ham and smoked sausage.

// www.aliani-casadelparmigiano.it

BUY A MASK

If you purchase a high-quality mask made from clay or papier mâché, you have a true souvenir. The best two mask suppliers of the city are: Atelier Marega or Magie di Carnevale, where you will also find porcelain dolls and costumes.

DAYTRIPS

TO THE LAGOON ISLANDS

Venice is not the only rewarding island of the lagoon. Murano is known for its glass blowers, whom you can watch at work. Burano, on the other hand, has a long tradition of lace embroidery. Moreover, the colourful fishermen houses represent the perfect choice for photographs. Torcello was once a bishop's residence.

NOT TO BE MISSED

ROAMING THROUGH LA GIUDECCA

Opposite the Sestiere Dorsoduro lies the archipelago Giudecca, which was originally called "Spinalunga" because of its fishbone shape. Once the centre of life for the patricians, today it is a valued living area for the Venetian population. In the west, at the end of the 19th century, the German architect Ernst Wullekopf designed in neo-Gothic style Molino Stucky, the former grain mill with attached noodle factory. In the centre of the island rises the Church of Il Redentore, whose construction Andrea Palladio led from 1577 to 1592.

TAKE A BACARI TOUR

Bacaris are small pubs. From mornings until late in the evening, you can have a drink and nibble on snacks at one of the standing tables. Since there are many bacaris in the Rialto area, you can explore them as part of a tour.

SAVOURING DELICACIES WITH VENETIANS AT VINI DA GIGIO

The small bistro located in a former wine shop is easily overlooked by tourists. The locals are more than grateful for the typical regional cuisine, which is based on fresh seasonal ingredients.

DECORATING CARNIVAL MASKS AT CA'MACANA

In the small shop, the masks are all handmade. Do not only browse, but become active yourself: first, a little bit of theory, then paint and decorate your own mask from papier mâché!

EXPLORING THE CANAL LABYRINTH WITH THE BRAGOZZI

Bragozzi are wooden sailboats, which were used in the past for fishing in and around Venice. Thanks to the shallow hull, you can traverse the lateral arms of the lagoon where other excursion boats cannot reach.

#52 VIENNA

VIENNA IS A CITY STEEPED IN HISTORY. THE ROMANS SETTLED HERE, AND LATER ON POWERFUL EMPERORS REIGNED FROM HERE, WITH THE RICH KINGDOM EXTENDING ITS HISTORY OVER MANY CENTURIES. ITS POETS AND THINKERS, MUSICIANS AND PAINTERS CONQUERED THE WORLD WITH GROUNDBREAKING IDEAS AND WORKS. TODAY, VIENNA IS A PULSATING CENTRE IN THE MIDDLE OF EUROPE, WITH ITS IMPERIAL SPLENDOUR, BIEDERMEIER IDYLL AND THE DYNAMIC RHYTHM OF THE PRESENT BLEND IN A UNIQUE MANNER. THE CITY GROWS AND THRIVES, IT IS FASHION AND TRADITION CONSCIOUS AT THE SAME TIME, NOT TO MENTION IT OFFERS FRESH AIR, WATER AND GREEN SPACES, PUBLIC TRANSPORTATION AND SECURITY, ALL OF WHICH CONTRIBUTE TO A VERY SUPERIOR QUALITY OF LIFE.

Left: St. Stephen's Cathedral is often referred to as "Preached in Stone". Approximately 230,000 bricks cover the roof of the "Steff".

Right: The Museum of Natural History does not house only artworks from seven millennia, from Ancient Egypt to the end of the 18th century, but it is a work of art in itself. The stairwell – which was painted by Ernst and Gustav Klimt and others – is dominated by a marble Theseus Group by Antonio Canova.

○ THE STATE OPERA
Exquisite Opera culture of the worlds highest standard offers the „First House on the Ring". Here, night after night, the best singers and conductors in magnificent outfits prove their skills.

○ ALBERTINA
The Palace accomodates the biggest graphic collection in the world with approximately 44,000 watercolours and drawings, as well as 1.5 million graphic prints.

○ NATIONAL LIBRARY
One of the most important libraries in the world with more than 6.7 million objects, including unique manuscripts and early printed books. The highlight of the European Baroque architecture is the cupola-crowned ceremonial room. It serves as a regular venue for interesting themed exhibitions.

○ HOFBURG
The Viennese Hofburg was the centre of the Habsburg Empire for more than 600 years, but above all, it was the main residence of the imperial family, and it can be visited today. Today, the Austrian Federal President, as well as several ministers and state secretaries work here inside the magnificent state rooms.

○ HOUSE OF MOZART
The famous composer lived in this house between 1784 and 1787. Since the anniversary year in 2006, there has been a permanent exhibition about the period. You will find portraits, music prints, autographs and much more here.

○ ST. STEPHEN'S CATHEDRAL
Vienna's most important place of worship and the city's landmark, visible from afar, is affectionately known by the locals as "Steffl": a marvel of stonemasonry with more than 750 years of history.

○ IMPERIAL GRAVE
The Habsburg rulers and their closest relatives have been buried in the cellar vaults, under the Capuchin Church, since the 17th century.

○ MUSEUM OF ART HISTORY
Visitors are drawn to the art gallery with artworks from five centuries, among others, by Martin Schongauer, Cranach and Dürer, Brueghel, Rubens and Rembrandt, Tintoretto, Tizian or Velázquez; moreover, you should also check out the Coin Cabinet, the top-of-the-class Egyptian-oriental collections, as well as the collections of sculpture, decorative arts and antiques.

WHY VISIT IN WINTER? IT IS TIME FOR THE BALLS! FROM JANUARY TO MARCH, AROUND 450 BALLS ARE HELD EACH YEAR. THE PRELUDE IS THE BIG NEW YEAR'S BALL IN THE HOFBURG; IN COUNTLESS OTHERS SUCH AS THE FLOWER BALL, THE HUNTER'S BALL OR THE CANDY BALL CAN BE DANCED UNTIL SPRING. THE BALLHOUSES INCLUDE THE HOFBURG, A SYMPHONY FROM MARBLE PILLARS AND HUGE CHANDELIERS, VARIOUS CONCERT HALLS AND THE VIENNA STATE OPERA. AN OBSESSION OF THE VIENNESE IS TO ALIGN THE BALLS OF VARIOUS PROFESSIONAL ASSOCIATIONS, SO ONE IS JUST BUZZING WITH LAWYERS OR VIENNESE COFFEEHOUSE OWNERS. ANYONE WHO KNOWS HOW TO DANCE AND DRESS CLASSY (TUXEDO OR BALL GOWN) CAN BUY TICKETS TO THE BALLS. A DANCE LESSON IN ADVANCE IS RECOMMENDED EVEN FOR THE EXPERIENCED, BECAUSE THE VIENNESE STYLE IS INCREDIBLY FAST. THE DANCE SCHOOL ELMAYER OFFERS BALL-BLITZ-COURSES.

○ MUSEUM OF NATURAL HISTORY

The 39 rooms hold one of the biggest natural science collections of Europe with minerals and meteorites, fossils, skeletons as well as contemporary flora and fauna. Highlights include, among others, the Stone Age statuette of "Venus of Willendorf" and the "Viennese Herbarium", with approximately 13,000 volumes, presenting sample plants from all over the world.

○ BURGTHEATER - IMPERIAL COURT THEATRE "THE BURG" IS THE UNDISPUTED NUMBER ONE AMONG THE LOCAL-STYLE THEATRES. THE ENSEMBLE IS AMONG THE BEST OF THE GERMAN-SPEAKING THEATRE WORLD. THE CONSTRUCTION IS ALSO INTERESTING FROM AN ARCHITECTONIC POINT OF VIEW.

○ THE NEW CITY HALL

The magnificent construction of the Gothic-style New City Hall took place between 1872 and 1883. The arcade court, the grand staircase and the ballroom can be visited as part of a tour.

○ THE VOTIVE CHURCH

It is not without reason that it is also called the "Dome of the Ring Street": the Votive Church, consecrated in 1879, is considered worldwide as one of the most important Neo-Gothic religious constructions.

○ NASCHMARKT

The biggest food market within the inner city – it dates back to the later 18th century – stretches from the Kettenbrücken Alley to Karl Square over approximately 500 metres wide. On the eastern end of the market, close to the Secession, the goods and shoppers are the most exquisite. In the middle of the market, you can inhale exotic scents and find many international specialties. On Saturday mornings, in this area, a farmer's market is organized, with a giant flea market right next to it.

○ SECESSION

In the years 1897 to 1898, Josef Maria Olbrich created this exhibition building for the »Vienna Secession« - an avant-garde artist group that had separated themselves from its conservative colleagues organized in the Artists House. It is one of the major works of Viennese Art Nouveau.

Left: At the affable suburban Balls and „Gschnasen" (fancy dress balls) – this is the Viennese name for a joyful costume party – there is no strict dress-code. The only specification is to try and dress as originally as possible. At the representative events, however, the elegant wardrobe is required – the ladies in a floor-length evening dresses, while the men wear a smoking or dress coat.

○ CHURCH OF ST. KARL

It was founded in 1713 by Emperor Karl VI, being commissioned on the occasion of surviving the plague epidemic. Its creators, Fischer von Erlach senior and junior, united classical forms of Greek, Roman and Byzantine architecture.

○ MUSEUMSQUARTIER

The Museumsquartier was opened in 2001, at the junction of the 7th and 1st districts. It unites the Baroque structures of the former imperial stables with postmodernist architecture and it is among the ten biggest cultural centre of the world, with the Art Gallery, the Museum of Modern Art and Leopold Museum.

○ HUNDERTWASSERHAUS

In an inconspicuous alley in the 3rd district, there is that strange house, which ranks among the most visited attractions after St. Stephen's Cathedral and Schönbrunn Palace. Its maker, Friedensreich Hundertwasser, offered a visual harmony, transforming all of his ideas into reality: he interspersed walls and edges with curved lines and irregularities, created crooked floors, planted trees on balconies and roofs and decorated the façades with brightly-coloured drops, curls and tile mosaics.

○ BELVEDERE PALACE

The Belvedere Palace, which was designed by Lukas von Hildebrandt, is one of the most important Baroque works Vienna has to offer. The Summer Palace consists of two Castles and it was erected between 1714 and 1723 for the legendary military General and Conqueror of the Turks, Prince Eugene of Savoy. In the staterooms, artworks by Waldmüller, Klimt, Kokoschka & Co. testify to the blooming of the 19th and 20th centuries painting styles.

Top Right: The New City Hall is a special jewel of the Ring Street architecture. It is located directly opposite from the Burg Theatre and it was built in a neo-gothic style, with lancet windows, loggias, balconies, a central arcade courtyard (81 x 35 metres) and an abundance of sculptural decorations.

Bottom Right: Hundertwasser designed both the Hundertwasser Krawina House as well as the Museum Kunst Haus of Vienna on the Unteren Weißgerber Street as a sort of a three-dimensional manifesto against the norms and regulations of the modern architecture, which he considered to be "soulless and dreary".

GOING OUT

Café Landtmann //This spacious, elegant Ring Street café represents a preferred meeting point for politicians, media people and actors from the nearby Burg Theatre.
// www.landtmann.at

Ubl // Traditional Viennese restaurant with home-style cuisine, typical pastries and open-air dining. Here, you can feel like a celebrity.
// Pressgasse 26

Gulaschmuseum // Here, you can enjoy approximately 15 versions of the spicy dish with paprika and meat that was imported from Hungary to Vienna centuries ago, and with many other varieties being invented here.
// www.gulaschmuseum.at

Figlmüller // The schnitzel from Figlmüller is one of the biggest and most delicious in all of Vienna. Thin and tender and cooked in three different hot pans.
// www.figlmueller.at

○ CENTRAL CEMETERY

The central burial ground of Vienna is located in the South-East District of Simmering, halfway between the City and the Schwechat Airport. It was opened in 1874 and it is spread over a surface of 2,4 square kilometres, with more than 300.000 graves, in which approximately three million people have found their final peace.

○ SCHÖNBRUNN PALACE

The icon of the imperial, baroque Vienna par excellence is the Schönbrunn Palace, located in the residential district of Hietzing. As a feudal creation of the early 18th century, it reflects the passion for architectural exuberance, which, after the triumph over the Turks, inspired the aristocratic builders. Up to 1918, Schönbrunn was the summer residence of the Habsburg family. Today, in the peak season, there are up to 11,000 visitors arriving daily to visit the magnificent imperia apartments, the historic horse-drawn carriages in the Wagenburg (Museum of Carriages), the Palm House and the Zoo.

○ PRATER

The Prater offers an oasis for relaxation and fun. This woodland and meadow landscape, almost 15 kilometres long, located between the Danube and the Danube Canal, was once an imperial hunting ground. Joseph II made it accessible to the public in 1766. The area is crossed by tributaries as well as by a widespread network of cycling and walking paths offering amateur athletes the perfect infrastructure. In the western, peri-urban area the so-called Wurstelprater attracts with beer gardens, amusement arcades and ghost trains, as well as diverse high-tech slings and roller coasters. And, do not forget, there is also the Ferris wheel – 67-metre high, with a spectacular iron structure, from whose wagons you can enjoy the magnificent panorama of Vienna.

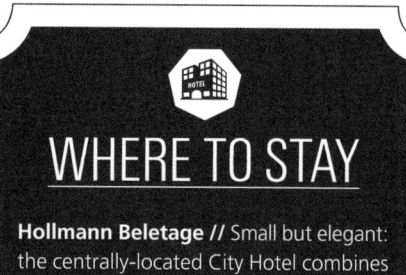

WHERE TO STAY

Hollmann Beletage // Small but elegant: the centrally-located City Hotel combines true Viennese charm with a modern design. There are 16 tastefully-decorated rooms in total, guaranteeing a pleasant stay.
// www.hollmann-beletage.at

Imperial // So to speak, the Rolls Royce among Vienna's posh hotels, also known as "the first house of Austria", in which the republic accommodates its official guests. Period furniture, old masters, precious chandeliers and carpets turn the former state palace into a habitable museum.
// www.imperialvienna.com

Levante Parliament // Located directly behind the City Hall and the Parliament, this Design Hotel opened in 2006. From outside, it appears rather inconspicuous but, inside, it is very tastefully decorated, offering art for connoisseurs, and especially for the ones who know the Savoir-vivre. // www.thelevante.com

SHOPPING

○ K.U.K. HOFLIEFERANTEN

On Kärntner Straße, Gerstner and Schlumberger offer exquisite confectionery and fine sparkling wine. A shop which resembles a fairyland. You can also enjoy a delicious breakfast here.

○ LODEN PLANKL

The oldest relevant business in Vienna produces jackets, trousers and traditional costumes made of cashmere wool, high-quality fabrics, cotton, leather, linen and, of course the loden cape.

○ RING STREET GALLERIES

Ideal for window shopping on rainy days: two elegant, covered passages only a minute away from the Opera in the eastern direction.

NOT TO BE MISSED

A WALK THROUGH THE VIENNA WOODS WITH SUBSEQUENT REFRESHMENTS

In addition to Castles, Palaces and Churches, there are wine taverns called »Heurige« in the natural paradise Wienerwald. Classic grape varieties: Zweigelt, Zierfandler or Rotgipfler. The venerable winegrowing village Grinzing at the foot of the Kahlenberg is the most famous wine tavern in the Vienna area. Its upscale venues usually offer guests a garden with atmosphere, a rich buffet and live music in the form of original Viennese songs.

SAVOUR SPECIALTIES IN A VIENNESE COFFEEHOUSE

Whether a Kleiner Schwarzer (Little Black) or Wiener Melange (Vienna Melange) – a piece of Sacher cake is part of the deal. Best at Café Hawelka, where Udo Jürgens and Elias Canetti once sat. A traditional address for those who love exquisite coffee houses is, of course, the Sacher Café, located on the ground floor of the posh hotel with the same name, placed directly behind the State Opera. Right next door, there is also the legendary chocolate cake, which you can take at home in a package suitable for travel.

LISTEN TO THE VIENNA BOYS CHOIR

Boys have sung in the Viennese court since the 14th century. Today, there are four choirs, with approximately 100 boys, aged between 9 and 14. Clear voices and the joy of singing can be enjoyed in the Chapel of the Imperial Place or in the House for Music and Theatre.

STROLL THROUGH THE KARMELITER-MARKT

You will search in vain for plush and fast food here. The Karmelitermarkt is modern, stylish and very trendy. There are organic shops and bistros to discover here.

TAKE A TRAM TOUR AROUND THE RING STREET

It starts at Sweden Square (Schwedenplatz) and takes you past the most important tourist attractions. Screens and headphones replace the travel guide.

INDEX

PICTURE CREDITS

IMPRINT

MONACO BOOKS is an imprint of Kunth Verlag GmbH & Co KG
© Kunth Verlag GmbH & Co KG, Munich, 2018
Concept: Wolfgang Kunth
Editing and design: Kunth Verlag GmbH & Co KG

Text: Monika Baumüller, Dietmar Falk, Robert Fischer, Christiane Gsänger, Stefan Jordan, Daniela Kebel, Ute Kleinelümern, Hildegard Kretschmer, Andrea Lammert, Norbert Lewandowski, Michael Müller, Christa Pöppelmann, Gabriele Redden, Oliver Renzler, Iris Schaper, Annika Voigt, Karin Weidlich, Walter Weiss
Translated by Ulrik Eeg for Anubis Consult Co., Ltd.

For distribution please contact:
Monaco Books
c/o Kunth Verlag GmbH & Co KG
St.-Cajetan-Straße 41
81669 München
Tel. +49.89.45 80 20-0
Fax +49.89.45 80 20-21
www.kunth-verlag.de
info@kunth-verlag.de